ICT and Language Learning

Also by Marie-Madeleine Kenning

CHANGING LANDSCAPES IN LANGUAGE AND LANGUAGE PEDAGOGY: Text, Orality and Voice (*co-editor with M-N. Guillot*)

PROMOTING LEARNER AUTONOMY IN UNIVERSITY LANGUAGE TEACHING (*co-editor with E. Broady*)

COMPUTERS AND LANGUAGE LEARNING: Theory and Practice (*with M.J. Kenning*)

AN INTRODUCTION TO COMPUTER ASSISTED LANGUAGE TEACHING (*with M.J. Kenning*)

ICT and Language Learning

From Print to the Mobile Phone

Marie-Madeleine Kenning
University of East Anglia

palgrave
macmillan

First published 2007 by
PALGRAVE MACMILLAN
Houndmills, Basingstoke, Hampshire RG21 6XS and
175 Fifth Avenue, New York, N.Y. 10010
Companies and representatives throughout the world

PALGRAVE MACMILLAN is the global academic imprint of the Palgrave Macmillan division of St. Martin's Press, LLC and of Palgrave Macmillan Ltd. Macmillan® is a registered trademark in the United States, United Kingdom and other countries. Palgrave is a registered trademark in the European Union and other countries.

ISBN-13: 978–0–230–51707–3 hardback
ISBN-10: 0–230–51707–2 hardback

This book is printed on paper suitable for recycling and made from fully managed and sustained forest sources. Logging, pulping and manufacturing processes are expected to conform to the environmental regulations of the country of origin.

A catalogue record for this book is available from the British Library.

A catalog record for this book is available from the Library of Congress.

10 9 8 7 6 5 4 3 2 1
16 15 14 13 12 11 10 09 08 07

Printed and bound in Great Britain by
Antony Rowe Ltd, Chippenham and Eastbourne

For Michael

Contents

List of Tables ix

Acknowledgements x

1 Technology as an Agent of Change **1**
Introduction 1
Pervasiveness of technological determinism 3
Myth number one: technology determines its own uses and effects 6
Myth number two: the changes brought by technology are inevitable 9
Myth number three: inventions as revolutions 12
An inherently complex situation 17
Outline of the book 21

2 ICT and Communication **23**
Introduction 23
Evolution of means of communication 26
Communication as a system 27
Communication characteristics 38
Communication in everyday life 53
Discussion and conclusion 58

3 ICT and Language **61**
Introduction 61
ICT and the causes of language variation and change 63
ICT and the direction of change 66
ICT and the factors involved in language change 69
Processes at work: levels of causality 78
Differential effects 86
Language spread 94
Conclusion 100

4 ICT and Education **103**
Introduction 103
ICT and the purpose of education 104
ICT and paradigms of educational organization 107

ICT and the teacher's role 110
ICT and educational content 116
ICT and literacy 118
Educational technology: strengths and weaknesses of individual media 126
Conclusion 133

5 ICT and Language Learning **135**
Introduction 135
Motivation and goals 136
ICT and methodological changes 142
Educational technology in language learning: historical overview 151
Development of a new rationale 155
In search of a principled approach 160

6 Case Study: the Telephone and Language Learning **171**
Introduction 171
Milestones in telephone history 173
The telephone in everyday life 176
The telephone in education and language learning 188
Conclusion 194

7 Conclusion **195**

References 198

Index 215

List of Tables

2.1 Channel possibilities for receiver (R) and source (S) 50
5.1 Summary of main strengths and weaknesses of individual media 162
5.2 Assessment of individual media 163
6.1 Communication characteristics of different forms of telephone interaction 179

Acknowledgements

I would like to acknowledge my debt to all those who read and commented on early drafts of the manuscript. I thank two anonymous reviewers who provided very helpful comments on four of the chapters. I am grateful to my husband Michael for all the conversations we have had about technology and language learning, for reading the entire script, and for offering guidance and expert advice. I am indebted to and thank Mary Fox, so often my first reader, for her patience in answering my questions about the English language, for the encouragement that she gave me, and for her help with the production of the typescript. Finally, I would like to thank Jill Lake of Palgrave Macmillan for her assistance and support.

1 Technology as an Agent of Change

Introduction

This book addresses two questions: what has been the impact of the evolution of information and communication technology (ICT) on the experience of the language user/learner through the ages? What can we infer from this about how best to use ICT in language learning today? It is based on the idea that the interplay between ICT and language learning goes beyond the exploitation of technology for language learning purposes to encompass other dimensions of the effects of ICT. The exploration of this idea is what sets the present book apart from other treatments of ICT and language learning. It also provides the framework for my enquiry.

Making use of ICT when learning a language at the beginning of the twenty-first century is, for most members of affluent societies, an obvious, normal course of action. Just as technology has become woven into the fabric of everyday life, so language study has come to rely on forms of technological enhancement, from audio and video recordings to World Wide Web (WWW) resources. This has not always been the case, nor does it apply to everyone today. But the fact that there are people in some parts of the world who learn foreign languages exclusively through direct contact with tourists is likely to be regarded by the digitally rich as a sign of deprivation, and, crucially, as a phenomenon liable to be put right eventually. The current prevailing assumption is that improved access to ICT will lead to its application to language learning and to the expansion of the dominant paradigm of wealthier countries.

The kind of informal language learning found today among Egyptian caleche drivers, Indian camel guides and Nepalese trek porters was a common occurrence in former times and raises some interesting questions on the relationship between technology and language learning. At an individual level, informal face-to-face learning without recourse to any form of ICT is undoubtedly very different, experientially, from formal language education. In addition, there are differences on dimensions such as motivation and outcomes (with some instances of spontaneous face-to-face learning proving very successful in terms of their objectives). At subject level, the availability and use of educational technology have traditionally been approached as opportunities to enhance learning: 'With each technological shift, each new software or hardware, new challenges are presented for teachers to improve delivery and enhance learning' (LanguagesICT, 2004). With the spread of digital technologies, the integration of ICT has almost become a kind of moral imperative: 'It is appropriate that teaching and learning should reflect these profound changes and that we should take advantage of them to enhance teaching and learning and, of course, to raise pupils' achievement' (LanguagesICT, 2004).

Notwithstanding its high visibility, the pedagogical exploitation of technological developments is only one aspect, itself many-sided, of the interaction between ICT and language study. As well as impacting on how languages are taught, information and communication media also influence language learning indirectly, through their impact on communication and on language. As the changes that follow technological advances filter through to language education, they affect not only how language is learnt, but also what kind of language is or should be learnt. Reading a book, conversing face to face, making a telephone call and writing emails require different kinds of competence and language. What difference does it make to be exposed to, or have to produce, language face to face compared to using one or other of the media currently at our disposal? What has been the effect of technological innovations on communicative practices and what are the implications for language learning? Has technological progress had a significant impact on language? What part has it played in the evolution of language pedagogy? These are some of the questions raised in this book. To raise them is important, not only because they have tended to be neglected, but because they invite us to investigate the role that technology has played in the past, what the gains and pitfalls have been, and whether there are discernible patterns or trends that might guide future developments. To ask such questions can not only help us learn from the past. It can also serve to pinpoint concerns and issues which risk being overshadowed by practical considerations in the face of a rhetoric based on potentials and economic arguments rather than empirical evidence. As Chapelle (2003: 35) points out, 'the public discourse on technology offers better data for critical discourse analysis than wisdom about learning'. Many of the alleged benefits of technology-enhanced learning have yet to be substantiated. If we are to make informed choices we cannot avoid questions such as: what constitutes effective use for each of today's media? Are new opportunities necessarily a good thing? Is there a danger that the opening up of possibilities may result in the curriculum being skewed towards a certain skill?

While there are valuable insights to be gleaned from the adoption of a socio-historical perspective, I entirely agree with Warschauer's suggestion:

> 50 years after the computer was invented, we do not have old language learning plus the computer, but we have a different language learning. If we are to fully understand the interrelationship between technology and language learning, researchers have to investigate the broader ecological context that affects language learning and use in today's society, both inside and outside the classroom. (Warschauer, 1998: 760)

I therefore combine the diachronic and the synchronic. Taking a panoramic view of language study from the printing press to the mobile phone, I approach the intersection of ICT with language learning from four complementary vantage points which provide alternative windows and a progressively narrowing focus. Inevitably, my exploration raises general questions about the relationship between ICT and other social phenomena that go beyond language education. It is appropriate, therefore, to begin by situating my enquiry within the wider context of the debate over the impact of technology on society and to address the controversial issue of technology and social change. I start by examining the tendency to view technology as all-powerful. Next I focus on three recurrent themes in the literature: technology determines its own uses and effects; the changes brought by technology are inevitable; major inventions constitute revolutions.

Pervasiveness of technological determinism

It is easy at a time of rapid technological developments, to perceive social change as the result of technological advances. This is not a new phenomenon but goes back a long way. Typified by McLuhan's writings, including pronouncements such as 'it is the medium that shapes and controls the scale and form of human association' (McLuhan, 1964: 16), the tendency to imbue technology with power and to place it at the centre of the historical process represents a deeply ingrained trend. According to Smith (1994: 2), 'The intellectual heritage of technological determinism can be traced to the enthusiasm and faith in technology as a liberating force expressed by leaders of the eighteenth-century Enlightenment.' Since that time, optimism has waned and even, occasionally, turned into pessimism in the wake of misuse or accidents, but the impression that technology has its own momentum and drives history continues to be widespread. Postman (1987), for instance, laments the changeover from the 'Age of Typography' to the 'Age of Television' and its impact on the content and meaning of public discourse. He deplores the fact that since the invention of the telegraph, the news is primarily made up of items which can be talked about but cannot result in meaningful action.

The main leitmotif of technological determinism has been the impact of technology on political systems and the social fabric of communities: 'Socially, the typographic extension of man brought in nationalism, industrialism, mass markets, and universal literacy and education' (McLuhan, 1964: 184). There is also a tendency to hold technology responsible for changes in social and cultural practices. In a comparative discourse analysis, Sasseville (2004) shows how texts from pedagogical and educational publications make use of figures of speech that highlight the inevitability of social change and the transformative power of technology. ICT is said to be revolutionary, its power is deemed limitless, and its use in education is often regarded as unavoidable. In a similar vein, rhetorical analysis shows that strains of technological determinism often permeate early academic discourse about hypertext: 'Technology is credited, for instance, with transforming discursive behaviour, social relations, the function of the discipline of English, or even patterns of human thought' (Haas, 1996: 191). This poses the question (to be addressed in Chapter 5): is there any evidence that technology has ever induced a paradigm shift in language education?

In a persuasive analysis, L. Marx (1994: 251) presents technological determinism as having arisen from a revision of the ideology of progress: 'The simple republican formula for generating progress by directing improved technical means to societal ends was imperceptibly transformed into a quite different technocratic commitment to improving "technology" as the basis and the measure of – as all but constituting – the progress of society.' Faith in technology can be seen as epitomizing the optimism of Enlightenment rationalism. But, by substituting technical advances for political aspirations as the main agent of change, it raised the status of technology to a point where it could seem to possess power over history and opened the way for a sense of history as technology driven. This impression makes worse the feeling of pessimism engendered by what Postman (1987: 70) refers to as 'a great loop of importance': our exposure through the mass media to an abundance of news about which we can do nothing except pass them on as more news. Hence the loss of a sense of control over the contingencies of life.

There are several reasons for the continuing pervasiveness of technological determinism. One is the vagueness of the term 'technology'. First attested in 1615 with the meaning 'A discourse or treatise on an art or arts; the scientific study of the practical or industrial arts' (*Oxford English Dictionary*, 1989), the word 'technology' was first used to refer directly to the 'practical arts collectively' in 1859, but does not seem to have gained wide currency until the middle of the twentieth century. In its current usage, it may refer to a particular practical or industrial art, to a type of firm or industry or its products, or be used in an inclusive, collective manner. This indeterminacy paves the way for reification. Because of their intrinsic visibility and tangibility, material artefacts attract attention, and thereby invite interpretations in which, correctly or incorrectly, technology finds itself equated with hardware. The process is self-perpetuating and generates more interpretations that steer people towards tools and devices rather than towards other meanings.

A second, related, factor promoting technological determinism is the opacity and complexity of the social realities behind the concept of technology. Unlike concrete objects, the managerial and financial components of technology are not readily identifiable. Like what lies under the tip of an iceberg, they are hidden from view, and their interpenetration makes them difficult to separate out. Their importance is therefore liable to be underrated and their effect overlooked, unless explicitly mentioned. This makes hardware stand out all the more, and increases the chance of technical developments being turned into autonomous entities capable of creating change. It is also the case that technological determinism fits in conveniently with society's desire to find simple explanations, as exemplified in the political arena by the propensity of certain figures to impute all difficulties to a single cause, typically the presence of immigrants.

It is a common mistake to equate chronological sequence with causation and to attribute changes that follow a particular event to that event. No one would dispute that technological inventions introduce new conditions. But this does not mean that technology is all-powerful and responsible for change, even if our use of language and our tendency to assimilate technology to hardware seem to imply this kind of simple causal relationship. Although difficult to avoid, statements that make technology or technological artefacts the subject of an active predicate have treacherous implications. Snyder (1998: 133) points out that when people say that hypertext transforms education, 'a complex event is made to seem the outcome of a technological innovation'. There are three major problems with such sentences: they portray change as stemming from qualities inherent in the technology; they present it as inescapable; and they exaggerate its importance. Even if it remains implicit, the unavoidable conclusion is that society is caught up in a process of cumulative changes with social consequences that are so far-reaching as to be quasi-irreversible. The myths spread by the popular discourse of technological determinism form the themes of the next three sections.

Myth number one: technology determines its own uses and effects

Contrary to the impression conveyed by technological determinism, technology does not determine its own uses and effects. To begin with, technological innovations do not simply appear out of the blue, but are the outcome of the endeavours of human beings who designed them with certain uses in mind and some idea of their effects on society and on individual lives: 'Until now, at least, no technology, no matter how ingenious and powerful, ever has initiated an action not preprogrammed by human beings' (Marx and Smith, 1994: xii). This is where real life departs from science fiction scenarios in which machines wrench decisions from human beings. And if, as is prone to happen, inventions come to be used for purposes and in ways other than those planned by their designers and developers, the change, like the advances themselves, is due to human intervention and ingenuity, albeit at a later stage in the historical process.

What technology does is create conditions offering new opportunities for action liable to be seized and exploited, ignored, resisted, or even rejected. Taking the telegraph as an example, it is undeniable that significant changes took place in the lives of news reporters following the introduction of telegraphic services. But the reason why practices changed was not technological in nature. Changes occurred as a result of commercial decisions and competition between newspapers, just as competition obliged proprietors to upgrade their printing plant in order to produce their paper faster and cheaper (Chalaby, 1998: 43). The contribution of the telegraph consisted in allowing change to take place by making certain things unnecessary. It removed the need for reporters to work through their notes in a shaking train carriage or stagecoach on their return from some important speech or event and it made it unnecessary for newspapers to keep correspondents in important news centres (Smith, 1979: 126). There were clear economic benefits to the new arrangements, and it is this that prompted their implementation. Under different circumstances, with different priorities, as when existing practices are retained in order to avoid redundancies, the new arrangements might not have been put in place. In other words, the advantages of speed, convenience and cost-effectiveness were part and parcel of a particular socio-economic system and they might have been disregarded in a different social, cultural and political context.

This is not to say that ignoring technological advances is without peril. But here too it is incorrect, however tempting, to make technology responsible for the consequences. For instance, despite what some accounts seem to imply, the responsibility for the rapidly diminishing influence of monastic institutions in the sixteenth century does not lie in the invention of printing as such. What put an end to the communities' social and cultural supremacy was their failure to adapt to the new environment and to reconsider their involvement in text copying, binding and the making of pens. Whether at the level of the individual, of groups or of societies, sociocultural change is never the direct outcome of technological progress but is mediated through human agency. The virus that interferes with a computer program was sent by someone, while at a societal level the history of technology shows the importance of the role played by human-based factors such as state control. The spread of technology-enhanced language learning is no exception.

A further problem with the idea that technology determines its own uses and effects is that strictly speaking, it is not technological innovations that have an effect, but their adoption. According to Rogers (1983), what happens to an innovation can be decided in one of three ways:

> (1) *optional innovation-decisions*, choices to adopt or reject an innovation that are made by an individual independent of the decisions of other members of the system, (2) *collective innovation-decisions*, choices to adopt or reject an innovation that are made by consensus among the members of a system, and (3) *authority innovation-decisions*,

> choices to adopt or reject an innovation that are made by relatively few individuals in a system who possess power, status, or technical expertise. (Rogers, 1983: 37)

In order to spread, technological innovations require a receptive environment. In all of the cases above, the perceived attributes of the innovation must bring benefits that are seen as aligned with other social trends and expectations. For example, the case for technology-enhanced language learning has received much impetus from the spread of computer technology outside the classroom and from the new status of computers as household objects. In a technologized world, there is increased pressure to resort to ICT, independently of the inherent merits of the case.

That innovations can only succeed if they fit in with the social matrix is demonstrated by the time it took for the press to take root in China and Japan. Whereas Europe already had flourishing newspapers by the 1750s, the press did not develop in the Far East until the late nineteenth century. Ascribing the delay to the existence of information systems that, unlike those of Europe, did not aim to place local events within a wider context, Smith (1979: 15) concludes:

> The evolution of the press in the Far East, therefore, though it seems at first sight to be an exception, actually bears out a general rule: the newspaper developed interconnectedly throughout the world as a form dependent on printing which emerged from the economic and political conditions of Europe and spread only in so far as those conditions spread to other societies.

Similarly, recent evidence shows that success or failure to bridge the digital divide depends on the ability of projects to consider the special characteristics of the community in which computers are put. An infusion of computers and Internet connections is not of itself sufficient. Without a well-thought-out educational program, installing computers may achieve no more than provide people with a high-tech toy for playing games (Warschauer, 2003).

Rogers (1983: 210–40) goes on to identify five attributes predictive of rate of adoption. They are:

- relative advantage (e.g. perceived as conferring social status)
- compatibility (i.e. perceived as consistent with the existing values, past experiences, and needs of potential adopters)

- triability (i.e. innovation is perceived as one which you can experiment with on a limited basis)
- observability (the degree to which the results are perceived as visible), which are all positively related to the rate of adoption, and
- complexity (i.e. the innovation is perceived as difficult to understand and use), which is negatively related to adoption.

It is acknowledged, however, that these findings may not be generalizable throughout all societies. Furthermore, the attributes of the device represent only one element in an intricate web of interdependent factors and processes. To the political and social influences referred to above must be added economic considerations, especially when a technology has close, direct competitors. Whatever its appeal, an innovation is unlikely to spread unless correctly priced. Thus, the popularity of the short message service (SMS) in Britain is arguably due at least as much to its affordability as to its convenience. This also makes it quite attractive as a potential educational tool, a topic which is given further consideration in Chapter 6.

Technological innovations are undoubtedly instrumental in ushering in change. Without the telegraph, reporters would have gone on travelling up and down the country. They would probably have done so at increasingly greater speed and in increasingly greater comfort, but they would have had to continue to travel. The telegraph made it possible for them to stop. It did not cause change to occur; it merely provided the potential for change. Rather than actively causing change, technology acts as a trigger or as a catalyst: 'At [...] moments of transformation, the impulse, often very powerful, can be technological, but what saves the process from determinism is that thousands of small and particular choices are made by individuals and institutions to channel that force to shape society and its institutions' (O'Donnell, 1996: 39–40).

Myth number two: the changes brought by technology are inevitable

It follows from what has just been said that there is nothing inevitable about the changes brought about by technology. They may be presented as automatic by promoters of technology, but if the effects of technology depend on the rest of the social matrix, they cannot constitute the ineluctable consequences of intrinsic technological features.

The invention of the printing press provides a good illustration of this:

> Let me begin by underscoring the fact that the historical record makes unquestionably clear that the most distinctive features of what we have come to refer to as 'print culture' – that is, the stabilization of written culture into a canon of authored texts, the notion of the author as creator, the book as property, and the reader as an elective public – *were not* inevitable historical consequences of the invention of printing during the Renaissance, but, rather, the cumulative result of particular social and political choices made by given societies at given moments. (Hesse, 1996: 21)

It might be objected that the changes brought in by technology are inevitable in a broader sense. That is to say, that inevitability does not necessarily imply a one-to-one correlation between technology and certain effects. Rather, that given a particular kind of social matrix, technology will have certain effects. For instance, that in a technologically rich society, language learning is bound to rely on ICT. The problem with this argument is that, besides diluting the concept of inevitability, it is only valid at a macro level. As soon as you go below that macro level, for example to when and how technology is used, differences begin to appear which may not be traceable to a particular source. This takes away the inescapability of the process. In fact, the consequences of technological advances are intrinsically difficult to identify and measure. They are not always evident and open to external scrutiny, they are often confounded with other effects, and they are prone to provoke subjective and value-laden judgements.

Fuelled by the discourse of technophiles and technophobes, the impression of an inevitable process also comes from human beings' difficulty in imagining that events could have unfolded differently from the way they have done. In a paper on the genesis of a case of homosexuality, Freud warns against the danger of perceiving developments as continuous and inevitable when undertaking retrospective analysis:

> So long as we trace the development [of a mental/psychological process] from its final stage backwards, the connection appears continuous, and we feel we have gained an insight which is completely satisfactory or even exhaustive. But if we proceed the reverse way, if we start from the premises inferred from the analysis and try to follow these up to the final result, then we no longer get

> the impression of an inevitable sequence of events which could not be otherwise determined. [...] In other words, from a knowledge of the premises we could not have foretold the nature of the result. (Freud, 1920: 226–7)

Freud goes on to state that we do not know the relative strength of different factors. This only appears at the end, when the strongest win.

Perceptions of the impact of technology are not immune to the fallacy of 20/20 hindsight. Looking backwards, what happened is seen as the only possible sequence of events. Yet, as shown by Pool's study of the predictions made during the early years of telephony, those who witness the introduction of an innovation are often blind to the 'inevitable' changes about to be unleashed. Pool (1983) chronicles how contenders in the telephone business held different views and made opposite prognoses regarding, for example, the likely speed of telephone penetration, or whether or not rural areas needed a special kind of low-cost phone system.

Some forecast uses for the phonograph as part of the telephone system that proved too costly or that were pre-empted by radio. Few had the foresight of Bell, who correctly foresaw long-distance telephone communication as early as 1878. Scepticism about the significance of telephony was widespread, not least among the officials and engineers of the Western Union who in 1876 told Bell: 'Mr Bell, after careful consideration of your invention, while it is a very interesting novelty, we have come to the conclusion that it has no commercial possibilities' (Allen, 1990). Clarke (1992: 213) tells two anecdotes that show how little sense Bell's contemporaries had of the potential of the telephone and its future social impact. The first is the reaction of William Preece, the chief engineer of the British Post Office, when news of Alexander Graham Bell's invention reached the United Kingdom: '"The Americans," he said loftily, "have need of the telephone – but we do not. We have plenty of messenger boys...."' The second is the prediction made by the mayor of an American city, who thought the telephone a marvellous device: '"I can see the time," he said solemnly, "*when every city will have one*."' Similarly, Dominick (1996: 180) reports that radio was initially regarded as a competitor to the telephone and telegraph industries, adding, tellingly: 'The fact that it was public, that everybody could receive it with the proper equipment, was looked upon as a drawback. No one could quite understand why anybody would want to send messages to a large group of anonymous individuals.' There is a general feeling among language professionals that the introduction of the WWW represents a momentous event for language learning, but the exact nature of the changes that lie in store is far from evident, although they will almost certainly acquire an aura of inevitability once they have taken place.

Admittedly, the fact that IT futurology is a risky business does not constitute evidence that the effects of technology are not inevitable. It is quite possible for incorrect predictions and unforeseen consequences to have been caused not by uncertainty, but by a mix of incompetence and shortage of visionary power, by an inability to take stock of the situation and imagine accurately the shape of things to come. It is hard, nevertheless, to reconcile unpredictability with inevitability, as inevitable events can usually be foretold. Summer follows spring year after year, and barring some awful catastrophe, will continue to do so. Furthermore, inevitable events are impossible to avoid or prevent. This is clearly not true of the effects of technology, which, as implied by the previous section, are open to manipulation, as well as to the influence of social pressures and developments in other fields. This is the reason behind the inclusion of a wild card category in British Telecom's Technology Calendar for 1997–2045. Made up of events that could happen at any time and interfere with predicted developments, it comprised, *inter alia*, stock market crash, life expectancy approaches 100, rise of an American dictator, and asteroid hits earth (Atwell, 1999: 13).

Myth number three: inventions as revolutions

A third feature of technological determinism is the presentation of inventions as revolutionary phenomena. Revolutions are instances of great change that disrupt and contrast with the gentle unfolding of evolutionary processes. They introduce, or seem to introduce, major historical discontinuities. They are both momentous and sudden. Overuse of the term in recent times has led to its losing much of its force. A Google search on 'language learning + revolutionary' will yield dozens of hits, most of them related to software. Even if the majority of these claims, perhaps all, can be safely dismissed as 'hype', there remains an issue about how the term 'revolution' is to be understood in a language learning context. Too often in the past, it has been applied to the introduction of an innovation without specifying the precise nature and scope of the resulting changes. Whatever pedagogical uses it was put to, the language lab 'revolution' could not have changed the whole of language education. It could only affect a small part of what is involved in language learning. This illustrates a tendency found in language education just as much as elsewhere to make excessive claims and generalize on the basis of important, but nevertheless limited effects. This is compounded by focusing on process rather than outcomes, and emphasizing attitudes and feelings over language competence (Knobel et al., 1998: 47).

In addition, the magnitude of the changes introduced by technological advances is often much less great than implied by the term 'revolution'. In portraying innovations as revolutionary, the popular discourse of technological determinism conveys the impression that technological advances introduce radical changes. However, it is common for innovations not only to employ, but to be dependent on, earlier technologies. English computers, for example, make use of the Qwerty keyboard of typewriters. Second, technological developments rarely sweep away what was there before. By and large, they alter what exists rather than kill it. Although there are instances of defunct technologies (e.g. telegrams), as a rule new technologies do not make established technologies obsolete. Rather, they add to the range of opportunities available and provide new contexts of use for the older technologies. As Ong (1967: 88–9) writes: 'The media in their succession do not cancel out one another but build on one another. When man began to write, he did not cease talking. [...] When print was developed, man did not stop writing.' We see this at work in the fallacy of the forecast paperless office, in intertextuality and the synergies between the media (e.g. film of the book, book of the film, etc.), and in the blossoming of multimedia.

Culturally, the effects are often modest at first, with some realignment and reshaping of practices rather than an abrupt break with the past. Witness the conservative content of early printed materials and the gradual disappearance of letter conventions from emails. Many of the changes brought by computer technology are cosmetic, with a great deal of repackaging of ideas that existed before. Nevertheless, the prospect of change tends to arouse fear, as illustrated by the early history of radio. Reith (1924), the first Managing Director of the British Broadcasting Corporation (BBC), documents how the arrival of radio met with opposition from theatre owners, concert givers and managers, who were sufficiently concerned by this new competition to warn artists and conductors that they would be blacklisted should they participate in broadcasting. Newspaper owners too perceived radio as a threat. Because of their concern that news bulletins would deprive them of their readership, licence to broadcast was only given by the Post Office after an assurance had been received that the first bulletin would not be read before 7 p.m. Newspapers have, of course, survived competition from radio. Similarly, television and video have not put an end to cinema going. Rather, the media have come to coexist in a state of complementarity and interdependence, with discussions of films on radio and television increasing cinema attendance, and television advertisements and cinema trailers promoting the sale of video cassettes. This symbiosis was anticipated by Reith (1924: 111–12), who, while acknowledging that radio would alter the position of newspapers, saw news bulletins as likely to push up sales: 'Suppose a speech of first-rate importance on some vital and highly controversial subject is delivered. [...] The whole country can hear it, and hear it direct from the lips of the exponent. People realize that it is something out of the ordinary, and they expect to see it reproduced, amplified, commented upon, in their newspapers.'

As far as speed is concerned, the tendency to focus on the consequences rather than the genesis of inventions leads to underestimate the time span over which an innovation has been developed. Upon inspection, many so-called technological revolutions turn out to result from the coming together of a number of factors and discoveries that have been at work or developing for some time and that coalesce to produce a leap forward. If they seem to appear out of nothing, it is because their origins receive little attention and precursory signs are ignored. In fact, the way has been prepared by the prevailing conditions. In a fascinating chronicle of the history of the development of new media, Winston (1998) shows that technological ideas are grounded in scientific knowledge and that inventions are the results of a long evolution. The process starts with someone getting an idea, formulating the problems involved, and thinking of a solution. But it may take more than a decade before a device is built: 'A German thought of the telegraph in the last years of the 18th century, three decades before the first working device. A Frenchman hypothesized the telephone in 1854, more than 20 years before Bell' (Winston, 1998: 5). 'Ideation' as Winston calls this stage, leads to the building of prototypes, and if prototypes meet favourable social factors, they undergo further refinements and are transformed into 'inventions', moving out of the laboratory into the world at large. The long gestation period explains why it is common for inventions to occur simultaneously in a number of places, as exemplified by the history of the telephone, with Bell and his rival Gray filing patents for a speaking electric telephone on the same day in 1876. Gestation is something that takes place away from the gaze of the general public, which often only becomes aware of the new machine at the very end of the process, when confronted with the finished product in the marketplace. It is easy to see how, in the absence of information, there may be a propensity to underestimate development time. The result is a distorted view of the history of technology favourable to the adoption of a revolutionary model.

It is not only the developmental phase that finds itself shortened in people's perception of inventions. The speed of the resulting changes also tends to be exaggerated. It is commonly said, for example, that Gutenberg's invention caused a revolution. It is certainly true that the printing press represents an extremely significant landmark in the history of ITC, but it took centuries for its effects to become widespread. In fact, as Haas (1996) underlines, it was not until the advent of the steam press in the first half of the nineteenth century, that is to say, over three centuries later, that the development initiated by Gutenberg began to have a substantial impact on the mass of the population. Briggs (1977: 46) makes a similar point in relation to the telephone: 'Just as the great inventions of the late eighteenth century transformed factory production only in the nineteenth century, so the inventions of the late nineteenth century transformed home life styles only in the twentieth century.' In addition, as exemplified by the case of print, inventions often undergo some significant improvements before reaching a mass audience. Unless accompanied by a change in terminology (e.g. mobile rather than telephone), these improvements will often be overlooked so that the introduction of the original invention will be credited with effects that are connected with subsequent developments. In this respect, and without denying that it is difficult nowadays to imagine language teaching without recordings, one may question whether it is justified to talk of a 'tape recording revolution' (Green, 1996), given the many refinements that have been made to recording devices.

Changes sometimes appear novel and unique when they are not, because antecedents and parallels have been ignored. The World Wide Web is a case in point. Winston (1998: 243) is one of many to underline that the idea of interconnectivity has been around for a long time. Similarly, the impact of the Internet is not without precedents. The way in which it has shrunk the world has a parallel in the effect that the telegraph had on Victorian society, providing coverage of the Crimean War in the 1850s and instant news of the eruption of Krakatoa in 1883. As Standage observes:

> Today, we are repeatedly told that we are in the midst of a communications revolution. But the electric telegraph was, in many ways, far more disconcerting for the inhabitants of the time than today's

> advances are for us. If any generation has the right to claim that it bore the full bewildering, world-shrinking brunt of such a revolution, it is not us – it is our nineteenth-century forebears. (Standage, 1998: 199–200)

Until the invention of the telegraph, sending information quickly over distances greater than the range of the human voice (1 or 2 kilometres) involved the use of signals such as puffs of smoke during the day and beacon fires at night, or the use of flags or semaphores. As well as depending on good weather, the first two options were restricted to prearranged messages (like the 'we've got a Pope' indicating a successful outcome in papal elections). Signalling by flags or lamps gave more possibilities, but was limited in range and content and, again, required good visibility. Complex information could only be transmitted by carrying messages physically, which took time. What was truly groundbreaking about telegraph technology was that 'it permitted for the first time the effective separation of communication from transportation' (Carey, 1989: 203). The difference made by the telegraph became dramatic after the laying down of submarine cable networks: 'Up to the 1830s, a letter posted in England took five to eight months to reach India; and due to monsoons in the Indian Ocean, it could take two years for a reply to be received. In the 1870s, a telegram could reach Bombay in five hours, and the answer could be back on the same day' (Thompson, 1995: 154).

The ability to communicate swiftly over long distances had many social and cultural consequences. It meant that news about the price of commodities could spread quickly so that prices no longer depended on local factors of supply and demand but responded to national and international forces. It facilitated the establishment of standard time zones. It enhanced the coordination of military, especially naval, operations and it contributed to the strengthening of imperialism, helping 'the transition from colonialism, where power and authority rested with the domestic governor, to imperialism, where power and authority were reabsorbed by the imperial capital' (Carey, 1989: 212). More importantly from the perspective of this book, the telegraph impacted on news distribution, practices and forms. It introduced a concern to be the first to report an event and the use of non-chronological formats (Bell, 1996: 3). This trend represents a major feature of the cultural environment in which languages are used and learnt in contemporary society and as such has the potential to affect what is taught.

An inherently complex situation

In overemphasizing the part played by technological artefacts in the evolution of society, technological determinism is guilty of reductionism and reification. What is a complex web of subtle interrelationships is reduced to simple causal links. Given the importance that machines have come to assume in everyday life, the impression of technology-led changes is understandable, but no less deceptive for being so. While it is true that innovations can spark or fuel change, they do not account for change or guarantee it (Kaufer and Carley, 1993: 99). Whether the seeds of change that innovations contain will develop and grow to produce change depends on the terrain. For a proper assessment of the role of innovations to be made, they must be placed within the sociocultural landscape of the time. Specifically, an understanding of how ICT affects communication can only develop by locating advances within the social, cultural and political context, which, together with technological conditions (the set of available technologies and their distribution in a society), makes up the context of any communication. A context that is dynamic and in constant evolution.

In the face of the controversy surrounding the role of technology, Misa argues that the degree of stress laid on technological change in historical interpretations depends on the level of the research: 'Machines make history when historians and other analysts adopt a "macro" perspective, whereas a causal role for the machine is not present and is not possible for analysts who adopt a "micro" perspective' (Misa, 1994: 117). However, while the micro level avoids the danger of determinism, it tends to be overcomplex and messy. Consequently, Misa advocates a middle-level methodology focusing on institutions and organizations. In a similar vein, Marvyn argues that:

> The early history of electric media is less the evolution of technical efficiencies in communication than a series of arenas for negotiating issues crucial to the conduct of social life; among them, who is inside and outside, who may speak, who may not, and who has authority and may be believed. Changes in the speed, capacity, and performance of communications devices tell us little about these questions. (Marvyn, 1988: 4)

Chief among the organizations with a say in decision-making is the government. History abounds in examples of how state intervention can accelerate or suffocate developments. Many countries, for instance, took a raft of measures in the first phase of the history of the press to bring printing under state control. In Britain, a limit was placed on the number of master printers and a 'surveyor of the press' with power to pursue unlicensed works was appointed. The common desire to maintain a firm grip on print manifested itself in different ways, with individual countries taking diverse positions regarding what could be printed, especially when religious publications were concerned. Catholic countries took a strict line. Bibles in the vernacular were rarely sponsored by Catholic rulers and their publication could lead to persecution and imprisonment. In contrast, Protestant monarchs not only allowed vernacular versions of the Bible, but they sometimes commissioned them. King Christian II of Denmark (1481–1559) ordered the first translation of the New Testament into Danish after his conversion to Lutheranism and James I of England gave instructions for the official translation of the Bible into English that bears his name.

Instead of, or as well as, having recourse to direct legislation, political elites can take economic measures such as the imposition or abolition of taxes to support or restrict developments. Thus the abolition in 1855 of the stamp duty on British newspapers after a vigorous campaign against what was regarded as a tax on knowledge led to an increase in circulation for existing papers and was followed by an upward leap in the number of newspapers. A recent example of direct state intervention with significant consequences for communication is the government support given to the French electronic network Minitel through the offer of a free terminal to every French household. Launched in 1982, Minitel provided online access to a number of services (phone directory, mail-order transactions, train ticket purchases, etc.) and became very popular. However, its success was arguably double edged. While it had the advantage of getting the French used to online services, it also delayed the deployment of the Internet in France. The education sector is another frequent candidate for governmental intervention, with, for example, the offer of incentives to promote the computerization of education. In the UK, what had begun as sporadic grass-roots initiatives in the late 1970s and early 1980s was taken over by central government, with state intervention moving from a strategy of influence (schemes and subsidies) to a strategy of control (introduction of the National Curriculum, inclusion of information technology as a component part of all foundation subjects). According to Boyd-Barrett (1990: 4), 'No other educational technology, save perhaps the book, has been the object of so much political concern.'

While political elites and official circles are in a position to support or thwart developments, the fate of an innovation and its societal effects are subject to a multitude of other influences. The sociocultural landscape is too variable and multifaceted to be described exhaustively. But to take an example, the societal influence of print involved factors as diverse as the cost of paper and production, government policy, the development of distribution systems, pricing, taxes, ease of borrowing or buying books, the amount of leisure time, and the value put on literacy.

With so many contributory factors the part played by technology and its impact are bound to vary, not only from one innovation to another, but also across different environments. Hence the variations observed in the take-up and use of specific technologies in different countries and the creation of different cultures of use. By the same token, the involvement of so many interdependent factors will produce variations in the pace of change. As noted above, change is often progressive and incremental, gathering momentum through a cumulative process. Irrespective of its importance, the invention of the moveable type press was only a first step. It would take further technical improvements and the conjunction of certain social trends before the printing press really impacted on society. But change can also be rapid and striking, if several mutually enhancing developments happen to coincide. Thus, for Graddol (1996: 206), 'The key to understanding the impact of the telegraph and how English grew up around it as the global lingua franca for trade, international news and technology itself lies in simultaneous and related developments in the political, technological and economic spheres.' The current situation is another example of convergence between trends, with the coming together of social, political, economic and cultural factors and representational, communicational and technological developments (Kress, 1998: 54).

As well as being compounded with other influences, the effects of an innovation may not be easily observable or felt, making them difficult to measure. Such is the case with the long-term cognitive outcomes of educational applications, hence the scarcity of reliable evaluation studies. Moreover, judgements concerning consequences are inevitably made against one's frame of reference, and as such largely subjective. Thus, as Kress (1998) points out, the characteristics of email language (e.g. greater informality) can be interpreted in various ways. Giving priority to technology, they will be explained in terms of speedy communication. Whereas if one gives priority to the social, email is seen as producing new relations involving greater proximity with one's interlocutors. This greater proximity then promotes the reshaping of language in the direction of speech-like forms. If, however, technology is viewed as enhancing and reflecting linguistic and social change, rather than precipitating it, email language will be presented as part of a general tendency towards less edited and more personal forms of writing (Baron, 2003: 88).

Although technology does not dictate the future, technological artefacts cannot be considered to be neutral. It is not the case that they offer an open range of possibilities for action. Rather, they possess a set of affordances, that is to say they have an inherent potential, that allows, or even encourages, certain types of action and at the same time sets limits on what can be done (Hutchby, 2001: 26–33). Notwithstanding this inherent bias, it is possible for the potential of innovations to remain unexploited. On the other hand, as demonstrated by the use of the short message service (SMS), ingenuity may successfully circumvent the shortcomings of an artefact. In education, affordances point to certain pedagogical applications rather than others. To the extent that different media possess distinct, albeit often overlapping sets of affordances, they will permit or hamper different kinds of applications. But this does not mean they must be used in a particular fully predetermined way. Moreover, neither their affordances nor the pedagogical applications for which these pave the way will necessarily be perceived instantly.

It follows that, in the words of Castells (1996: 5), 'technology does not determine society. Neither does society script the course of technological change, since many factors, including individual inventiveness and entrepreneurialism, intervene in the process of scientific discovery, technological innovation, and social applications, so that the final outcome depends on a complex pattern of interaction.' Similarly, within the relatively new field of social informatics, the study of ICT in social, cultural and institutional contexts, ICT is considered as equally important as human social factors, with which it meshes and interacts to shape developments. While the ways in which technological artefacts are used are shaped by their affordances, there is no compulsion for them to be used in these ways and lead to certain pedagogical applications. The study of the impact of technological progress on communication, language, education and language learning undertaken in the next chapters should not therefore be taken as implying that the consequences under discussion were the necessary and inevitable effects of the innovations that preceded them. In fact, it will be seen that significant events were often the result of the confluence of several developments, social and intellectual as well as technological. My aim is only to document and shed light on an aspect of the evolution of society that, as yet, has received little attention, but that can contribute to making more informed decisions in the use of ICT in language learning.

Outline of the book

The remaining chapters in this book fall into three groups, with Chapters 2 and 3 outlining the changing context of language learning through a discussion of relevant aspects of the embedding of technology in daily life, while Chapters 4 and 5 focus on education, and Chapter 6 presents a case study of the telephone.

Chapter 2 considers the impact of ICT on communication. Following a brief review of the evolution of means of communication, most of the chapter is devoted to the analysis of key components and dimensions of communication, and their significance for language users. Attention then turns to the ways in which people communicate in modern society and their use of the media. The chapter ends with a discussion of the relevance of communication patterns.

The focus in Chapter 3 is on language itself, with a discussion of the contribution that ICT makes to language change and language spread. Questioning the view that language change takes place exclusively through accommodation during face-to-face interaction, I outline how ICT relates to external factors affecting language change, and argue for a finer analysis of the interrelationship between ICT, language variation and language change based on the notion of levels of causality. I then proceed to examine a range of linguistic innovations that suggest that it is possible for the media to be a contributory factor in certain circumstances. This is followed by a discussion of the part of ICT in language spread. The chapter concludes with an assessment of the implications for second language (L2) users and language learners.

Chapter 4 approaches the evolutionary dimension of the intersection of ICT with language learning from an applied perspective, in terms of the influence of ICT on education. As the chapter progresses, the focus narrows from general matters such as the part played by technology in the emergence of new educational paradigms, and the interface between technology and the teacher's role, to specific issues such as the effect of technological innovations on the conceptualization of literacy.

With Chapter 5, the discussion closes in on language learning. Consideration is given first to the influence of ICT on language learning motivation and goals, and then to the interrelationship between media use and methodology across the ages. The chapter then explores the use of educational technology in foreign language education, including the affordances of contemporary media and the aspects of language competence that they best address.

Chapter 6 brings together the various strands of the previous chapters with a case study of the telephone, a technology that not only has a comparatively long history, but shares in the rapidly developing interest in the use of mobile technologies in language learning.

2
ICT and Communication

Introduction

In this, the first of two chapters on the context of language learning, I consider the impact of ICT on communication. I begin by outlining how technological features affect communication variables and then discuss some relevant aspects of communication in everyday life.

It is not uncommon to overlook the ease with which human beings adapt to transformations in the communication landscape. Over recent decades, technological advances have introduced means of communication that not so many years before belonged to the realm of science fiction. Gradually, despite the fact that change involves the acquisition of new knowledge and skills, many people have succeeded in integrating new communication patterns and processes into their daily life. They now routinely make use of email, mobile phones and the World Wide Web (to quote only three examples) to communicate with others or look for information. It is only when you pause to consider how different current practices are from the situation 20 or 30 years ago, that you fully appreciate the number and extent of the changes that have taken place in the manner, range and scope of social interactions, and human beings' remarkable ability to alter their communicative behaviour in response to new conditions.

As communication patterns evolve, so do the abilities required by L2 users and learners. However, the evolution of communication is something that language education still has to engage with fully. The profession has embraced technological and social developments to the extent of making use of the media as teaching and learning tools and promoting a limited set of authentic applications such as email exchanges. Communication skills have been included among the key skills that formal education has been charged to develop. But, with a few exceptions such as Little (1998), Warschauer and Healey (1998) and Chapelle (2003), little attention has been given by applied linguists and foreign language teachers to what communication entails in contemporary society, and to the implications of changing communication patterns for the conceptualization of communicative competence.

When the concept of communicative competence first rose to prominence in the 1970s, interactions with the L2 community were largely confined to written correspondence and to face-to-face transactions in the course of trips abroad. In line with Hymes's original formulation, which defined communicative competence as 'competence as to when to speak, when not, what to talk about with whom, when, where, in what manner' (Hymes, 1972: 277), face-to-face interactions provided the basis which the concept was predicated on. The new emphasis on communication brought about a paradigm shift in language teaching which has served the subject well, but in recent years thinking has failed to take sufficient notice of developments in the world around. Communicative competence theory has ceased to be societally grounded in that it no longer reflects the events and practices of communication in today's society, where communicative effectiveness goes far beyond the ability to handle conversations and conventional written texts.

In a text published a decade ago, Little writes:

> In the very near future we shall need to ask ourselves to what extent we can still talk of second language learning taking place at a distance from the target language community; and we shall also need to consider whether the capacity to interact with and via information systems should be included as a routine part of the behavioural repertoire towards which many, perhaps most, second language learners should aspire. (Little, 1996: 211)

Today, the very near future that Little refers to no longer lies in the future. As underscored by the Common European Framework's suggestion that 'users of the Framework may wish to consider and where appropriate state: which media the learner will need/be equipped/be required to handle a) receptively b) productively c) interactively d) in mediation' (Council of Europe, 2001: 95), it is not possible to continue to ignore the technologization of everyday communication and the commonplace nature of transnational communication.

Several things are needed. To begin with, we must have a more comprehensive definition of communicative competence on the lines proposed by Savignon (1983: 303), who describes communication competence as 'functional language proficiency; the expression, interpretation, and negotiation of meaning involving interaction between one or more persons belonging to the same (or different) speech community (communities), or between one person and a written or oral text'. Next, we need more information on the nature of the capacity that underpins the use of different media, both in general, and from the particular perspective of the L2 user. Although the emergence of new forms of communication seldom poses serious challenges to expert users of a language, it should not be taken for granted that the same applies to less expert users. Witness the fact that, unlike literate native speakers, L2 users seldom deal with similar oral and written texts with equal ease. If the purpose of language learning is to develop the ability to use language in a way that approximates the way language is experienced in the real world, we need to know how technology affects communication processes. For example, what are the particular conditions and constraints associated with a given media? Are they unique to this media or are they shared with other media? How do they impact on participants? Do they make the participants' tasks as receivers or producers of language more difficult than in face-to-face or less difficult? What implications are there, if any, for less proficient language users? We also need to build a picture of current communication practices. What use is made of the opportunities offered by new communication environments? What patterns of communication do people actually enter in on a day-to-day basis and for what purposes? What place do face-to-face interaction and mediated communication occupy in people's lives and relationships? How is this affected by the ability to communicate in more than one language?

The aim of this chapter is to shed light on such questions by bringing in relevant findings by scholars with germane interests. Communication is a popular study topic. According to the *Encyclopaedia Britannica*, it has attracted the attention of specialists in some 40 disciplines, from psychologists, to social scientists, to mathematicians and engineers. Inevitably, this level of interest has led to the development of different concepts and analyses of communication, making the term a slippery one. From this wealth of approaches, I pick out a number of descriptions and findings that seem to have particular significance for language learning, focusing on those aspects considered to be most pertinent. After a brief overview of the evolution of means of communication, I explore three key components of communication systems: the channel by which information is conveyed, the source of the message and the receiver. To avoid the ephemerality of an analysis based on the media themselves at a time of rapid changes and increasing convergence, communication is analysed in terms of a set of five parameters applicable to all communications: space coordinates, time coordinates, range of symbolic cues, interactivity and action orientation. Attentions then shifts from the communication process to the forms assumed by communication in contemporary society. Having sketched out a broad picture of media use, I consider the potential effect of established or incipient bilingualism. Lastly, all the threads are brought together in a general discussion of pedagogical implications.

Evolution of means of communication

There are grounds for claiming that, taking a bird's-eye view, one of the most striking aspects of the evolution of means of communication is the increasing pace of technological advances. Whereas four centuries separate the invention of the printing press from that of the telegraph, the telegraph, the telephone, radio, film, television and computer technology have all been developed within 150 years. Clarke (1992: 20) underlines that on her accession to the throne in 1837, Queen Victoria relied on the same means of sending messages to the outlying parts of her empire as Julius Caesar. She had no faster means of transport than galloping horses and sailing ships. Yet, in a relatively short space of time, electricity was to transform communication by doing away with 'the ancient barriers of time and distance', with first, the introduction of the telegraph and Morse code in the 1840s, and then the invention of the telephone in 1876. Motion pictures started being shown to paying audiences in the 1890s, while the first public radio broadcasting station opened in Pittsburgh in 1922. Regular TV transmissions date back to the 1930s. Further landmarks include the laying of the first submarine telephone cable in 1956, the launching into orbit of the first efficient civil telecommunications satellite, Telstar, in 1962, and the use of lightwave or fibre optic communication from 1977.

Following Rogers (1986), the chronology of human communication may be divided into four eras: writing, printing, telecommunication and interactive communication, with telecommunication covering one-way, one-to-many mass media like radio, film and television, as well as one-to-one media such as the telegraph and the telephone, whereas interactive communication refers to newer developments with two main characteristics: some degree of interactivity resembling a two-person, face-to-face conversation, and the ability to exchange a special message with each individual in a large audience. How to encapsulate the essence of such a diversified field is the subject of the next sections.

Communication as a system

One of the earliest and most famous attempts to capture the fundamentals of communication was what has become known as the Lasswell formula. According to Lasswell (1960: 117 (1948)), communication can be described by answering the following question: 'Who, says What, in Which Channel, to Whom, with What effect?' In other words, communication involves a communicator, a message, a channel, a receiver, and has an effect. In the humanities, an influential model has been Shannon and Weaver's (1949) schematization of the communication process as a system consisting of five discrete parts: an information source, which produces a message, a transmitter (encoder), a channel, a receiver (decoder), and a destination (the person or thing for whom the message is intended). Reference should also be made to Saussure's (1972: 27 (1916)) 'speech circuit', in which two people are shown linked by dotted lines representing sound waves. As the complexities of communication have become better understood, the number of components has tended to increase. Jakobson's (2000 (1960)) model of speech events has six factors, while Hymes (1972 (1964)) has eight, as does Dominick (1996). The subdivisions and names vary according to the perspective from which communication is approached. Dominick's model, for instance, comprises a source, a process of encoding, a message, a channel, a process of decoding, a receiver, the potential for feedback, and the chance of noise.

Transmission models such as Lasswell's, and Shannon and Weaver's, have been shown to have a variety of shortcomings (Chandler, 1994), notably the fact that they are based on a simplistic conduit metaphor. But whether communication is viewed as a process by which a source sends a message to a destination on whom it has an effect, or as a negotiation and exchange of meanings involving diverse interactions, it is useful for analytical purposes to isolate certain key elements without which communication cannot occur. This is not to deny the dynamism and fluidity of communication, and the interdependence of the various component parts. As will become clear, the elements discussed below are actually intertwined and do not operate independently. They have been selected, and are focused on here, because they are essential to communication and have special significance in an L2 context.

Channel

General observations

Terminology is a constant problem in the communication literature and the range of terms employed to refer to the way in which a message travels from sender to receiver is a good illustration. In common with a number of scholars, Shannon and Weaver use the term 'channel', which they define as the medium used to transmit the signal from transmitter to receiver. Other scholars use mode for this, but medium/media is also used. In general, channel tends to be found in texts oriented towards engineering, and to refer to physical instantiations (e.g. light waves), whereas mode occurs more in texts concerned with meaning and semiotics, and has to do with sensory activity (e.g. sight). Nevertheless, one finds numerous references to 'the visual channel', in addition to uses such as 'television channel'. As for medium, this is used with a variety of meanings, ranging from the generic meaning of an intervening substance to more specialized uses as in 'mass media'. To add to the complexity, mode is sometimes used (e.g. in Kress and Van Leeuwen, 2001) to denote a specific kind of meaning making (e.g. speech, music, sounds), rather than what addresses a sense organ. This is the meaning with which mode is used here. However, to try and avoid confusion, I do not follow Kress and Van Leeuwen's practice of calling the means by which the message presents itself to the receiver media, preferring to reserve the term for technical media such as radio and print. For what addresses a particular sense, I copy French practice and use channel (French *canalité*). This leads to the making of a distinction between multichannel and multimodality, with multimodality regarded not in terms of channels, but of codes (Fowler, 2000: 31).

Of our five senses, the most commonly resorted to in human communication are hearing, sight and touch. Smell and taste are mostly exploited for obtaining information about the world. Where impairment precludes the use of a particular channel, communication occurs via other channels: sign language relies on sight, while Braille uses touch. One important feature of human communication is that it is generally multichannel. This has always been the case, since the use of more than one channel is a characteristic of face-to-face interaction, which, despite the rise of mediated communication, remains the primary mode of communication. Not only because of its earlier occurrence both biographically (as infants we learn to combine communication by touch, sight and sound) and historically (face-to-face communication preceded other forms of communication by thousands of years in the history of mankind), but because face-to-face is the form of communication that people turn to when faced with crucial tasks (Boden and Molotch, 1994: 258).

The fact that communication tends to be multichannel does not mean that the contributions of the various channels and modes involved in a given interaction are of equal importance. In face-to-face, most of the information typically comes from the auditory channel, via speech, even if we occasionally give priority to the visual, as when we infer from someone's glum expression that they are not telling the truth when claiming that they are fine. This leads to concepts such as 'oral culture' and 'primary orality', to denote cultures where the auditory/vocal channel plays a major role in the transmission of knowledge. 'Primary orality' implies 'a culture totally untouched by any knowledge of writing or print [...] by contrast with the "secondary orality" of present-day high-technology culture, in which a new orality is sustained by telephone, radio, television, and other electronic devices that depend for their existence and functioning on writing and print' (Ong, 1982: 11). In the context of this book, the existence of multichannel and/or multimodal communication (since different modes may be transmitted through the same channel or through different channels) raises a number of interrelated questions. For instance, what are the essential differences between the channels? What are the semiotic potentials of each channel and mode? What does each channel or mode do best? Which makes for more effective communication?

Distinctive characteristics of particular channels and modes

One major difference between the channels lies in the way they are organized. Thus the sequential, temporal organization of sound contrasts with the simultaneous, spatial organization of the visual. This makes the visual vastly more efficient for carrying and processing large amounts of information (Kress, 1998: 55), although the increase in efficiency varies with the mode that is used. For instance, owing to its intrinsic linearity, written language does not convey information with the same efficiency as pictures or diagrams.

The relative inefficiency of the written language comes to the fore when ordering certain items via the Internet. Finding out what cheeses are available in a supermarket only requires a quick glance at a cheese counter or at the appropriate shelf. Internet ordering, by contrast, currently involves wading through a long list of products, besides giving no information on texture, freshness, etc. It should be mentioned at this point that it is not uncommon for the graphic properties of the written language to be overlooked, and a spurious contrast to be set up between the written and the visual, as if written language was not perceived visually. Such is the case when the term 'visual' is used as shorthand to refer to non-linguistic pictorial uses of the visual channel, which ignores the fact that both sign language and writing are apprehended through sight, and are therefore visual.

It is undeniable that some channels and modes are more suited to the expression of certain meanings than others. Instrumental music, for instance, lends itself better to the communication of feelings than to the communication of facts. In a similar way, there are times when, as the saying goes, a picture is worth a thousand words. Lemke illustrates this as follows: 'You cannot readily describe in words the shape of a draped bolt of fabric, but you can gesture that shape and you can draw it (if you have the necessary skills)' (Lemke, 1998: 291). The reason why gestures and pictures are better suited to conveying shapes lies in their superiority at conveying differences of degree. Language, on the other hand, operates mainly by classifying things into mutually exclusive categories.

But there is more to the consequences of the organization of different channels and modes than this opposition between analogue/unsegmented and digital/segmented representations. For instance, as a temporally, sequentially organized mode, speech lends itself to the representation of sequences of actions and events that can be arranged as a narrative. In other words, the inherent logic of speech is to orient us towards things that happen and the order in which they happen. By contrast, the spatial and simultaneous organization of the visual means that it is inherently suited to the display of salient coexistent elements in the world (e.g. objects, people) and the spatial relations between them (Kress, 1998: 68–9).

Where verbal, vocal and kinesic or visual resources are available, as in face-to-face interactions, we find them making different kinds of contribution, described by Schneller as follows: 'Abstract and logical elements rely mostly on the spoken word; emphases, attitudes, and emotions are mediated mainly by paralanguage and/or facial expressions; the transmission of request and commands, the various stages of greeting, and the regulation of turntaking are commonly performed by gesture' (Schneller, 1988: 154). Once engaged in communication, effectiveness depends on the exploitation and combination of the specific semiotic opportunities offered by the channels and modes available, as when we use gestures and facial expressions that reinforce, illustrate or specify the verbal message. However, effective and efficient communication also requires the correct decision to be made earlier on, when selecting how to communicate (assuming there is a choice). Unfortunately, at this earlier stage, semiotic potentials often have to compete with factors such as cost and convenience. In some cases, semiotic potentials may not even be considered. Yet certain messages are clearly better served by some modes than by others. It may be tempting to send an email to a colleague rather than go down to the end of the corridor to speak to them, but emailing may diminish the effectiveness of our communication, or lead to unnecessary friction if we are conveying criticism. Because 'this is the fourth time I have asked for this information' can be modulated in face-to-face interaction in a way it cannot be in written form, it is less liable to provoke hostility when delivered orally. It is also more likely to get you what you want. Within the realm of education, as Halliday (1994: 71) points out, experienced teachers know that some things are more effectively learnt through talk, while others are probably best presented in writing, and they juggle the modes or mix them. Science teachers, for example, will often write formulae on the whiteboard while simultaneously reading them aloud and adding some oral comments that combine to create a multifunctional discourse (Royis and Parpette, 2000).

ICT and the relative position of language

Among the effects that ICT has had on human communication patterns over the past 6000 years are shifts in the balance between different communication channels and modes. The first major shift occurred with writing, which, according to Ong (1982: 81–2), 'initiated what print and computers only continue, the reduction of dynamic sound to quiescent space, the separation of the word from the living present, where alone spoken words can exist'. The introduction of the telephone at the end of the nineteenth century and the subsequent diffusion of radio brought in a shift in the other direction, towards oral communication. The effect of the next major innovations was to be more ambiguous. Superficially film and television would seem to have caused the pendulum to swing back towards the visual. But both media are also heavily dependent on sound, especially speech. This can be seen in the demise of silent films and the poor relation status of subtitles, with many productions being dubbed rather than subtitled. It is also evidenced by the high profile of dialogue in low-level soaps, which cannot afford the expensive shots and visual effects of more upmarket series. Meanwhile, radio plays live on, despite the absence of visual input. Similarly, computers seemed, at first, to usher in a return to the visual and the written, but technological advances have expanded the range of what is feasible, not only visually, but also through sound.

As the balance between communication modes changes, so does the position of language. To take a simple example, it is possible to learn to dance by following written descriptions of the steps involved. But it is much easier to do so with diagrams that illustrate the various positions. Demonstration videos showing the steps in slow motion, as well as at normal speed, make life even easier. By enhancing the meaning potential of the visual, film increases the representational superiority that pictures have over words to encompass not only position and postures, but also movements and gestures. As long as pictorial representations require expensive equipment or special skills, their superiority in certain domains poses no real threat to the supremacy of verbal communication. With the rise of computer graphics, video and animation, this is no longer the case.

The growing importance of pictures in today's society is sometimes viewed with concern, just as fears have long been expressed in certain circles over the possible adverse effects of cartoons, the amount of space allocated to photographs in the popular press, and the supposedly pernicious impact of television. But it has also been welcome as a development liable to redress what is regarded as an unfortunate bias towards the written language with a dampening effect on some human potentials (Kress, 1998: 75). What is incontestable is that the rise of pictorial representations is challenging the pre-eminent position of language and altering the relationship between language and pictures. As such, it is a development that is bound to affect language learning.

The influence of technological conditions on the ups and downs of individual channels and modes can be seen in the education world, where the work now produced by students is visually far superior to the assignments handed in by their predecessors. Not that improvements are wholly attributable to the existence of better materials and facilities. They are partly due to a growing awareness of the communicative benefits arising from the use of colour, careful layout, and other means of enhancing aesthetic appearance, awareness which in turn derives from, and contributes to, the growing attention paid to the visual. As seen in the last chapter, and as argued by Bolter (1996: 254), it is impossible to separate technological constraints and social construction. While it is true that the affordances of a technology both impose limitations on its uses and pave the way for certain applications, there are still many different choices open to each culture or group.

To take print as an example, there is more to the ascendancy of verbal texts in early printed books than the inability of the printing press to deliver the magnificent, colourful, richly adorned designs produced by scribes and monks. Although the high standard of manuscript illuminations could not be equalled, it was possible to use woodcuts, and, later on, etching, if one wanted to include pictures. Combining type and images was done in some works. Botticelli, for example, produced woodcut illustrations for Dante's *Divine Comedy*. But the integration of pictures made printing more complex and costly. Significantly, the issue was not just a practical and/or financial one. The relegation of pictorial elements also had to do with their function, and with the way they were regarded. Early illuminations had been a critical part of the text, but in the eleventh and twelfth centuries, images became subordinated to the text, with the latter becoming the main conveyor of meaning (Olson, 1994: 112). Apart from being used for disseminating portraits of saints and works of art, picture reproduction became associated with domains whose need for illustrations was paramount, such as herbals and cartography. The relative neglect of the semiotic potential of pictures, after the extensive use that had been made of pictorial communication through stained glass windows and sculptures during the Middle Ages, was part of the intellectual climate of the time. Humanist scholars are said to have snubbed illustrations, regarding them as a means to instruct people who were too ignorant to read the text (Febvre and Martin, 1976: 98). Pictures would acquire a pivotal role with the spread of satirical prints in the seventeenth and eighteenth centuries, as well as in narrative strips and picture stories. But it is only recently that they have been fully rehabilitated, being first given an explanatory, subordinate role, before being acknowledged as having a distinctive, complementary contribution to make to communication.

Comparing science textbooks from 1936 and 1988, Kress (1998) notes that, in 1936, language is the vehicle providing all the information that is judged relevant, and images assume the role of illustrations repeating that information. In 1988, language no longer conveys all the information, and images are used to communicate what the world is like. In other words, there has been 'a move *from the narrative to the display*' (Kress, 1998: 72). Duplication and redundancy have been reduced. Images do not simply take up more space. The meanings they carry are independent from the words in the text and can only be recovered from the images themselves (Gee, 2003: 13). In a similar vein, Clément (2000: 31) observes that stories in digital books are mainly told through pictures, together with a sound track that includes music and noises as well as spoken words.

All this has implications for language and, consequentially, for language learning, which will be considered in subsequent chapters. For the moment, one should note that the distinctive, complementary functions of speech and written language in multimedia products, as highlighted, for instance, by Mochet and O'Neil (2000), require not only familiarity with different types of register, but also the ability to deal with language under both forms. It is not enough to have good reading comprehension skills or good listening comprehension skills. In order to use the products effectively, it is necessary to be able to handle both modes. Not merely because the information is not repeated (unrecorded written texts, recordings unaccompanied by transcripts), but because verbal information is sometimes used as a support for other expression forms. For example, where oral texts fulfil a cohesive function, video images will not form a coherent whole if you do not understand the spoken segments that link them together.

Finally, besides being viewed and exploited differently at different moments in time, semiotic potentials are not used in the same way across all cultures. These fluctuations have implications both for our concept of literacy and for our approach to language learning. Are we to limit our horizons to language as a verbal code, or should we broaden them to encompass non-verbal communication? Since the processing of speech and writing calls for distinct types of skills, should we not take account of the kind of profile that media associated with different modes of communication have in the target community when deciding on the type of practice to be offered to language learners? This is not to say that such considerations should constitute primary criteria, only that they should inform decisions. To probe further into these issues, two other components – source and receiver – need to be examined.

Participant roles: source and receiver

It is easy to identify the source and the receiver in a dyadic situation such as a conversation between two friends: the source is the person currently speaking and the listener is the receiver. But things are not always so simple. People may think that they can tell the source of a newspaper article by the name of the journalist appearing at the top or bottom. If so, they are being deceived by their ignorance of media practices. In fact, the text of articles is frequently the work of many hands. It is likely to have gone through a series of stages involving deletions, additions and other types of alteration by various kinds of editor, to follow an imposed editorial style, and to rely on a limited set of preferred phrases and expressions. There is a sense, of course, in which all language is heteroglot (Bakhtin, 1981: 291), carrying echoes of previous uses, as formulae are recycled, quotes embedded and people parodied. But what we have here is different, in that the composite character of the news is largely the result of deliberate interventions by multiple parties. It confirms that, as argued by, among others, Hymes (1977: 54), Goffman (1981) and Levinson (1988), more categories of participant roles are required than are provided by traditional descriptions.

Although hidden in the case of a newspaper article, the need to decompose the concept of source (or speaker) is clear in the case of a television newsreader looking at a script or an autocue. Outside technologically mediated communication, evidence that the prototype notions of source and receiver each subsume several concepts can be found in those situations in which the speaker or receiver acts as an intermediary, i.e. as a spokesperson or, more generally, as a messenger charged with relaying some information. This is, in a way, not unlike what happens with ICT and the distinction in Shannon and Weaver's model between information source and transmitter, and receiver and destination, or, in Dominick's version and terminology, between source and process of encoding, and process of decoding and receiver.

Goffman (1981: 226) observes that the term 'speaker' is used in three senses. The most common meaning is 'animator', the person who utters the words. A second meaning is 'author', the person who composes the text that is uttered. A third is the meaning of 'principal', the person whose position and belief the words reflect. These roles are conflated in simple situations, but can be distributed over several people. Inspired by his knowledge of news language production, Bell (1991: 37) adds editor to Goffman's list, a modification which exemplifies how the evolution of technology and technological practices may invite us to reconsider and revise existing descriptions. In a news media context, the principal is the person who sets editorial policy, the author generates language, the editor cuts and modifies the language, and the animator is responsible for the phonological/graphological transmission of the message. In some situations, including news production, the four roles may be united in one person, but the subdivision foregrounds the complexities of what happens in any communication. With respect to the receiver, Bell (1991: 91) again recognizes four kinds of role, but in this case the roles are not cumulative. The first is addressee, who is the party known, ratified and addressed by the speaker. Auditor refers to third persons known and ratified, but not addressed. Overhearer designates third parties known to be there, but who are not ratified participants, while eavesdropper applies to parties whose presence is not even known.

Both the participant roles of speaker (or source/addressor) and receiver (or hearer/addressee) and the subcategories they can be broken into can have one or more incumbents simultaneously. Besides the one-to-one encounters of canonical face-to-face, standard telephone calls, faxes, etc., one finds one-to-many, many-to-one and many-to-many. One-to-many occurs when a speaker addresses a group, as is the case with lectures, speeches, sermons, board meetings and, crucially, the mass media. The transmission of messages directed at large audiences is, in fact, a defining characteristic of mass communication, and the enormous importance of the media in our daily lives makes one-to-many a frequent configuration. By contrast, many-to-one is fairly infrequent if 'many' requires concurrent participation, thereby excluding situations in which a source acts on behalf of a group or institution. In spoken interaction, many-to-one implies a chorus. This may be people who have memorized the same text, or are reading a text aloud together, as in the recitation of prayers. Or it may be individuals responding together to a question addressed to them as a group, e.g. 'Anyone know the time?' In written interaction many-to-one implies a degree of collaboration that prevents attributing any section of a message to a single individual. When the audience is a group, many-to-one becomes many-to-many. But many-to-many may also be a new possibility offered by computer mediated communication (CMC), for example mailing lists and bulletin boards, in which everyone can intervene at once and is free to decide what to pay attention to (Quaterman, 1993: 55). By contrast, telephone conference calls only allow one person to speak and be heard at any given time, so that despite appearances, the interaction is actually one-to-many.

Two questions, in particular, arise for language learners and language teachers from participant roles. The first is the relative emphasis to be put on the two roles, including the amount of time and energy to be devoted to the enhancement of skills and abilities specific to each role, e.g. the acquisition of a good pronunciation. It can be argued that there is a tendency in language education to overplay production at the expense of comprehension, in the sense that even when a method allows language learners to delay production until they feel ready, the ultimate goal is still to achieve a certain level of speaking proficiency and, often, writing proficiency. In many cases, receptive skills are not tested separately (e.g. through comprehension questions to be answered in the first language), but form part of assessment formats that also call for productive skills (e.g. comprehension questions to be answered in the target language). Expressive skills, on the other hand, are the subject of independent tests such as essays. In the same way, research tends to concentrate on error analysis or on the use of technology to support production, as illustrated by the number of papers on the impact of word processing on writing.

There are at least three problems with this emphasis on production. First, it runs counter to everyday experience, since people spend more time in the role of receiver than in that of source when exposure to the mass media is factored in. Second, emphasizing production may not accord with the learner's personal objectives. Some people do not wish to become fluent speakers or to write in an L2. Their aim is to develop receptive skills in order to understand the dialogue of a film, the words of a song, or to gain access to works that have not been translated. Third, to lay stress on productive skills fails to take into account that comprehension is less demanding than production, requiring recognition, not recall, and overlooks the potential spread of 'bilingual' interactions, in which each side uses their own language (Hawkins, 1994: 121–2). Language alternation undoubtedly seems strange to monolinguals, but it is commonly found in multilingual settings, as well as in some tandem learning, and as such represents an interesting prospect calling for the fostering of comprehension. I do not mean to imply that language learning should, or ever can, only concern itself with receptive skills. I simply wish to suggest that the latter may not be receiving the right amount of attention.

The other question raised by participant roles, and especially by the practices of media text production mentioned above, relates to assessment procedures. It has already been mentioned that most media texts are collective products. Equally, it is standard practice for the published version of a scholarly text (such as the present book) to incorporate amendments made in the light of comments by readers of earlier drafts. Yet, despite moves towards group work and collaboration, students are often marked on what is supposed to be entirely their own work, and are often only allowed one attempt, at least at university level. It would seem to be in order to devise systems that come closer to what is done in academic and media circles. This may involve allowing students to present more than one version, or to seek advice from others (e.g. peers, native speakers), possibly with the proviso, when the work is to be graded, that interventions are acknowledged and appropriately documented.

Communication characteristics

Introductory comments

Focusing on the components of communication, as I have just done, has the disadvantage of presenting a snapshot frozen in time in which participants are allocated set and separate roles instead of portraying communication as it really is: an ongoing dynamic process between two or more parties. With this in mind, a modified version of the analytical framework proposed in Thompson (1995) is used below as a platform for mapping out the key dimensions of communication as an interactional process. The superiority of Thompson's model over others lies in the fact that it combines simplicity with coverage. It identifies a relatively small number of fundamental variables that can be assessed in terms of their significance for different types of language users. Three modifications are made to Thompson's model. The first consists in splitting Thompson's first parameter, space-time constitution, into two separate variables: space coordinates and time coordinates. This is done on the grounds that the two parameters, while having similar values in the canonical communication situation, are actually independent variables, since co-temporality does not require or imply co-presence. The second modification is the integration of participant roles, which is designed to bring to the fore the often different effects that the variables have on the source and the receiver, a point of crucial importance for L2 users. This is also the motivation behind the third modification: the replacement of dialogical/monological with the construct of interactivity, which covers feedback as well as reciprocity.

Space coordinates

It has become commonplace since McLuhan's (1964) seminal publication to regard the media as extensions of the senses. The media enable people to hear without being within earshot, and to see beyond their field of vision. They emancipate human beings from what with hindsight appears as constraints, but was probably unquestioned at the time, and accepted as part of the ordinary framing of everyday life.

One of the main differences between face-to-face and mediated communication is that whereas the former takes place in a shared spatial and temporal context, the media allow the context of production and the context of reception to be separated. As a result, communication can stretch across both time and space. As indicated above, the two disjunctions do not necessarily go together. Spatial separation can occur without a time gap between production and reception, while temporal separation does not preclude production and reception from taking place in the same location. Telephone calls are typical illustrations of the first scenario, leaving a note on a pad for someone to read exemplifies the second.

Although the notion of separation implies a pair of mutually exclusive alternatives (a context that is shared or one that is not), it also introduces the idea of distance, which is not a binary choice but a matter of degree. Spatial separation may involve distances of thousands of kilometres, but it also covers cases in which production and reception take place in close proximity, such as two adjacent rooms. The absence or presence of a shared context has consequences for language use, for example the use and interpretation of deictic expressions (e.g. 'here'). However, the main consideration from a language point of view is the distance between the two contexts. Contrary to McLuhan's claim about the abolition of time and space, physical distance continues to matter.

It is important to emphasize that distance represents a very different issue for technology and for language use. From a technological standpoint, there is a close correlation between distance and difficulties. Geographical obstacles such as mountains and lakes have undoubtedly faced the development of telecommunications with problems, but the main challenge and the main objective have been to establish communications over long distances. So much so that increases in reach, including the development of global networks, have been hailed as great successes. From a language use point of view, the matter is rather more complex. It is true that, as with technology, distance brings problems, because of the increased likelihood of encountering new phenomena: peculiar terms, expressions, gestures, accents, even an entirely different language. Prior to the development of mediated communication, exposure to new features would have been rare. It would have arisen from mobility, either one's own or someone else's. However, following the invention of writing and the development of transport, the exclusive link between travel and exposure to unfamiliar features found itself severed. Strange new features could now be encountered without actually moving, and the possibility of this happening would grow steadily in the wake of subsequent technological advances.

The heart of the matter is that linguistic difficulties do not grow along with distance. It is not the case that the further apart the production and reception contexts are, the more difficulties there will be. In the first place, linguistic and cultural differences (as distinct from difficulties) do not increase proportionally to distance. There is no doubt that, because people who live away from each other tend to develop different linguistic and cultural practices, distance tends to contribute to language variation. But distance is only one factor among many. The influence of other factors, e.g. natural boundaries, settlement patterns, political divisions, makes physical distance an unreliable indicator of linguistic and cultural distance. Furthermore, to the chagrin of traditionalists, the link between language and territory has been eroded by a massive increase in mobility and in mediated communication. Geography is being marginalized. One should add that there is no certainty that the parties in an exchange will be members of the local speech communities. They may just be passing by, as in communications with friends or family members on business or on vacation, or they may have moved to that part of the world from somewhere else. In short, distance cannot be equated with difference.

A second reason for the lack of correlation between distance and difficulties is that linguistic and cultural differences only represent *potential* sources of problems. The extent to which they are liable to interfere with communication will depend on two factors: the degree of linguistic and cultural distance between the participants' varieties, and the degree of previous exposure the participants have had to areas of divergence. Neither of these factors is directly related to physical distance. Nevertheless, distance remains important owing to its impact on language variation and on contacts. In one-way communication, the crucial factor will be the extent to which the receiver is acquainted with the variants used by the source. Where communication is two-way, the situation is more complicated, since either one or the other participant, or both, may not be accustomed to the other party's variety.

Because L2 users tend to be less expert than L1 users, and will generally have been exposed to a smaller range of varieties, unfamiliar features can be expected to be more numerous and troublesome when communication involves an L2. The issue looms particularly large in languages of wider communication in which more than one variety is frequently involved in mediated communication. This clearly has implications for language learning and teaching with regard to the number and kinds of variety which language learners should be introduced to.

Time coordinates

Like spatial separation, temporal distance between production and reception covers a spectrum of possibilities, from intervals of a few seconds to time gaps of hundreds, even thousands of years. As with space, separation is liable to confront the recipient of communication with unusual features. However, time coordinates also affect communication in another way, through their impact on encoding and decoding conditions. In what follows, I first consider the effect of language change on participants and then turn to the relationship between time and encoding/decoding.

Because language changes over time, any text produced in a different period is likely to contain features that are not those the recipient is used to. Language change is a gradual phenomenon that is more closely related to the passage of time than language variation is to physical distance. While the speed at which it takes place is variable, it is an inevitable continuous process. There is, consequently, a relatively straightforward correlation between temporal distance and the presence of features that are obsolete. Generally speaking, the older a text is, the greater the probability that it will contain archaisms.

This simpler relationship between distance and differences makes the occurrence of difficulties more predictable than with physical distance, as does the comparative uniformity of exposure that receivers will have had to archaisms. Familiarity with certain aspects may vary from one individual to another, especially when texts date back to a point within the lifetime of some individuals. Nevertheless, there is not the diversity found with geographically based features. Since language change is relatively slow compared to the time frame of most communicative events, being faced with differences caused by the age of a text is only likely when communication spans significant periods of time. Overall, archaisms are not a common problem on a day-to-day basis. First, because they are confined to one-way communication. Second, because communication tends to revolve around contemporary texts.

The second effect of the temporal dimension, the impact of transmission speed on encoding and decoding conditions, is of greater practical importance. As can be seen by comparing letter correspondence, email exchanges and chatting on the Internet, transmission speed can have a dramatic impact on communication. Even slight hold-ups can disturb interactions. This is the reason why telephone conversations over unidirectional links, which contain breaks in signals that are liable to be interpreted as end of turn pauses, tend to be more difficult to manage than telephone calls over bidirectional links. In a similar way, transmission delays can be a problem in synchronous multi-party CMC and contribute to the distinctiveness of CMC discourse (Murray, 1989, 2000). When the source's message does not appear on the receiver's screen as it is being typed, but only when it is sent, communication proceeds in bursts interspersed by blanks when anyone can seize the floor. This produces unusual turn sequences, as when the source unexpectedly continues in their role after asking a question, in a manner reminiscent of an impatient interlocutor unable to wait for people to reply. Where there are several parties, transmission delays produce multiple interwoven strands that can be quite disconcerting and allow the more skilful to pursue more than one conversation. To manage this requires some expertise, but not as much as taking part in two simultaneous conversations in real life.

It is possible to liken face-to-face interaction to a couple dance in which the tempo is set by the source, in the same way that the man is the leading partner in a waltz or a tango. In face-to-face, production and reception take place not only virtually simultaneously, but in a lockstep fashion. Reception must keep up with production, while the latter must meet certain norms or expectations (see, for example, Guillot, 1999: 27–46). The penalty for failing to maintain the required pace is a breakdown in communication. The occurrence of the two processes within a single time frame and the fact that these processes involve improvised immediate responses to a changing situation, in other words on-the-fly processing, are crucial aspects of face-to-face interaction. Their combined effect is to create a state of dynamic dependence between production and reception which is a distinctive feature of synchronous communication. There is no time for preparation in synchronous communication, although it may be possible to think in advance of what to say, or to look up and rehearse certain phrases. But once under way, the process must rely on automatized skills, as help cannot be sought either from declarative knowledge or from outside sources such as more expert users, reference works or concordance programmes. Pressure is usually less when communication is written rather than oral, but the need to maintain a certain tempo tends to remain.

In asynchronous communication, on the other hand, the time lag between production and reception gives the two processes a measure of independence. Uncoupled, production and reception no longer have to be coterminous and it becomes possible for semiotic practices that take place together in synchronous communication to be disaggregated. This means that the original discourse may be recorded and transmitted faithfully, or may be distributed in an edited form, as discussed by Kress and Van Leeuwen (2001). In the same way, the received product may or may not be processed as it stands. The first scenario will require participants to operate in real time, and therefore on the fly, the second will reduce the need for rapid spontaneous encoding or decoding. Two sorts of mutually compatible transformation can be used to reduce the demands placed on participants. First, the time taken by production or reception can be stretched or compressed to suit the individual. This typically happens with writing or reading a letter, but is becoming increasingly possible with recordings, which, with the right equipment, can be played back at slow speed or speeded up. Second, production and reception may be turned into discontinuous processes, with interruptions that lessen the load, as when people compose or decipher a text in stages rather than at one sitting. They can also be undertaken more than once. As for the extent to which opportunities for reducing the load arise, this will vary with the medium and with technological progress, notably the existence of facilities for eliminating errors and for removing traces of the editing process, and access to sophisticated playback mechanisms.

For many people, the example that springs to mind in relation to asynchronous communication is letter correspondence. It is therefore apposite to mention that although reading and writing have traditionally been assumed to be inherently self-paced (unless of course subject to artificial time limits), recent developments have shown this not to be the case. In fact, the reason why writing and reading do not usually call for rapid encoding and decoding has less to do with the nature of writing and reading per se than with the materiality of the products on which texts have been inscribed. Stone, parchment and paper are all static media and it is this that gives participants time. When a dynamic medium is used, as with subtitles, computer games and enunciator panels, participants have to operate on the fly. As illustrated by Kress's (2003) account of watching his son and his son's friends playing with their Playstation, this kind of reading requires very different skills from traditional reading:

> There is a musical score, there is rudimentary dialogue, and there is writing – usually as in comic strips, in a box above the rest of the visually saturated screen. The speed at which the written text comes and goes can be adjusted. The pace at which it is set by the players is always too fast for me to read: I can never follow the text fully. Occasionally I have attempted to test whether the players have read and followed the written text, and have found each time that while they have, I have lagged behind. (Kress, 2003: 174)

As will be discussed in the next chapter, the impact of the temporal dimension on encoding and decoding conditions in turn influences language use. Predictably, this impact is crucial for language learners, for whom the temporal dimension represents a major variable. The following quotation shows that the difference between the situations that demand on-the-fly processing and those that do not can be keenly felt by an L2 user: 'In face-to-face meetings, non-native speakers of English always feel strong time pressure to understand and speak in real time. For me as a non-native speaker, email is a more satisfactory medium of communication because email allows me to take time to read and compose the messages' (Ishii, 1993: 150). This ushers in a dilemma for the teaching profession with regard to how much time should be spent on automatization and how much on declarative knowledge, reference skills and learning strategies. It is not a question that can be addressed in the abstract, as the answer will depend on the learner's objectives.

Range of symbolic cues

One of the characteristic features of face-to-face interaction is the exploitation of an array of non-verbal cues that serve to expand and modify the verbal content. These cues, which can have a range of functions, include non-verbal auditory cues (e.g. prosodic features), visual cues (e.g. facial expressions, gestures), and, albeit less frequently, tactile cues (physical contact of some kind). Taking gestures as an example, gestures can be used to reinforce or clarify the meaning of what is said, for instance by pointing to a building while stating 'she has gone to the bank'. Alternatively, they may complete a sentence, as in the following example, in which the speaker uses a gesture to replace what might have been a complex descriptive phrase:

> A young girl was discussing some other young people she knew of. She indicated that these people were not very desirable, at least not in her view. She said, 'Their parents are professors but the kids are /GESTURE/' – completing her sentence by rapidly moving both hands forward, splaying out her fingers to the fullest as she did so, and concurrently producing a 'disgust' facial expression. (Kendon, 1988: 135)

It is also possible for gestures to add something new to a well-formed, seemingly complete sentence. In Kendon's next example, which involves a psychiatrist discussing difficulties in taking a history from a patient, the speaker's words 'and she moved very rapidly from one area to another', are accompanied by a rapid back and forth movement of the hand. Kendon describes the hand movement as 'a visual representation not just of moving from one place to another, but of moving back and forth, of vacillation between topics' (Kendon, 1988: 135). In other words, the gesture specifies the type of movement involved. Kendon stresses that gestures do not always depend on the verbal context. An example of an independent gesture would be the 'drink' gesture implying 'I want a drink' or expressing an invitation such as 'Let's go for a drink'. Lastly, it must be borne in mind that while gestures are universal, their emblematic meanings and, consequently, their interpretation vary across cultures. This can give rise to misunderstandings and is particularly important for immigrant groups. Schneller (1988) presents the results of tests involving Ethiopian newcomers to Israel which showed that nearly 70 per cent of 26 typical Ethiopian emblems such as the use of four stretched fingers put diagonally over the lips, which is intended to mean 'Be quiet!' or an audible intaking of air, exposing the teeth, which is intended to mean 'Sorry', were misunderstood by a group of 46 college students, selected from 14 different cultures. Schneller comments: 'Modern education emphasizes the importance of second language instruction. These studies should include the NV [non-verbal] dimensions of communication as well, at least the passive level of "reading ability". This would be of particular importance for S.L. [second language] training in immigrant or multicultural societies' (Schneller, 1988: 167–8). Acquiring linguistic skills is not enough for intercultural communicative competence.

Predictably, the array of symbolic cues available in a given situation is related to the channels available. While face-to-face interaction tends to be better endowed than mediated communication, the latter sometimes affords opportunities to include devices that are not normally employed in face-to-face, such as written transcription (e.g. subtitles) or a window with sign language translation. The use of multiple symbolic cues has a number of advantages for participants. Multiple cues can reduce ambiguity. They allow the receiver to assess what is really going on, including whether the speaker is giving an accurate, reliable account. They help regulate turn-taking and contribute to building up the interpersonal relationship. Conversely, reductions in the range of symbolic cues mean additional work for the participants, who have to resort to their own resources in order to interpret the messages conveyed (Thompson, 1995: 84). There is an obligation for the source to include contextual information necessary to frame the discourse. For example, in a conventional telephone conversation, callers will start by identifying themselves (Schegloff, 1977). In face-to-face communication, identification and recognition would normally be accomplished through visual cues. Another effect of the reduction in cues is that turn-taking is unlikely to be as smooth as in face-to-face. All this can make mediated communication difficult to handle, especially for L2 users. Telephone calls, for instance, are routinely experienced as problematic by students, who need the support given by gestures and lip movements.

This is not to say that access to more cues is always helpful. It is only beneficial when verbal and non-verbal cues convey the same or similar messages. Otherwise the receiver will tend to be confused, unable to decide which channel or mode to trust. Interlocutors whose body language conflicts with what they say, as with the grim looking person who claims everything is fine, make you suspect that they are not telling the truth. In a similar way, television pictures of marginal relevance can constitute a hindrance for those who find it difficult to understand what is being said. To take an actual example, showing a sunny beach in a report describing how the employees of a travel firm in trouble may not have a sunny future is more likely to perplex, by evoking holidays, than help. Similarly, research into media effects suggests that recall and potential learning by audiences are determined by narrative and message structure in general, and by the meaningful integration of verbal and visual elements in particular (Jensen, 2002: 145). In education, the presence of multiple cues will tend to be beneficial, but again only if the modes work together: 'A simple rule of thumb is that, where there is a complementary relationship between the information in different channels or modes, then this can contribute to learning. However, where there is no relationship between the information in one mode and that in another mode, then what is irrelevant becomes noise and distracts' (Tiffin and Rajasingham, 1995: 93).

Interactivity

The term 'interactivity', as used in this study, covers two distinct variables: reciprocity and simultaneous feedback, which are examined in this order below.

Reciprocity

Reciprocity has to do with whether or not participants take turns at acting as source and receiver. If they do, the interaction is said to be reciprocal. If they do not, it is non-reciprocal. Other terms used for the same feature are two-way or dialogical instead of reciprocal, and one-way or monological for non-reciprocal. It is important to stress that reciprocal does not imply total symmetry in the sense of equal participation by the two parties. However, it does involve some switching of positions. In this, it contrasts with feedback. Feedback keeps the roles as they are, as shown by the fact that to refer to A receiving feedback from B (or to B giving some feedback to A), is to see the communication process from A's perspective, not from B's. It makes A both source and beneficiary. Berlo (1960: 111–12) gives the following explanation: 'Feedback provides the source with information concerning his success in accomplishing his objective. In doing this, it exerts control over future messages which the source encodes.' The point being made is that although receivers are not the main protagonists, they are far from being passive participants. They react to what they hear (or read), agreeing or disagreeing with it, adding to it, feeling sympathy and so on. This responsive attitude is something that the speaker expects (Bakhtin, 1986: 68–9). In reciprocal communication, the listener eventually becomes the speaker and responds verbally. Meanwhile his or her reaction frequently manifests itself, through facial expressions, gestures or sounds, and, if available to the speaker, will be taken into account. As we speak, we continuously monitor the verbal and non-verbal feedback from our partner(s) and often modify our message in the light of what we see and hear. This is one of the reasons why people feel less inhibited when using basic CMC (i.e. without a webcam), sometimes sharing with strangers that they cannot see things that they would not dream of disclosing face to face.

Reciprocity correlates strongly with one-to-one (point-to-point) communication and, prior to the development of Internet Chat and instant messaging (IM), also correlated very strongly with oral communication. Face-to-face conversations are typically reciprocal, as are telephone calls. Mass communication, on the other hand, is monological, even when it includes phone-ins, since only the caller experiences the exchange as reciprocal. For the rest of the audience the information continues to flow in the same direction. Answerphones also lack genuine reciprocity and initiate a kind of pseudo-dialogue.

Reciprocity has both advantages and disadvantages for the participants. The role of source is a demanding one and can be quite taxing for people with limited linguistic proficiency. On the other hand, reciprocity gives opportunities for meaning to be negotiated. It allows participants to direct the exchange and alter its course, to ask for clarification, to avoid or repair breakdowns in communication, and to request a different pace. Such opportunities do not exist with one-way communication. Their absence may not be too much of a problem when communication is written and involves a static medium, since the participants can try and resolve difficulties by consulting reference works or other sources of help. But it can be a major obstacle in the case of broadcasts, especially when they are live and not recorded.

One difficulty peculiar to reciprocal communication is the different conventions governing turn-taking in different situations and communities. Mey (2001: 277) points out that

> silence, or the absence of spoken language, [...] can be used in a variety of ways, and is given varying values across cultures. If we consider the mechanism of 'turn-taking' in CA [Conversation Analysis], we will see that the rules that allow a speaker to 'jump into' the ongoing conversation at a 'transition relevant point' [...] vary from culture to culture.

The different expectations of English and Athabaskan speakers provide a striking example. While for English speakers a silence of more than one and a half seconds represents a legal point of entry, for the American Indian speaker this silence has the normal duration of an 'inter-sentence', but not an 'inter-turn' pause (Mey 2001: 277–8). One can easily imagine the consequences of this level of discrepancy. Yet cross-cultural differences have tended to be overlooked by language pedagogy, and it is only in the past decade or so that the place of pragmatics in language teaching has begun to receive adequate attention (e.g. Aston, 1995; Rose and Kasper, 2001).

Simultaneous feedback

Whereas reciprocity is concerned with role alternation, simultaneous feedback refers to the availability of in-role opportunities that enable the source to evaluate the effect that their message has on the recipient and modulate their behaviour accordingly. In other words, simultaneous feedback enables the source to take self-corrective action. In the present work, feedback refers therefore to what the source can garner without relinquishing their role as source and does not include the evaluative response that the receiver may proffer once they become source.

Two important points need to be made about simultaneous feedback. The first is that simultaneous feedback is independent from reciprocity. The other is that for simultaneous feedback to be possible, there must be channels through which the receiver is accessible to the source. Note, incidentally, that what matters is the potential for simultaneous feedback, not whether the receiver actually manifests any emotion or reaction. Once again expectations come into play, so that not to do anything may be significant. Since there is no live link between production and reception when they are separated in time, feedback is bound to be nil in asynchronous communication. Where production and reception take place simultaneously, feedback will depend on the number of channels available, with particular reference to auditory and visual presence (audibility and visibility). This gives four main scenarios applicable to both one-way and two-way communication:

(a) the source can both see and hear the recipient
(b) the source can see the recipient, but not hear them
(c) the source can hear the recipient, but not see them
(d) the source can neither see nor hear the recipient.

An important factor in two-way communication will be whether transmission and production can take place simultaneously in both directions (full duplex) or whether it is only possible for signals to flow in one direction at a time (half duplex). In the first case, the source and receiver are in the same position. They will, for instance, both hear each other, as with national landline telephone calls. On the other hand, where communication is half duplex, it will only be possible for one of the participants to be heard or seen. For instance, with phone calls made with mobiles, the receivers' vocal reactions will stop the speaker's voice from getting through.

It is worth emphasizing at this point that the discussion of symbolic cues in an earlier section referred to what was communicated by the source to the recipient. What are being considered here are cues going in the opposite direction, from recipient to source. Moreover, it should be stressed that the channels available to the two participant roles do not necessarily match. Given that the recipient must be able to either hear or see the source for any communication to take place, this yields a set of 12 theoretical possibilities regarding the visual and aural channels, three of them symmetrical, the other nine asymmetrical (see Table 2.1, which omits the four cases when the recipient can neither hear nor see). Not all 12 possibilities are currently readily available, but technological progress is gradually turning them into real affordances. Where the recipient is visually present to the source, the latter will be able to take account of gestures and facial expressions. Where they are auditorially present, the source will be helped by the interjections, grunts, exclamations and

Table 2.1 Channel possibilities for receiver (R) and source (S)

	R		*S*	
	Hear	*See*	*Hear*	*See*
1	√	√	√	√
2	√	√	√	X
3	√	√	X	√
4	√	√	X	X
5	√	X	√	√
6	√	X	√	X
7	√	X	X	√
8	√	X	X	X
9	X	√	√	√
10	X	√	√	X
11	X	√	X	√
12	X	√	X	X

other expressions of assent, dissent, surprise, etc. typical of interactional situations.

Action orientation

The final parameter, action orientation, relates to the extent to which communication is oriented to specific others rather than to an indefinite range of potential recipients. In face-to-face and mediated interpersonal communication the receiver is typically selected by, and known to, the source. How well they know each other will vary, but in his or her discourse, the source will take account of their respective statuses, their past history together, prior statements, and any form of feedback available. A conversation between people with a great deal of shared context and knowledge, e.g. spouses or close friends, may begin with a question such as 'What was the result?' that would be opaque to an outsider. However, due to the high profile of the event that is being referred to in the interlocutors' lives, the receiver will normally be able to infer the intended meaning. By contrast, in mass media communication, the receiver consists of a large, heterogeneous, scattered audience. Given that, as a rule, the audience will have chosen to engage with the reading matter or broadcast, recipients will share a common interest in the topics under discussion. Nevertheless, the audience will not be uniform, as its members are likely to differ in age, gender, occupation, level of education, as well as in other respects.

The difficulty of addressing a remote, heterogeneous audience is illustrated by an anecdote from the early days of the BBC:

> Early experiments with broadcast talks showed that it was useless to address the microphone as if it were a public meeting, or even to read it essays or leading articles. The person sitting at the other end expected the speaker to address him personally, simply, almost familiarly, as man to man. This led to further experiment. Should broadcasters speak impromptu? How else could this personal spoken speech be maintained? And yet, without a carefully prepared and timed talk, how could a speaker be sure of getting all he needed to say, in its right proportion, into his fixed space of time? (Matheson, 1933: 75–6)

Since Matheson's time, the shift away from distant and authoritative relationships towards more informal, interactive styles has continued. It is exemplified by the introduction of phone-ins that help redress an in-built imbalance between broadcasters and audiences. The outcome is that the audience have the impression of being treated as individuals rather than as a collective, a phenomenon which Scannell describes as follows: 'The hearable and seeable effect of radio and television is that "I am addressed". This means that *I* am addressed, and not someone else. In listening to radio I do not feel I am an eavesdropper, as if I had accidentally got a crossed line and was tapping in on a private conversation' (Scannell, 1996: 13). In TV broadcasts, this feeling of something akin to personal communication is reinforced by, among other things, the look-to-camera (and therefore towards the viewer) of the television newscaster reading an autocue. It helps explain how some members of the audience come to feel they know a screen personality and form non-reciprocal ties of emotional intimacy with them. Reality TV has the same kind of effect, with perhaps more justification.

The dependence of action orientation on interlocutor knowledge means that the more opportunities there are for participants to gather information about one another, the more interpersonal specificity is able to grow. Evidence of the dynamic nature of interpersonal specificity can be found in the way in which electronic conferences develop, with participants accommodating and emulating each other (Davis and Brewer, 1997: 32). Two factors influence the evolution of interpersonal specificity within a communicative event: interactivity and range of symbolic cues. The relationship between interactivity and interpersonal specificity is a straightforward one, as reciprocity and simultaneous feedback both provide participants with information about their interlocutor that they can use to adjust their own input. Symbolic cues are a slightly more complex case in that the additional information given by multiple cues is only useful for the development of interpersonal specificity if combined with reciprocity (i.e. whoever acts as recipient has access to multiple cues) and/or feedback potential (when the source too has access to multiple cues). When multiple cues are not associated with reciprocity and/or feedback potential, the benefits associated with having a wide range of cues are entirely confined to the receiver and, therefore, cannot influence the source's discourse.

From an L2 perspective, the advantage of interpersonal specificity is that where the receiver's language proficiency is known to depart from the norm (e.g. children, people with certain impairments, L2 users), interpersonal specificity will cover the kind of linguistic accommodation that produces motherese, caretaker talk, foreigner talk discourse. This minimizes the chances of a communication breakdown, and is helpful to less expert users. On the other hand, from a language learning point of view, it is essential that there should still be enough novel features to permit acquisition to take place.

Concluding remarks

It can be seen from the above that most communication parameters have both advantages and drawbacks of varying significance. The one exception is action orientation, where interpersonal specificity appears to be consistently beneficial to participants by lowering task difficulty (as assessed by what is required of participants). Stress must be laid on the fact that we are dealing with interacting dimensions. That is to say, the importance of the effect of a particular variable tends to be affected by the other variables. Language variation, for example, will usually be more of a problem in synchronous interactions when communication takes place on the fly than when communication is asynchronous and allows reference works to be consulted. In addition, the extent of the problem will vary with the range of symbolic cues, and with the degree of interpersonal specificity. This opens the way for pedagogical applications in which variables are manipulated systematically in order to produce learning experiences of an appropriate level of difficulty.

Finally, doubts must be expressed as to the robustness of certain categories, such as the conventional distinction between synchronous and asynchronous communication. Given that synchronous communication is not simultaneous, but only virtually simultaneous, it is not clear at what point synchronous communication becomes asynchronous. One way of resolving the issue is to interpret synchronous as implying the parallel development of two processes that unfold in a fixed relationship to each other. But this would make listening to a live recording in deferred time an instance of synchronous communication. The best solution is probably to define synchrony in terms of the necessary availability of the participants for the whole of a communicative event, which excludes the deferred time example. Equally, it is possible to argue that the distinction between reciprocal and non-reciprocal is often a function of the timescale on which one operates, and depends on what is used as the unit of analysis. Using a short timescale involving single texts, reading and writing a letter will be classified as a form of asynchronous, non-reciprocal communication. Zooming out, it becomes part of a reciprocal activity known as correspondence. The same might be said of texting, which, when one considers the speed at which certain people exchange texts, does not seem to warrant its traditional label of asynchronous non-reciprocal communication. In fact, even email seems to be becoming a pseudo-synchronous means of communication, expected by some people to deliver rapid, almost instant responses. Overall, the analysis underscores the distinctive concerns of a technological perspective and a language use standpoint, and confirms that what is considered central to one may not be as important to the other.

Communication in everyday life

As a relational phenomenon, communication is necessarily subject to societal and social influences. Like so many other aspects of life, the types of communication that people engage in are shaped by the kind of institutions that structure their society, and by current trends in individual interactions. The impact will vary according to personal circumstances, including whether communication is in L1 or L2, but use cannot but be affected by the backdrop against which individual practice develops. Where people are able, or are learning, to use more than one language, media use, like the lexicon of bilingual infants, will be spread across the languages. The balance will not be the same for everyone, but it can be safely hypothesized that the overall usage, as well as the distribution across languages, will be affected by what happens around the person concerned. It would be foolish to expect the use of L2 media to replicate either the use of media in the L2 community or an individual's use of L1 media. It would be equally foolish not to expect the use of media in the L2 community and personal media history to have some bearing on the use they make of L2 media. In this section, I consider the place of mediated communication in contemporary life. I begin by examining some relevant media research findings, and then move on to discuss the potential impact of bilingualism on media use.

The development of devices that are easy to carry and can be used outdoors as well as indoors, has helped mediated communication become more visible. There can be no doubt that the media are part of the fabric of daily life and that the reception of media products has become more than ever 'a routine, practical activity which individuals carry out as an integral part of their everyday lives' (Thompson, 1995: 38). According to Castells (1996: 333), media consumption in urban societies is the second largest category of activity behind work and is the predominant activity at home. Media use is not necessarily an exclusive activity, but can be mixed with other activities, such as eating or home tasks. This is particularly true of radio, which is frequently used for background noise, but it also applies to television and telephones, especially mobiles, and the Internet. It is a consumption pattern that is very frequent among the 16–24s, who regularly use a combination of media. Internet use is most frequently combined with listening to the radio (40 per cent), with having the TV on not far behind (32 per cent). Mixing Internet use with reading a magazine is much less frequent (6 per cent), just above mixing Internet use with reading the paper (5 per cent). By contrast, when listening to the radio is the main occupation, 30 per cent also use the Internet, 33 per cent read a newspaper and 32 per cent read a magazine (EIAA, 2006a).

It is not surprising, therefore, that the past few years have witnessed a dramatic increase in media ownership. In 1999–2000, 95 per cent of British households had a telephone, 44 per cent a mobile phone, 86 per cent a video recorder, 32 per cent a satellite receiver, 38 per cent a home computer and 19 per cent Internet access (ONS, 2000: 146). By 2002–3, the figure had risen to 70 per cent for mobile phones, 90 per cent for video recorders, 45 per cent for satellite receivers, 55 per cent for home computers, and it had more than doubled to 45 per cent for Internet access, with a 1 per cent decrease for telephone ownership (ONS, 2004: 152), presumably owing to the diffusion of mobile telephony. Significantly, statistics for video recorders and home computers have only been collected since 1985, while data for mobile phones, satellite receivers and Internet connection only goes back to 1996–97 in the case of mobile phones and satellite receivers, and to 1998–99 for the Internet.

In contrast, the proportion of British households with durable goods such as washing machines and microwaves has remained stable. Across the globe, the most accessible information and communication technology is still radio. In 1997, there were 418 radio broadcasting receivers per 1000 inhabitants in the world, against 240 television receivers, the highest ownership being found in Oceania and America (over 1000), the lowest in Africa and Asia (216 and 255), with Europe occupying the middle ground with 418 (UNESCO, 1999). Everywhere radio was more common than television. However, other technologies are gaining ground. There are no roads in Namche Bazaar, a large trekking village at 3400 m altitude in the Himalayas. But in 2001, there were already three cybercafés and a Sky dish, although the former were, admittedly, mainly patronized by tourists sending emails home.

The growing importance of the media in modern society has been accompanied by changes in use, and, in the case of the mass media, in the types of programmes that are broadcast. Media consumption has been the object of much scrutiny, not least by advertisers keen to maximize cost-effectiveness. Research has shown that consumption patterns vary from country to country, across the population, and within the lifespan of an individual. At an individual level, patterns laid down in childhood and early adolescence tend to be carried into adulthood, so that, by and large, high media users continue to make more use of the media than low users. At the same time, use varies with age as well as with technological and social change. For instance, Rosengren (2000) reports that the introduction of cable television and the video cassette recorder into Sweden initiated a change from a system characterized mainly by supply/output control to a system increasingly characterized by demand/received control. These structural changes in turn led to an increase in the amount of television watched by adolescents whose tastes were better catered for. Rosengren (2000: 158) comments on the increase in these terms: 'This is a finding interesting *per se*, but above all it teaches us that many results from the social and behavioural sciences are somewhat less general than sometimes assumed. *To a considerable extent, they are dependent on the time and space in which they have been collected.*' As evidenced by recent research on changes in media consumption patterns by women across 10 European countries (EIAA, 2006b), local variations are to be expected and, as Rosengren acknowledges, do not negate the existence of broad trends: 'The phenomena of individual mass media use, its causes and consequences are so general all around the globe [...] that the general tendencies [noted in Sweden] should be much the same in many or most other industrial or post-industrial societies' (Rosengren, 2000: 154).

Research has shown that media use is partly contextual and unplanned, and partly a goal-directed, purposive behaviour based on expectations. The media are known to fulfil a range of needs. They are used, for example, to obtain information, for recreational purposes (e.g. relaxation, stimulation), or to postpone getting on with chores. There is a degree of specialization, with, for instance, people turning most frequently to radio and recordings when they want to relax (Dominick, 1996: 50). For years, the media with the highest profile has been television, which has become 'the command centre of the new epistemology' (Postman, 1987: 79). There are several reasons for the centrality of television. They include the vast amount of television that people watch, the usefulness of television as a source of relaxation and entertainment, and its importance as a window on the world and a source of information on current affairs and political figures. But the central position of television also stems from its influence on contemporary culture and from what Fiske (1987) refers to as 'vertical intertextuality', that is to say its relations with texts that refer explicitly to it. Of prime importance here is the role of television programmes as topics of conversation. As shown by the viewers' diaries analysed by Gauntlett and Hill, 'talk about, and stemming from issues raised in, television programmes is a part of many people's social lives' (Gauntlett and Hill, 1999: 139). This is corroborated by Pile's (2001) findings, with 55 per cent of respondents stating that they often have interesting chats about programmes. Soap operas are particularly liable to stimulate talk, provoking discussions similar to those revolving around real human beings. Equally, by defining certain issues or programmes as worth talking about, television helps establish the agenda of political and cultural discussions, so that lack of access to television, in so far as it adversely affects people's awareness of current issues, constrains their ability to join in conversations. However, the centrality of television may be a temporary state of affairs, and must be set against the growing importance of the Internet and the increasing ease with which it can be accessed.

The paradoxical value that television has acquired as a topic of conversation creates a symbiotic relationship between TV and conversation in which they mutually support and enhance each other. It also testifies to the enduring importance of face-to-face interaction that remains '*the* fundamental mode of human intercourse and socialization' (Boden and Molotch, 1994: 258). Further evidence of the primacy of face-to-face can be found in the inability of the telephone to entirely satisfy people's need for interaction. As Moores argues:

> The fact that the telephone can be used as a 'sociable medium' [...], as a means of maintaining friendships or for kinkeeping purposes, is evident in the advertising slogans which are employed by the telecommunications industry – 'it's good to talk', 'reach out and touch someone'. [...] However, we must not automatically assume that this mediated communication will always be a satisfactory replacement for physical copresence with known others. (Moores, 2000: 142)

Telephone calls, like emails, IM and Chat, do not take away the desire to be physically close to others, and are not adequate substitutes when matters become sensitive, complex or uncertain. Hence the occurrence of requests to 'upgrade' to co-presence: 'let's meet and discuss this', etc. The superiority of face-to-face is also demonstrated by the amount of time that top managers spend in co-presence, while their involvement in oral communication in general testifies to the value that is put on talking to people. Managers are said by Boden and Molotch (1994: 272) to spend about 50 per cent of their time in face-to-face interactions and more than 75 per cent of their working day engaged in meetings, telephone calls and casual conversations. The fact that the most important exchanges among the most consequential actors involve face-to-face is not without interest to language learners, since it indicates that the acquisition of oral skills can enhance career prospects, in addition to improving interactions with users of the target language.

As far as the impact of additional languages on media use is concerned, the ability to understand and/or speak more than one language can be regarded as introducing an additional potential decision point that may be located upstream or downstream from medium selection. That is to say language choice may take precedence over medium selection or, on the contrary, come second. In addition, the earlier decision may limit subsequent options or may leave them open. The distribution between languages will depend on three interacting factors. The first is language expertise. Generally speaking, one would anticipate that low competence acts as a deterrent to media consumption, as with the members of the Russian and Arabic minorities in Israel studied by Adoni et al. (2002): 'In Israel's multimedia environment, the two minorities were highly exposed to all the main communication media and the major determinant factor in people's choice of media seems to have been their dominant language' (Adoni et al., 2002: 425). However, findings involving members of established minorities in a particular country may not be true of a different kind of L2 user or in a different country. The second influence over language distribution is place of residence. Patterns of media use are likely to be closer to those of the target speech community when users reside among that community, than when they live at home, or in some other country with a different language. The third main factor at work is the respective and relative status of the target and the native language. Given that the status of a language is related to its general diffusion and its presence in the media, a high-status language will tend to offer more opportunities for mediated communication than a low-status language. The key issue here is that the availability of choice introduces a competitive situation. The fierceness of the competition will differ from one pair of languages to another, and will be a function of the status of the two languages, with physical distance an additional parameter in the case of certain media (e.g. radio or terrestrial television). Even on its home ground, a language that is not a language of wider communication may offer relatively few occasions for mediated communication, if a high percentage of broadcasts and mediated interactions are in other languages. Such is the case in Finland, where 'on any day of the year, soundtracks in English comprise a major proportion of the broadcasting on all four national television channels. An examination of the nationwide television broadcasting in Finland during one week (15–21 September 1997) revealed that English language material accounts for just over 40 per cent of all broadcasting time on all channels' (Battarbee, 2002: 262).

Discussion and conclusion

It has been claimed that 'educational systems are preparing people for the past, for the ideas and attitudes and values of a way of life that is fading away and for work in areas of shrinking labour requirements' (Tiffin and Rajasingham, 1995: 71). Is this true of language education? What does language education currently prepare learners for? The view taken in this book is that if the aim of language learning is to produce all-rounded communicators, L2 users need to be able to handle both face-to-face and mediated communication and, relatedly, that this requires some modifications to our approach to language education. Specifically, greater account needs to be taken of mobility, technological progress, and the changes in communication that go with them. One can cite many facts in support of the need to rethink language learning, from the greater propensity of many ordinary citizens to go and live in another country, through people's desire to extend their horizons and feel part of a wider community (as shown, for example, by the preference of part of the British public for American or European television programmes that enable them 'to "reimagine" the boundaries of community' (Moores, 2000: 4)), to the large number of people involved in mediated communication with correspondents from a different language background. Furthermore, one can predict with a degree of confidence that as interactions on the basis of shared interests rather than physical proximity grow in number, mediated communication across linguistic boundaries will become even more widespread.

While the case for reappraising language learning is clear, what weight is to be given to the development of particular linguistic skills remains a thorny issue. From a quantitative point of view, current patterns of media use would seem to give priority to reception over production. High levels of mass media consumption, automatized calls, voice generation, the outsourcing of call centres, are all factors that put a premium on good comprehension skills. On the other hand, the significance of particular media cannot be assessed solely on the basis of quantitative measures. Activities involving production, such as texting, phoning others, or talking to them face to face, although taking less time overall in someone's life, may be far more important to them than the television programmes they watch. Ultimately, decisions as to what constitutes the right balance can only be taken on a case-by-case basis, in the light of people's motives for learning the language, the activities they are likely to undertake, and the knowledge and skills that these draw on. Attention must then be paid to the type of pedagogical intervention required, including assessing what learners might be able to pick up, what they need to be told explicitly, and how much repetition is desirable, if any. All this requires fine-grained investigations that have still to be carried out. It also requires open-mindedness on the part of language professionals.

The generic framework presented above is best regarded as offering a list of points that should be considered when attempting to answer questions on the conditions and constraints deriving from the use of a particular media, and their impact on participants. It is not intended to provide a means of mapping different communication practices in a detailed systematic and comprehensive manner, but rather to support a principled approach to the integration of mediated communication into language learning briefs. The main value of the analysis presented here lies in the insights that it provides on the many ways in which technological progress has brought about changes in the nature of communication. It gives credence to my claim that advances in ICT have led to a considerable diversification of communicative practices that challenges traditional notions of communicative competence. Technological advances have moved the goalposts: printing introduced expectations of literacy, and subsequent developments have followed suit. In the process, technological progress has arguably proved a mixed blessing, ushering in an outstanding expansion of communication opportunities, but also potentially enlarging the communicative repertoire that L2 users have to master.

In view of the number of possibilities, it is imperative to think critically about the kind of interactions that language learners might need to be prepared for, and to establish which aspects of proficiency most need to be fostered. Johnson (2001: 199) observes that learner communication needs depend on 'whether the main use of the FL is likely to be for international communication, or for communication within the borders of the country'. The distinction is important. It would be useful, for this reason, to gather language-specific empirical data on the relative significance of different forms of communication for different types of L2 users, so as to identify a range of scenarios representative of foreign and second language use in various linguistic and cultural contexts, including the opportunities and challenges that they offer.

3
ICT and Language

Introduction

In the previous chapter, I approached the context of language learning in terms of the impact of ICT on communication. In this chapter, I turn to a related aspect and focus on the relationship between ICT and language. As human beings' main means of communicating, it is inconceivable that language could be left untouched by changes that affect communication. Yet the part played by ICT in the evolution of language has been the subject of little systematic investigation. This neglect, or oversight, appears all the more surprising when one considers how frequently the media are blamed for a deterioration in standards. In recent years, concern over the allegedly pernicious influence of newspapers and television has extended to email and SMS, with email being 'accused of ruining letter-style writing and grammar', and SMS being 'portrayed as a prime menace to communicative skills' (Kesseler and Bergs, 2003: 75). However, the view that the media have a significant effect on language is not one shared by linguists, many of whom regard the influence of ICT as peripheral and superficial. The issue is addressed infrequently (Herring (2003) is one of the few exceptions) so that relevant evidence is sparse and dispersed. Characteristically, recent publications on language change tend to contain very few references to ICT. One possible explanation is that such books have their roots in historical linguistics, with its specific perspective on linguistic evolution and diachronic change. Nevertheless, the high profile of ICT, together with mounting evidence on the way in which the Internet stimulates linguistic ingenuity, would lead us to expect the impact of ICT on language change to be referred to more frequently than has been the case until now. If only because there is a prima facie case that ICT comes under, or at least has some link with, several well-known causes of language change.

This prima facie case provides the starting point for my exploration of the impact of ICT on the linguistic landscape. I concede that public opinion is often ill informed and that complaint letters to newspaper editors can be motivated by questionable convictions. Nevertheless, taken together with the discussion in the last chapter, the public perception of an influence arguably provides sufficient grounds for investigating the intersection of the media and language change, conceived broadly as including emergent as well as established change.

The aim of this chapter is not to determine precisely the role of ICT in the evolution of language. Rather, it is to bring together relevant evidence on the relationship between language variation and change on the one hand, and technological contexts on the other, and to analyse the repercussions for language users and language learners. Unlike specialist accounts of language change, the chapter does not set out to investigate the manner in which phonetic, morphological, semantic and other features of language change over time. Rather, it seeks to document and delineate the extent to which ICT is intertwined with change in a broad sense. More precisely, it is concerned with more than the slowly diffusing modifications that come to be integrated into the language system. It also encompasses synchronic phenomena that may not necessarily alter language in the long run, but which form part of users' everyday experience of language. In other words, it also considers variability and short-term changes.

In view of the lack of agreement over the role of ICT, the chapter concentrates on discussing the part played by past advances in altering the characteristics of language as it comes to be used by successive generations. After sketching the relevance of ICT to the causes of language variation and change, I examine whether the media help rein in language or, on the contrary, lead to diversification. This is followed by a discussion of the factors involved in language change that begins by focusing on the effect of the properties of ICT before considering the role of the social matrix. Attention then turns to the process of change and the controversy over the impact of ICT. The latter part of the chapter is more narrowly focused, and illustrates the influence of ICT on specific aspects of language and on language spread.

The relevance to language learning of a study of the interface between ICT and language change is self-evident. Anything that alters the linguistic landscape necessarily affects language users and language learners. However, the prime concern of language users and language learners is with usage rather than change. While the contribution that ICT makes to language change deserves attention, the issue of what leads changes to propagate within a language or across languages is at one remove from language learning. For this reason, most of the implications for language learning are dealt with in the conclusion, rather than being pointed out in the course of the discussion.

ICT and the causes of language variation and change

Causes of language change can be divided into two broad categories, according to whether they are language external or language internal. Fennell (2001: 7) lists language external factors as geography, contact with new vs old phenomena, imperfect learning, a substratum effect and social prestige factors, whereas internal factors comprise ease of articulation, analogy, reanalysis and randomness. What is noteworthy in Fennell's account of the forces that shape the evolution of language is the relevance of ICT to no less than three of the external factors. These are geography, contact with new phenomena and social prestige. The connection between ICT and these factors is outlined below.

Geography

The importance of geography for language change stems from the fact that distance and topographical features such as the presence of mountains, seas and plains, affect prospects for face-to-face interactions, and therefore language contact, between speech communities. In turn, language contact influences the evolution of language. Lack of contact results in divergence, while frequent dealings promote convergence.

Since the end of the nineteenth century, contact with people outside one's immediate circle, and therefore potential exposure to new forms of language, have come not only from trade, travel and migration, but from ICT. Over the years, this has happened on an increasing scale and more and more independently from geography, as discussed in the last chapter.

A first step was taken with the invention of writing, with print bringing further progress. Following the invention of the printing press, 'words no longer moved with the slow flux of migrating peoples, but travelled at speed across continents in the form of multiple first editions, rapidly acquiring currency and then permanency' (Hughes, 1988: 92–3). However, it is only since the diffusion of telecommunication that language contact has become truly freed from the stranglehold of geography through the severing of the link between communication and transport. This is highlighted by Headrick's (1991: 4) observation that 'whereas railroads and electric power reached their optimum efficiencies on a regional scale, telegraphs quickly became national and, in the case of submarine cables, intercontinental and even global'.

This is not to say that 'geography is history', as the slogan of the telecommunications industries proclaims. What we have is simply the arrival over the last century of new factors among the forces that operate to produce language change. As Carey (1989: 210) explains, with reference to the telegraph, technologically mediated communication had to take account of geographical variation and remove the local, the regional and the colloquial, if a story was to be understood across a wide region. While it is difficult to imagine geographical factors becoming a thing of the past, it seems likely that ICT will continue to limit their impact. It is highly probable, for instance, that Australia will not experience the amount of variation found in England, which is the product of the very different transport and communications conditions of former eras. Similarly, provided American and British people continue to communicate, their dialects are unlikely to drift so far apart as to become different languages (Trudgill, 1990).

Over the past decades technologically induced language contact has intensified with the diffusion of satellite television and the Internet. It seems to me that the emergence of opportunities for language contact that bypass geographical factors calls into question the suitability of 'geography' as an umbrella term. I would argue that the expansion of the forces shaping linguistic evolution warrants replacing 'geography' with 'language contact', since this is the prime common factor. More significantly, the downgrading of geography calls for looking into whether, and in what circumstances, established models of language change, such as the wave model, remain valid.

Contact with new vs old phenomena

Language changes in response to the evolution of society, adjusting to new events, artefacts and ideas, and to the declining importance of certain old phenomena. The linguistic consequences of inventions, and of the activities they give rise to, can be seen mostly in the area of vocabulary, with the coining of new words and with extensions in the meaning of established lexis. They also take the form of new jargons and varieties. It is well known that progress in medicine, biochemistry, physics, aviation, has led to the creation of thousands of new terms and the development of new specialized registers. A similar picture obtains with regard to ICT. At each stage appropriate nomenclatures have been devised through neologisms and borrowings, and the spread of the technology has been accompanied by the development of verbal means of managing and referring to the activities that it has spurred. In addition, because it is used to disseminate information, ICT contributes to the diffusion of linguistic change that reflects social and technological transformations outside its own field.

Social prestige factors

Social prestige is conferred by factors, and through processes, that sometimes remain unclear. Typically, however, linguistic forms employed by the higher classes will enjoy prestige imparted by the status of those who use them, and will be actively promoted by those in power. Vaugelas, the seventeenth-century grammarian who set out to define and describe *le bon usage* (proper usage), was quite adamant that the best French was not the language of the common people, but the French spoken by that part of the court that followed the usage promoted by esteemed contemporary authors. This is the kind of French that he held up as a model for others to imitate (Vaugelas, 1970 (1643)). The usual linguistic outcome of this propensity to view the language of the powerful in a positive light is that the variety of the dominant elite becomes the standard. But, as was the case with Vaugelas, other factors, perceived educatedness, the existence of a valued literature, etc. may play a part in the selection of the standard, and even sometimes have a dominant role. Honey (1997) argues that the prestige that came to be attached to Standard English had more to do with the influence of literature than with its association with London as the centre of culture and of political and economic power. Honey (1997: 81) does not deny that the link with London was instrumental in the rise of Standard English, but claims that the prestige enjoyed by what was to become the standard variety was primarily due to the existence of a revered literature that served as a model and object of study. It hardly needs stating that without the printing press, literary works would have had a much more restricted distribution. Since this would have limited their influence, an account such as Honey's that gives pride of place to literary works indirectly attests the role of technology in language change. Interestingly, Vaugelas explicitly acknowledges that good writing can be developed through reading, but insists that good speaking habits can only be acquired by frequenting the court.

All over the world, print has affected the fate of languages, helping to preserve and raise the status of some, whereas its absence had the opposite effect. Baron (1984: 123) notes that modes of communication which are given publicity or are valued as a source of prestige have the ability to influence the shape of other modalities. Cross-modal influences can be seen at work today in relation to CMC and SMS. Overall, ICT can be said to interact with social prestige in multifarious and complex ways, both because of its vehicular functions – there is no doubt that the recent increase in the borrowing of English terms by other languages is linked to the prestige of American culture, particularly pop music, a culture that has been brought to the rest of the world by modern media – and because the prestige of the new media is transferred to the linguistic forms that they help circulate.

However influential the dominant elite may be, it does not serve as a conscious, or subconscious model for everyone. What is perceived as superior and desirable varies across the population, and social elites compete with counter-elites for people's allegiance. The 'punk-rock' singers described by Trudgill (1983), whose pronunciation combined stereotypically American forms with stereotypically English working-class forms, coupled with a higher than usual number of non-standard grammatical forms like multiple negation and third person singular 'don't', constituted one such counter-elite and offered themselves as icons: 'The intended effect is assertive and aggressive. There is also clearly an intention to aid identification with and/or by British working-class youth, and to appeal to others who wish to identify with them, their situations and their values' (Trudgill, 1983: 155). When it transmits this kind of music, ICT makes those forms available to a wider audience, and presumably helps to raise their prestige in certain circles.

In a similar way, the airtime allocated to different languages or varieties on radio and television tends to both reflect and contribute to their relative social prestige. The situation is often delicately balanced and is open to multiple influences, so that it is liable to change with the passing of time, as illustrated by the growing presence of regional accents on British TV. National newscasters are no longer exclusively RP speakers, while regional news programmes tend to be broadcast in the appropriate regional accent (Fennell, 2001: 186–7).

ICT and the direction of change

The uneasy coexistence of elites and counter-elites that pull language in opposite directions exemplifies the kind of conflicting pressures that language is constantly under. In supporting adherence to a single norm, elites are trying to contain language, whereas by deviating from the norm, counter-elites bring diversity. In either case ICT helps the linguistic forms to circulate. Bakhtin (1981: 270–2) calls 'the historical processes of linguistic unification and centralization', such as the impact of social elites, 'centripetal forces of language'. Centripetal forces are forces aimed at creating and defending a common unitary language always threatened by 'centrifugal forces' that work in the opposite direction, i.e. towards decentralization and diversification. Centripetal forces pull language inwards towards homogenization, whereas, like counter-elites, centrifugal forces push language outwards towards variation. The former work to the advantage of language learners to the extent that they rein in language, promote regularity, and set clear boundaries and models. The latter introduce additional challenges and can be a source of confusion, but they give a degree of respectability to deviant language.

At an individual level, the tension between divergence and convergence takes the form of a balancing act between originality and intelligibility, as people try to be themselves and find their own voice without compromising communicational efficiency. Even on the Internet, a prime site of struggle between conformity and unconventionality, it is essential to exercise restraint and avoid too many idiosyncracies in order to be understood. This is one area where one suspects that the concerns of language learners will tend to diverge from those of expert users. Someone with limited ability to express themselves is more likely to be concerned with being understood than with appearing original, while unconventionality on the part of others will tend to represent an additional obstacle.

At the level of society, centripetal and centrifugal forces come in the form of social, political, economic and technological structures. In common with many other phenomena, ICT may create tendencies towards unification and towards diversification. Thus, according to Eisenstein (1979: 117), print promoted both expansion and pruning: 'Typography arrested linguistic drift, enriched as well as standardized vernaculars, and paved the way for the more deliberate purification and codification of all major European languages.' One also observes a twofold effect in relation to the diffuse networks of social interaction fostered by electronic media. By bringing together people from diverse backgrounds, electronic communication expands individual and collective linguistic competence. But inasmuch as people then accommodate to one another, electronic interactions also encourage uniformity of language patterns. This is not unlike what occurs with urbanization, where interactions between people from a variety of linguistic backgrounds increase exposure to other linguistic forms and at the same time promote the levelling of differences. Throughout the last 200 years, easier travel and communication have simultaneously expanded people's linguistic horizons and induced convergence:

> The steamship and the railroad, the automobile, and the airplane have brought people into contact with one another and joined communities hitherto isolated, while the post office and the telegraph, the telephone, the radio, the movies, television, and electronic data transmissions have been influential in the intermingling of language and the lessening of the more easily altered local idiosyncrasies. (Baugh and Cable, 1993: 196)

One major variable in all this is the scope for external control. With the exception of police states, interpersonal interactions are largely free from outside control. By contrast, mass communication is open to interference by the powers that be through the imposition of language policies and censorship, and/or selective appointments or patronage. Since intervention is motivated by the public nature of mass communication, the nature of the measures that are taken (and therefore whether they have a centripetal or centrifugal effect) will depend on the sociopolitical structure and the prevailing ethos. Reith (1924: 160–1), the first Director General of the BBC, was in no doubt that the corporation should act as a centripetal force and spread the King's English. He explains how a special effort was made to select radio presenters who could be relied on 'to employ the correct pronunciation of the English tongue'. The orthoepic objective is explicitly stated: 'There is now presented to any who may require it, an opportunity of learning by example.' As Leitner (1980: 81) remarks, in the 1920s, 'radio was looked upon as an active social instrument, and this included the propagation of "good" language'. Reith, who has in mind native speakers of English rather than foreigners, goes on to give the following illustration of the BBC's role as guardian of the language: 'It may have been observed that the verb "to broadcast" follows the conjugation of the verb "to cast", and hence not "broadcasted" but "broadcast" for the past tense. This was a decision of the B.B.C.! After all, it is our verb' (Reith, 1924: 162). The comment speaks volumes. Attitudes, however, do not remain constant over time. One suspects that radio newsreaders no longer wear a suit, as they used to do in the 1950s, and we have seen that RP is no longer an essential prerequisite for reading the news on the BBC. By giving a platform to speakers of non-standard varieties, the mass media help tilt the balance some way towards diversification, even if shared global experience of media remains essentially centripetal.

One can get an idea of how centripetal and centrifugal forces operate in an unfettered context by studying what happens in environments supposedly free from external control such as Internet newsgroups and discussion lists. What can be observed is not only the surfacing of linguistic conventions that help give a community of practice a distinctive identity, but also the monitoring of language usage by some moderators.

In all cases and contexts, centripetal and centrifugal forces remain subject to the restraining influence of the demand for functional efficiency. As stated above, for the telegraph, this meant the elimination of local terms. Eco (1995: 125) explains how, in the case of Italian television, concern for intelligibility has led the authorities to modify their strategy and cut out jargon:

> Broadcasters, acknowledging that some messages must, for the good of the community, be received as unequivocally as possible, have used their awareness of aberrant decodings to take the cultural circumstances of the audience more into account. This involved reducing the semantic gaps by adopting simpler language, respecting audiences' needs rather than talking over their head in a slang made up of in-jokes comprehensible only to those in public bodies and their political patrons.

ICT and the factors involved in language change

There is ample evidence that in language as in other spheres, change is frequently the result of the coming together of a number of factors. Thus, although print is often credited with having had a strategic role in the fixing of the English language, it would not have had the same stabilizing influence without the assistance of a special set of social and political factors. In general, the high degree of interplay between the various dimensions of life argues against a one-to-one cause-and-effect relationship between ICT and linguistic evolution. However, it is possible to evaluate the implications for language use of various aspects of ICT by historicizing technology. That is to say one can try and trace linguistic innovations back to their origins by putting ICT into its historical context, and then use the contexts to more fully understand technology (Haas, 1996: 205). This is what this section seeks to do in order to try and get a better idea of the role of ICT in language change. The impact of the properties of certain inventions on language change will be discussed first. The relationship between ICT and language change will then be approached using the social matrix as a springboard.

Properties of ICT and language change

As argued by Ong (1982: 82), the first landmark in the history of ICT is not printing, the first port of call in this book, but writing. Since printing would clearly not have had the same impact in the unlikely scenario of being developed before writing, and used only for the reproduction of diagrams and pictures, I will begin by taking a brief look at the effect of writing itself. In so doing, I hope to be in a better position to distinguish between changes attributable to the invention of the printing press, and changes that are ultimately due to writing.

It is a defining characteristic of oral cultures that information is passed on through face-to-face interaction. While it occasionally involves drawings and other forms of representation, the transmission of knowledge in an oral culture relies primarily on oral verbal communication. As a result, knowledge preservation and dissemination are heavily dependent on memory constraints. Few of us are happy to deliver a speech or an oral presentation without notes, and this gives us some appreciation of the limiting effect of having to rely exclusively on memory. Necessity and practice undoubtedly combined to make our ancestors more expert at learning by heart than we are; in fact, according to recent research, considerably more so (Olson, 1994: 98). Nevertheless memory capacity remained a problem. Because of the difficulty of formulating and recalling abstractions orally, knowledge was encapsulated in myths and legends (Havelock, 1963). Rhythm, parallel terms, mnemonics and rhyme were used to lessen memory load and guard against variation and inconsistencies. Knowledge had to be constantly repeated using formulaic language (Ong, 1982: 24). It is important, however, not to overestimate the reliance of oral cultures on linguistic mnemonic devices. As studies of African and South American oral traditions have revealed, oral cultures also enhance recall through rituals and physical artefacts, such as the knotted cords of variable colour of the Inca. For this reason, many anthropologists now think that there is not as great a divide between pre-literate and literate cultures as was once thought (Olson, 1994: 98–105).

One of the main effects of the invention of writing was to drastically decrease the importance of memory by allowing the dissemination of knowledge via a text. It also entailed a change in channel which was to have major consequences. Let us suppose for a moment that, rather improbably, mankind had invented some sort of audio recording device instead of writing. What effect would this have had? Obviously, it would have allowed speech to be stored and played back. But this would not have been very much of an improvement, since texts could already be heard more than once by asking the source to go through them again. Nor is there any reason to suppose that learning by heart did not entail a fair amount of rehearsing, as it does now, and did not prompt requests for certain passages to be repeated. And since repetition was probably provided as and when required, the process was altogether more efficient than trying to locate the relevant bit of information you do not remember by playing the text back on a cassette recorder or CD. Like writing, an audio recording device would have made the acquisition of knowledge a more autonomous enterprise, and this lessening of dependence on others may have led to greater originality of thought and language. But it would not have brought any fundamental change to language itself. The reason why writing had such an impact on language is that it involved a shift from the aural to the visual.

What is it about the visual channel that makes such a difference? First and foremost, in the technological environment of the time, the move to the visual created different conditions for the production of language. It permitted what can be called 'leisurely' production as opposed to the on-the-fly, time-pressured conditions associated with speech. Writing on parchment or paper allows the source to take their time, whereas speech requires a reasonably quick tempo, at least in a conversational context. It is true that speech is not always spontaneous, in which case words can be put together in a more leisurely manner. But they then have to be memorized, which reintroduces the limitations of human memory. In addition, when recorded on a static material, written text, unlike speech, is not evanescent. It becomes recoverable. This makes it easier to take stock, or to compare alternative turns of phrase. Even with a cassette recorder or CD, trying to compare the wording of sentences without recourse to writing is a bit like trying to decide which of ten similarly priced violins sounds the best. After three or four, you become virtually incapable of recalling what each instrument sounds like.

By creating conditions favourable to the formulation of complex arguments, the invention of writing helped push back the frontiers of knowledge: 'The large-scale accumulation of exact knowledge which makes possible elaborate and dispassionate causal analyses and sharp abstract categorization depends absolutely on writing. Astronomy, mathematics, physics, grammar, logic, metaphysics and all other abstract knowledge remain mere potentials of the human mind until some use can be made of script' (Ong, 1967: 203). A playback machine would not have had these far-reaching effects. What applies to encoding also applies to decoding. As we know from experience, abstract reasoning and long utterances with multiple embeddings are much easier to grasp in written than in spoken form:

> We are still largely in the dark about the exact processes and mechanisms that determine the cognitive handling of spoken and written discourse, but the evidence is very clear on the existence of major differences between the two types of discourse. Analytical considerations, as well as experimental and clinical evidence, are compelling in their unanimity that many dissociations exist in the way the mind deals with the two language modalities. What is not yet known – or not known clearly – are the exact physiological and psychological causes and concomitants of these dissociations. (Jahandarie, 1999: 196–7)

Reference was made in the last chapter to the fact that writing does not automatically guarantee time to think. Although it is usually possible to process language in a less hurried manner when writing than when speaking, how much opportunity there is for mental planning and reflection depends on the communication situation. In multi-participant electronic chatrooms, for example, contributors must post their messages up quickly if they are not to be left out. The result is a discourse made up of fast, brief and fairly superficial responses that is far removed from carefully crafted prose. Even the ubiquitous answerphone has an effect on language use. The durability of the recording and the lack of opportunity for negotiating meaning make many people choose their words more carefully than in an ordinary telephone call. The decisive role of production circumstances and their interplay with the visual and oral channels are stressed by Biber (1995: 151) in his analysis of variation in English. At one end of the spectrum are highly interactive, affective registers produced under real-time constraints that have the linguistic characteristics of 'Involved Production' and may be spoken or written. At the other are informational written registers produced with maximal opportunity for planning and revision that have the linguistic characteristics of 'Informational Production'. In between lie intermediate registers, both written and spoken, that combine varying degrees of interpersonal or informational purposes with a range of possibilities for careful production.

Print and writing have much in common. Both fix texts in the state in which they are. Both give texts durability by extending the length of time they remain available. Both make the reproduction of texts easier by allowing faithful copies to be made. But in each case print scores higher. With regard to the fixing of texts, print proved better by lessening the risk of errors or variations during the duplication process. Whereas with hand-copying no two copies were exactly alike, printing helped produce copies that were identical, or nearly identical. As will be seen, the effect was not immediate, and early printed books often show divergences due to the practice of correcting proofs during the production process. Moreover, pirate copies often put inaccurate texts into circulation. Nevertheless, Briggs and Burke's (2005: 56) verdict is that 'these qualifications do not overturn the moderate argument that the [printing] press favoured the relative fixity of texts'. Second, print improved durability. Depending on the quality of the paper and the binding, individual copies may not necessarily have been more long lasting than manuscripts, but the ease with which text could be reproduced gave it greater permanence. Above all, printing changed the way in which we conceive the preservation of text (Landlow, 1996: 29–30). With manuscripts, texts were preserved by restricting membership to slow down degradation, whereas in the case of print, text preservation is achieved through dissemination and an extended readership. Digitizing text takes the process further, and permits unconstrained reproduction with little effort and no ill effects on means of duplication. Lastly, the printing press made the production of multiple copies a far less laborious and less expensive operation. This enabled individual readers to access a greater number of books, and every book to reach more readers. The compounded effect of these factors was to permit the circulation of texts on a scale hitherto impossible. By 1640, more than 20,000 titles in English had appeared in England, ranging from pamphlets to huge folios. Through the reproduction of a text in thousands of copies, there now existed a powerful force for spreading certain linguistic forms throughout all the territories in which the language was understood (Baugh and Cable, 1993: 195–6).

Over the course of history, the impact of technological progress on language has manifested itself in various ways, depending on which attributes exercised an influence. For instance, the small size of the screen and keypad of mobile phones, together with the 160 limit on the number of characters that can be sent in one batch, have prompted a new kind of shorthand that compresses information in a small space: 'TB' for 'text back', 'L8' for 'late', etc. Processing facilities such as spellcheckers and grammar checkers inherently foster standardization, while the unidirectionality of media like email tends to lead to the omission of the phatic comment clauses (e.g. 'mind you', 'you know') of face-to-face conversations (Crystal, 2006: 43).

As a result of its properties, a media will have a built-in bias towards certain uses, as well as affinities with certain kinds of texts and therefore certain kinds of language. Print, for example, is intrinsically suited to the delivery of a narrative or a complex sustained argument, so that fiction and treatises are well served by books. On the other hand, tool-like texts that are dipped into for specific information and/or incorporate a large number of cross-references (e.g. telephone directories, railway timetables, repair manuals, encyclopedias) are enhanced by digitization and hypermedia. However, associations between a particular media and a certain type of text or language are never permanent. Nor are tastes uniform among the public. People who have grown up with answerphones are not reluctant to leave recorded messages. If they have switched from phoning their friends to leaving them text messages, or to communicating by email, it is not because they feel uncomfortable ringing people up or speaking to an answerphone, but because text messages and email are more convenient or cheaper. Their lack of concern is interesting, because it demonstrates the interdependence of different types of influences (technological and non-technological) within the social matrix. It is to the analysis of this interdependence that I now turn.

The social matrix

It hardly needs stating that the materialization of any potential that ICT may have to influence linguistic evolution depends on how widespread the new medium becomes, and how quickly it is adopted by a significant segment of the population. The rate of adoption of an innovation has been found to be affected by many factors, notably cost, public perception of its inherent and relative advantages, and the increasing pressure to adopt an innovation as more of those in your interpersonal networks do so (the diffusion effect). In addition, there may be a centralized legitimizing source helping or hindering diffusion. In the past, national governments have often exercised control over which innovations to diffuse, how to diffuse them and who to diffuse them to. The slow development of the telephone in France in the 1880s is a case in point. The French government, viewing telecommunications as the preserve of the state and a means of spreading its influence, was so little interested in the development of a system liable to encourage reciprocity and dialogue that the potential for introducing two-way dialogue was lost. The telephone 'was usually presented as a new channel for "monologue", meant to "transmit speeches, sermons, lectures", as a forerunner of radio, a new means of diffusion, another one-way-system' (Attali and Stourdze, 1977: 103).

This is a telling illustration of the way in which governmental policy can affect the balance between interpersonal and mass communication and, in so doing, influence the kind of language people are exposed to. Where, as in the example above, the balance tilts in favour of one-way communication, the effect is to give those in authority enhanced opportunities to intervene in language matters. All over the world, it is common for governments to see their remit as including the way in which language is used, and engage in language planning. Characteristically, the establishment of strong centralized monarchies in England, France and Spain between 1600 and 1800 increasingly led to the promotion of linguistic unification (Harris and Taylor, 1997: xviii). Not all governments favour official monolingualism, but all are called to take decisions involving language, and this often works to the advantage of a particular variety that becomes the standard variety. This variety is then taught in schools and to foreigners.

Historically, the vehicular function of print has tended to serve standardization through the privileged exposure it gave to certain forms. As readers saw a given spelling or structure time and time again, they came to regard it as the norm. By the middle of the sixteenth century, the dialect spoken in the financially and culturally dominant area in which most of the early presses were located had established itself in England as the common dialect of educated people (Honey, 1997: 74). It became the language of traditional ballads and narratives, and the language of the church or chapel. Far more people could read than is generally thought to be the case. As Vincent (2000) points out, although mass education did not emerge until the nineteenth century, any adult who could make out an alphabet was able to undertake instruction in basic literacy. In addition, there is plentiful evidence of serendipity learning by children, who picked up rudimentary skills when playing or working around adults.

As well as being a vehicle for language forms and promoting the standard variety by osmosis, print was used to promote the ideology of the standard in a deliberate fashion through the publication of works aimed at reducing language variation. Western European countries in the sixteenth, seventeenth and eighteenth centuries saw the publication of various proposals for spelling reforms, grammar books and national dictionaries, including the *Vocabolario degli Accademici della crusca* (1612), work of the national language academy of Italy, used as a model by other states, *Le dictionnaire de l'Académie française* (1694), and Samuel Johnson's *Dictionary of the English Language* (1755). When undertaken early and endorsed by institutions dedicated to regulating the language, attempts to remove irregularities and to stipulate what should be said (rather than record what was said) succeeded in bringing in a degree of systematicity. When attempts at harmonization occurred late, codification found itself hampered by established conventions. Johnson (1755) admits having been 'often obliged to sacrifice uniformity to custom', writing 'convey' and 'inveigh', 'deceit' and 'receipt', 'fancy' and 'phantom'. Notwithstanding these inconsistencies, Johnson's work became the accepted standard for private spelling and thereby helped fix English (Scragg, 1974: 82). In the nineteenth century, the replacement of dialect by the standard language would be assisted by the development of railways (making communication easier and faster), the depopulation of the rural areas (reducing the number of dialect speakers), and the spread of formal education. As we have seen, the new mass communication media of the twentieth century would initially be pressed into the service of the standard, while developments in mediated interpersonal communication, which, in a free society, can only help stabilization by circulating forms within a self-regulating system, were sometimes viewed with suspicion.

Even when a high degree of standardization has been achieved, those in power will find themselves confronted with a whole range of issues calling for linguistic engineering, from the safeguarding of standards and the monitoring and improvement of literacy levels, to the introduction of changes in keeping with social trends. ICT will often be used to attain these ends, while also acting as a target. Censorship in the West has lost much of its former strictness, but language continues to serve as a criterion for deciding whether films are suitable for certain age groups. Films shown on terrestrial television may be edited for language and are often accompanied by warnings that they contain swearing. Measures have also been taken that ban the use of sexist or racist language. Other measures supposedly promote the use of plain language in official communications. Again, regulations can only really apply to mass communication, but even there, deregulation and the advent of communication systems bypassing national agencies are eroding the state's sphere of influence. In an article describing the characteristics distinguishing independent radios in Italy from the state monopoly radio prior to the reorganization of the latter in 1976, Eco (1995) relates how the independent radios' use of local varieties surprised audiences, destroying the feeling of radio as a kind of official voice. Eco (1995: 226) stresses that selection still occurred, since the choice of contributors depended on the ideological outlook of the radio station. But it involved very different criteria from those of the state radio, hence the impression of a lack of censorship. Thirty years on, power over language in the media has moved further away from government departments and appointed representatives. Satellite television, email and desktop publishing are reducing the ability of the state to direct the kind of language people hear or read (or learn). This does not mean the end of all controls, at least in the case of satellite television, but, in so far as it allows language to adapt spontaneously to the new conditions brought by technological advances and other social changes, it seems to make for a more natural linguistic evolution. Baron's (2000: 215) hypothesis that 'unmonitored self-publication may come to redefine public standards of acceptability for the written word' may turn into reality.

In addition to highlighting that the impact of ICT on linguistic evolution is subject to outside influences like the educational context and government control, attempts to identify the origins of language change show that it is difficult to separate technical and cultural aspects of ICT. First, as the early use of the telephone as a broadcast rather than a two-way medium suggests, what we consider to be built-in properties may turn out to be imposed qualities. Second, it is possible for the same aspect of language use to arise from different circumstances or characteristics. We saw earlier how the small size of the mobile phone screen was conducive to the use of abbreviations. Similar pressures to make texts short exist in other media. Words may have to be cut to fit a newspaper column, or a small section of script dropped to fit a radio or television window. Information has to be compressed through devices like noun–noun sequences and appositive noun phrases (Biber, 2003). However, although the pressures seem to be tied to the materiality of the hardware, they actually originate in cultural practices. Despite appearances, a large part of what looks like fundamental constraints is not, in fact, of a technical nature, so that, as Crystal (1997: 392) notes, similarities between newspapers styles, for example, are largely superficial, and preferences vary enormously.

In helping to shape the communication tool that they use, ICT indirectly affects language users and language learners. The exact nature of the effect, both globally and in any given case, will vary according to circumstances. It will depend, among other things, on whether ICT, or a specific media, supports standardization or diversification. It cannot therefore be neatly summed up. All that can be said is that, as noted in the last chapter, variation tends to be more problematical for language users than language change. From this point of view, a key aspect of the impact of ICT is its growing ability to expose people to a host of language variants that compete for attention. This may initially prove unsettling and confusing, especially for L2 users, although the benefits and drawbacks will only be assessable in the light of other factors, such as the likelihood of face-to-face contacts with speakers of particular varieties. Conversely, where it helps standardization, ICT will tend to make life simpler for users, unless the selected variety differs from the one they speak. This may be a frequent occurrence with L1 speakers, inducing a sense of disempowerment. It is less likely to happen with L2 users, many of whom will have learnt the language in a formal context and been taught the standard variety.

Processes at work: levels of causality

It follows from the above that the role of ICT in the evolution of language varies from case to case, ranging from acting as a trigger, to a catalyst role and a disseminating device. What part ICT plays in a given instance is not always easy to decide. Crystal (2006: 41) is no doubt correct both in describing written language as unable to express all the intonational and other prosodic features of speech, and in linking the multiplication of emoticons to the immediacy of certain Internet interactions. But graphic ways of capturing prosody and paralanguage are not as new as he seems to imply when asking why smileys were not introduced before the development of Internet communication. ICT did not, in fact, initiate the use of emoticons. Informal letters have long contained crosses for kisses and various other means of compensating for absence. What ICT did was expand and standardize the use of graphic symbols by making them well known. As this case illustrates, the possible roles of ICT are not discrete, but merge into one another as ICT precipitates change and then spreads it. Furthermore, the role of ICT as a disseminating device is not confined to linguistic forms. ICT also disseminates ideas about language. Linguistic topics are popular, and the press and radio frequently carry debates or contributions from members of the public on linguistic matters (see Cameron, 1995).

How much the circulation of potential models impacts on language behaviour is unclear. Using diffusion success as a criterion, Milroy and

Milroy (1985: 347) propose the following tripartite classification of speaker innovations. Speaker innovations may

- fail to diffuse beyond the speaker
- diffuse into a community with which he/she has contact, but no further
- diffuse into a community with which he/she has contact and then subsequently diffuse from that community into other communities via a further innovator who has ties with both the relevant communities.

Only in the latter case is the result labelled 'linguistic change'. In common with a number of other linguists, Milroy and Milroy (1999) argue that the effect of ICT on language is not as great as people think, and that, although the media provide exposure to new or 'strange' features, these do not actually diffuse into new communities and therefore do not produce language change. They back up this claim by referring to research by Rogers and Shoemaker, published in 1971, which shows that interpersonal channels of communication are more influential than mass media channels in persuading people to adopt an innovation. Generally, mass media channels give rise to awareness of an innovation, but are not very effective in promoting adoption. Milroy and Milroy (1999: 25) go on to add that 'there is no reason to think that the diffusion of linguistic innovations will follow principles different from those governing the diffusion of other kinds of innovation', citing in support of their claim the lack of influence of the standard spoken language used by the BBC on the rate of adoption of that standard.

I wish to take issue with the idea that the diffusion of linguistic innovations is no different from that of other innovations. To begin with, awareness and adoption are insufficient as a conceptual framework to describe the effects of language contact. Secondly, Milroy and Milroy's choice of evidence relates to an area that is acknowledged to be resistant to change and is probably not wholly representative of language change. In addition, the percentage they give, i.e. around 3 per cent (Milroy and Milroy, 1999: 151), needs to be substantiated, and, as remarked by Honey (1997), even if people have not taken on RP in a wholescale fashion, they may have adapted their accent towards RP.

Adoption is an easy enough concept to apply to the language area. A linguistic novelty (novel at least to the individual) can be regarded as having been adopted if it appears in the language they produce, although we may wish to follow Trudgill and differentiate between accommodation and what Trudgill (1986: 40) calls, somewhat confusingly, 'diffusion': 'Diffusion can be said to have taken place, presumably, on the first occasion when a speaker employs a new feature in the *absence* of speakers of the variety originally containing this feature – when, in other words, it is no longer accommodation.' Awareness is a more complex issue. Awareness of linguistic diversity or linguistic similarity, be it the existence of another language or variety, or of prosodic, lexical or grammatical characteristics that may or may not match those of your own variety, is distinct from the ability to handle language, and brings us into the realm of metalinguistics. Moreover, unlike what happens, for instance, with the purchase of a piece of equipment, awareness is not a prerequisite to adoption where language is concerned. Language alterations can be a conscious process, but they also commonly take place subconsciously, without entering awareness. Lastly, to present the diffusion of linguistic innovations solely in terms of awareness and adoption is to leave out an important possible outcome, namely the ability to understand language items that you do not personally produce, or that you pronounce or use differently. Swear words are an obvious example.

What is uncontroversial is that ICT provides encounters with a linguistic range that surpasses what the most extensive travelling can deliver. While all media play a part in this widening of horizons, the role of mass communication is more obvious than that of mediated, point-to-point interaction. In a number of cases broadcast media have promoted a consciousness of the standard and helped to give it authority, while simultaneously enhancing people's awareness of linguistic diversity. Matheson (1933: 61) stresses how radio made people aware of the speech of others: 'By enabling a whole country or continent to listen to a disembodied voice, wireless concentrates attention on it – flood-lights it, as it were – bringing out every trick and peculiarity.' She reports that pronunciation phenomena arouse great interest and attention, and that listeners were keen to contribute evidence of local pronunciation of words and place names. This interest in linguistic matters and regional variation is still very much in evidence today.

Where differences are marked, exposure to unfamiliar features may induce awareness of variation that is not accompanied by comprehension. However, as people meet the new forms in a range of contexts and get used to them, comprehension difficulties diminish. The growing ability of the British to understand American films illustrates that ICT can enhance the chances of this happening. As Trudgill

(1990: 10) reminds us, until the 1930s, most British people had never heard an American accent. Consequently, when American talking films were first introduced into Britain, many complained that they could not understand them. American productions are now commonplace on cinema and television and people have ceased experiencing difficulties.

Apart from the fact that the media clearly have some impact on language, if only temporarily, there are a number of reasons for not rejecting the possibility that they may be a contributory factor in systemic language change. The first and by far the most important is the dearth of reliable evidence on the subject, at least with respect to certain categories of change. A second reason is the emergence of findings challenging paradigms based on mobility and contact, such as the presence of consonantal features typical of Southern English in the speech of non-mobile working-class adolescent Glaswegians (Stuart-Smith and Tweedie, 2000). Results of this kind have prompted speculations that broadcast media may play a role in language change, a hypothesis that is currently being investigated in relation to television in a project described as marking the beginning of systematic research into the relationship between television and language change (Stuart-Smith, 2004). That this should be the first project studying the impact of television on language is astonishing, but is paralleled by similar neglect of the relationship between interpersonal mediated communication and language change. This neglect is apparent in the way in which the prevalent orthodoxy is articulated. The basic premise is that language change occurs through accommodation, which requires reciprocal communication. However, accommodation is then linked to direct (as opposed to technologically mediated) contact rather than to interpersonal communication in general: 'It is *only during face-to-face interaction* that accommodation occurs' (Trudgill, 1986: 40, italics added). Whether an oversight or a flaw in the argument, the equation of reciprocal communication with face-to-face is questionable. While it is legitimate to distinguish between accommodation, and imitation and copying, which are taken to be the mechanisms at work with broadcast media, the definition of accommodation seems unjustifiably restrictive. Even if it is the case that accommodation does not occur to the same extent in mediated communication as in face-to-face – and one must not overlook the possibility that different forms of mediated communication may differ in this respect – the same basic mechanism of adjustment to the other participant or participants seems to be involved. To sum up, there are two separate but related problems with traditional accounts of language change: the linking of language change to a specific narrowly defined mechanism, and the probable underrating of the impact of broadcast media.

It is difficult to reconcile the idea that the contribution of the media to language change is confined to the spreading of some new lexis and idioms and fashionable pronunciations of individual words with the known effects of writing and printing on language. Pursuing Ong's (1982) point that writing transforms both speech and thought, Benczik (2003) argues that in making segmental language resources carry the full weight of the message, the imperfections of writing led to sophisticated semantic precision and the proliferation of word forms, as well as to greater syntactic complexity. These effects are said to have permeated speech, and to have been beneficial to thought. Conversely, the inability of written language to register suprasegmentals is regarded as having impoverished those components. Here Benczik adduces as evidence the greater intonational richness of languages such as Spanish, Italian and Russian, where writing was disseminated relatively late, compared to English and German, where writing was taken up on a large scale relatively early. He expresses concern that the end of print culture and the loss of position of writing as a transporter of communication will lead to a gradual impoverishment of language and have a negative effect on thought: 'Today, when writing seems to be losing its earlier hegemony over communication, the question arises as to whether this will lead to the erosion of human language, and also of human thought' (Benczik, 2003: 249). Even if the consequences are not as drastic as Benczik implies, language is bound to change as technological progress brings about different distributions of the communication load between the written word, speech and pictures.

While not everyone will go as far as claiming, as Benzick does, that communication technologies have played a key role in the history of language change, it can be argued that the majority view lacks strong supportive empirical evidence and convincing arguments. In particular, more careful consideration should be given to the interpretation of negative results, and to the multifaceted and heterogeneous character of any potential impact. The increasing distinctiveness of the dialects of inner-city African Americans, who are avid consumers of mass media, may well be proof that the media fail to cause linguistic change, as claimed by Chambers (1998), but this is not the only possibility. For instance, the programmes people watch or listen to may only partly be in Standard English, or there may be strong counter-pressures cancelling their effect. It is noteworthy that in a later work than the one referred to by Milroy and Milroy (1999), Rogers (1983) states:

> Mass media can:
>
> 1. Reach a large audience rapidly.
> 2. Create knowledge and spread information.
> 3. Lead to changes in weakly held attitudes.
>
> The formation and change of strongly held attitudes, however, is best accomplished by interpersonal channels. (Rogers, 1983: 198)

This suggests an alternative explanation for the phenomena referred to by Chambers, namely that the dialects of African Americans are too much entrenched as markers of social identity to be influenced by the mass media. If this is correct, it is not possible to rule out that the media may have an influence under other circumstances.

Similarly, Trudgill's argument that, if nationwide radio and television were major sources of diffusion then the whole country would be simultaneously affected, presupposes sameness of media consumption, which goes against established facts. One might add that simultaneous adoption is very unusual, even perhaps unknown, and would make the diffusion of linguistic novelties quite unlike that of other innovations, where there are typically early adopters, mainstream adopters and late adopters. It may be the case that the mass media have the potential of inducing a swifter pace of diffusion than other forms of communication, but not to the point of simultaneous adoption.

It is not uncommon for technological progress to call existing theories into question. This would seem to be the case here. The many questions that arise when examining the conventional approach to language change in the light of contemporary interactions suggest that the accepted paradigm needs to be revised. The idea that the media have a peripheral role must be submitted to close scrutiny, and the distinction between mechanisms must be endowed with a better intellectual and empirical basis. It is common experience that there can sometimes be a fine line between what is conscious and intentional and what is spontaneous and unconscious, between what belongs to copying and imitation and what represents accommodation. Even in face-to-face it may be difficult to tell unconscious accommodation phenomena from skilled deliberate attempts to match someone's verbal and physical behaviour in order to increase rapport, as recommended, for instance, by NLP (neuro-linguistic programming).

Without some sharply defined criteria, admittedly difficult to formulate given the lack of observability of the necessary data, it is not possible to characterize and compare modifications that take place in different technological contexts. How are we to classify changes in the forms of greetings, vocabulary, turns of phrase, abbreviations, found in emails and Chat? How can we recognize whether they are planned or spontaneous? Crucially, the fact that a particular mechanism has played a primordial role in the past does not guarantee that it will continue to do so against the backdrop of changing communication patterns. In particular, the formation of networked communities along non-geographical lines suggests that changes in the dynamics of underlying populations may no longer provide an adequate explanation of language change. In a changing world even change may change, witness the fact that the Middle English period saw major changes in grammar but, apart from the effects of the Norman Conquest, lesser changes in vocabulary, whereas the converse has happened since the invention of the printing press and the spread of literacy and formal education.

Given that people are daily exposed to multiple influences pulling in different directions, it seems unrealistic to expect the media to leave a clear imprint on linguistic behaviour. Rather, the media are likely to deliver a patchwork of influences that will occasionally coalesce into changes. Bombarding people with a particular advert is a common ploy in the publicity trade, which reckons that repeated exposure wears down people's resistance to a message and helps the diffusion of innovations. There is some evidence that frequent exposure can occasionally have the same effect on language, at least with regard to the use of imported terms and other forms of cross-linguistic influence such as loan translations. What specific circumstances lead to change is not known but the phenomenon itself is known to exist. Discussing how the constraint of lip movement synchronization has led to the use of peculiar Italian expressions in films dubbed from English, Ross writes:

> The need for a close match becomes particularly critical for short speech items, the most troublesome being short one-word expressions such as 'Great!' When Italians want to express similar approval, they normally say something like *Magnifico! Meraviglioso! Favoloso!* or *Splendido*! But none of these are successful translations for 'Great!' when lip and mouth movements are considered: they all have far too many syllables and start with very 'visible' sounds. Watch a few films or TV programmes in Italy that have been dubbed from English and you are bound to catch a *Grande*! Or a *Grandioso*! (grand) voiced over a 'Great!' (Ross, 1995: 46)

Ross adds that, although such expressions are not really suitable or natural, they have infiltrated the language and are beginning to be used spontaneously. He also suggests that the practice of translating 'Call me tomorrow!' by 'Chiamami domani!' instead of the normal 'Dammi un colpo di telefono domani!' or 'Telefonami domani!', which are too long and do not match the original track from a labial point of view, probably accounts for the increasing use of 'chiamare' in the sense of 'to telephone' in ordinary conversation. Again, it is difficult to be sure how voluntary the changes are, how they should be classified and whether they are representative. But they provide additional evidence of an influence.

Because factors such as increasing mobility, the development of new means of communication, and social pressures weave an intricate web of possible influences, it can be difficult to pinpoint exactly the trigger for, and contributory factors to, linguistic change. For the path of language change to be easy to chart, the diffused feature must be very prominent, or modifications particularly striking. Smileys are salient enough for their crossing from the Internet to informal letters to have been noticed and remarked on. Similarly, because new vocabulary items and catch-phrases tend to attract attention, people are aware of the role the mass media play in their propagation. For instance, most people in Britain are aware that the phrase 'the weakest link' has been given a new lease of life and new connotations by the popularity of the TV programme with that name. Whether the effect turns out to be long-lasting and anchors the phrase in the language system remains to be seen. Another instance of a clearly identifiable influence is the impact on journalism of the demand for economy that the telegraph imposed on telegrams: 'The desire for compression, to save money on the wire, led to shorter sentences and a greater emphasis of key-words. There is often a gain in simplicity and lack of padding; often a loss in the simplification of complicated issues, and in the distorting tendency of the emphatic key-word' (Williams, 1980: 219). Significantly, this occurred on a smaller scale in local papers, which made a lesser use of telegrams. There is also supportive evidence that the telegraph was instrumental in inducing Poe and Hemingway to pare down their writing style. In his autobiography, Steffens (1958: 834) recalls Hemingway enthusing about the cabelese on his return from the exodus of the Greek fugitives from Turkey and quotes him as saying some time later that he had to stop being a correspondent because he was getting too fascinated by the lingo of the cable. These are exceptions. Clear signs are rare and, in most cases, influences are subtle and hard to detect, so that changes cannot be traced to their source. In addition, the impact of ICT on language change varies not only from medium to medium, but across the various aspects of language structure and use, as illustrated in the next section.

Differential effects

The purpose of this section is to document in greater detail the effect of ICT on language. The section is not intended to provide an exhaustive treatment of the subject but aims to give an indication of the diverse ways in which ICT affects language. The areas selected have been chosen because they exemplify varying degrees of susceptibility to the influence of ICT. The omission of a particular area is likely to be due to the paucity of information and should not be interpreted as a sign of immunity.

Lexical and semantic change

One of the areas over which ICT is acknowledged to have some influence is vocabulary. In the first place, advances in ICT give rise to the formation of new words or extensions in meaning of part of the existing stock. Olson (1994) has discussed how 'putting the world on paper' required and triggered the elaboration of lexical and syntactic devices for representing the illocutionary force of utterances. Means of compensating for the loss of voice had to be devised to enable the reader to determine the speaker's communicative intention, whether the propositional content was intended to be taken as a claim, a tentative suggestion, an authoritative statement, and so on. Second, ICT helps disseminate new and unfamiliar forms and meanings beyond their original context, including items borrowed from other languages: 'Worldwide communication via the Internet, globalization of national economies resulting in multinational corporations, and commercial television with its advertisements and videoclips have led to a new dimension of lexical borrowings and code-switching, at least in the technical languages of business and commerce, computing, advertising, and youth language' (Busse and Görlach, 2002: 14). This is illustrated by Muhr (2003), who presents detailed evidence of the impact of German German television programmes broadcast via satellite on Austrian German. Examples include the emergence of the particle 'mal' in Austrian German and the replacement of some core lexical items with their German German equivalents (e.g. replacement of 'Verkhülung' (a cold) with 'Erkältung').

Each technological innovation has been accompanied by lexical developments. According to Crystal (1988: 212), as a result of the continuous flow of new words from the fields of science and technology since the seventeenth century, scientific and technical terms now make up over half the vocabulary of English. Some of the new terms are known only to specialists, but others have passed into common usage. Ayto's (1999) analysis of lexical growth areas in succeeding decades of the twentieth century shows that radio and film along with cars and aircraft dominated lexical innovations in the first half of the century, while computer and computer-related topics were the main source of growth in the second. ICT has been an extremely prolific source of new words or new meanings. Well-known examples from English include 'television', 'tape recorder', 'cassette recorder', 'videotape', 'computer', 'chip', 'mouse', 'memory', and the rapid spread of the 'e'-prefix (e.g. 'e-money', 'e-commerce', 'e-learning'), as well as new uses for words like 'folder' and 'save'. Some of these words have been taken over by other languages, while other inventions have led to the use of loan translations or calques and home-grown terms. Thus French has 'film', 'flash-back', 'star', 'superstar' from American English (Walter, 2001: 242) as well as 'programme', 'processeur', 'moniteur', 'base de données' (database), 'autoroute de l'information' (information (super) highway), 'balladeur' (walkman), all translated from, or modelled on, English, and the indigenous 'ordinateur' (computer).

The multiplicity of terms and meanings that have sprung up around ICT as opposed to, for example, washing technology, is an indication of the significant place ICT has come to assume in daily life. While it is the norm for inventions to bring new words or new uses of old words, some inventions have more influence on language than others. Not because they are intrinsically more important, but because they have a greater impact on the culture of the community into which they are introduced. Unless they break down, washing machines, tumble dryers and dishwashers only impact on a small part of people's lives. They are a relatively infrequent topic of conversation and have not brought many new words into the language. By contrast, television and computers figure prominently in people's activities. They are much talked about and have led to the coining of a wide range of terms, as well as to the extension of the meaning of a substantial number of established items.

Another aspect of the impact of ICT on vocabulary is the effect of ICT-related activities on relative frequency. The most obvious example is the semantic extension of words like 'mouse', 'file', 'directory' and their propulsion up the frequency ladder following the spread of computer technology. A more recent and somewhat different case is the increased use of navigation and orientation terms in entertainment products in which pictures and sounds take over the narrative functions traditionally assumed by the written text, for example video games.

As noted earlier, the increased contact with other languages and language varieties that ICT permits, has led, if not always to the adoption, at least to better comprehension of certain foreign or regional lexical items. Some English terms (e.g. 'weekend') have gained much currency in other languages, and British English has taken in a number of expressions that used to be regarded as Americanisms. Significantly, unless the instances of localization found in the American editions of the Harry Potter books and the use of a term like 'momentarily' to mean 'soon' in the film version of the first book represent exceptions – and there is no reason to believe that they do – the traffic of words across the Atlantic seems to continue to have the dominant West–East direction noted by Strang (1970). Strang gives a list of examples regarded as Americanisms during the Second World War that had already been absorbed 25 years later. They include 'bowling alley' (rather than 'skittle alley'), 'radio' (rather than 'wireless'), 'raincoat' (for 'mackintosh') and 'thriller' (instead of 'shocker'). Trudgill (1986: 41) provides more recent illustrations, including the use of 'hopefully' as a sentence adverbial and the expression 'a whole new ball game', together with the comment that 'it has to be assumed that radio and especially television play a major role in the diffusion of innovations of this type, though of course written American English and face-to-face contact with Americans will also be of importance'.

The traffic imbalance between American English and British English, and the adoption of German German terms by Austrian German speakers, illustrate how technology intersects with sociopolitical and economic realities to produce instances of language change that reflect and enhance asymmetrical power relationships. They exemplify the mix of forces at work in society and give an indication of the social dimension of the influence of technology on language.

Pronunciation

As will be apparent from earlier statements, the impact of ICT on pronunciation is a controversial issue. Reference was made to the fact that the BBC was originally cast as an agency for the diffusion of RP, supplying the public with models to imitate which they had previously had little access to. Increased exposure to RP, however, appears to have had little effect on the general public. Milroy and Milroy's educated guess of a proportion of speakers of RP of 3 per cent may underestimate the number of RP speakers. Even so, it is clear that the accent has not caught on in a massive way. This should not come as a surprise. Although RP was the norm in the public schools attended by some of the Lancashire employers of the second half of the nineteenth century, it seems to have taken several generations for it to take root (Joyce, 1991: 202). In a similar way, one regularly comes across people identifiable by their accent as originating from a different region or country from the one they have settled in. Their accent may not be as strong or pure as it once was, but it remains noticeable. If this can occur in the face of daily exposure to a different accent in the context of face-to-face interactions, it is unrealistic to expect a pronunciation heard on the radio or television to sweep away local practices throughout the country.

In general, the impact of ICT on pronunciation tends to be limited to the pronunciation of specific words or to particularly salient features, sometimes involving cultivated habits. Analysing the pronunciation of some types of British pop songs in the late 1950s, Trudgill (1983) found that they employed different accents when singing from when they were talking, using features stereotypically associated by the British with American pronunciation such as non-prevocalic /r/ in words like 'girl' and 'more'. Trudgill (1983: 144) ascribes this tendency to the cultural ascendancy of North America in the field of popular music which led singers to imitate American sounds when performing what was a predominantly American activity. In time, the tendency faded, a change which Trudgill puts down to the popularity of the Beatles.

In my view, the spread of American pronunciation trends among singers shows that ICT, which acquainted singers with the features they went on to incorporate in their singing, can lead to shifts in pronunciation when circumstances are especially favourable. At the same time, the fact that the tendencies were confined to the pronunciation singers used when they sang (and, one assumes, any karaoke-like performances by others), and did not spread either to their speech or to that of their audiences indicates insufficient desire to adopt the model among the general population. It is arguable that pronunciation normally involves firmly implanted patterns that are inherently difficult to modify. For any change to occur, the user must therefore have comparatively more to gain than with other language components. Where habits are less deep-seated, as in the case of learnt languages or borrowed items, changes in pronunciation may be easier to accommodate. In support, one might quote the fact that L2 users of British English seem to find it less difficult to change to an American pronunciation than to shed their original accent, and the evolution of the pronunciation of imported terms. Thus, the modern French pronunciation of 'club' has an [œ], which is felt to be closer to English than the [y] used in the nineteenth century, while the use of [ng] in words such as 'camping' in the post-war period has given way to the English pronunciation [ŋ], filling an empty place in the French phonemic system (Humbley, 2002). Similar changes have taken place in other languages: 'Since spoken English has become much more easily accessible, loanwords are now largely pronounced in a way that approximates to the etymon. This is certainly the case with new borrowings, but is also evident in corrections of earlier loanwords transmitted through texts' (Görlach, 2002: 3). There is no hard evidence that the media were implicated in the change, but they are likely to have been a significant factor.

Spelling and punctuation

Spelling and punctuation are traditionally considered as the areas in which standardization is easiest to achieve. Orthographic standardization is a gradual process on which ICT has tended to have a beneficial effect, even if, in Britain at least, stabilization initially suffered a setback after the introduction of printing, due to the lack of a tradition of uniformity in craft training or practices in the early years of the trade (Howatt, 2004: 10). Contrary to popular belief, standardization started well before the invention of the printing press:

> What has come to be known as the West Saxon scribal tradition produced in the late Old English period a remarkably rigid system in use throughout England. The success of the scribal tradition in stabilizing spelling cannot be overstressed. It came about at a time when the political situation was particularly favourable, for under the reign of Edgar (959–75) the country was united, prosperous and free from external attacks. (Scragg, 1974: 7)

Stabilization broke down with the political upheaval caused by the Norman Conquest, but was resumed in the fourteenth century. Early in the fifteenth century, the Chancery, which had been using Latin or French, once more began to have recourse to English, providing a lead for other professional scribes. One might have expected the spread of spelling consistency to be helped by the setting of the first English press in 1476, but in fact printing initially hampered the move towards orthographic uniformity. One reason for this is that Caxton relied on imported machinery and had to use foreign compositors incapable of regularizing the spelling of what they set in type. Moreover, spelling variants were technologically convenient, allowing printers to spell a word like 'bad' in a short form ('bad') to avoid line-breaks or in a long one ('badde') to fill out a line to meet a right-hand margin (Howatt, 2004: 91). However, matters gradually improved and 'by 1700 stabilization was complete' (Scragg, 1974: 80). As is well known, technological advances have introduced centrifugal tendencies into this relatively stable state of affairs. CMC has seen the elaboration of many new linguistic forms and norms. Some of these, for instance novel abbreviations such as 'lol' for 'laughing out loud', represent true innovations. Others are departures from standard orthography, with some deviant spellings becoming, according to Crystal (2006: 94), 'so widely used as to be virtually standard in this variety'.

As regards punctuation, Little (1994) describes how the conventions regulating punctuation in the written language that appears on television screens differ from those governing standard edited English. She notes that punctuation tends to be used sparsely, as the main priority is visual impact, and words, whether written or spoken, are incidental. After stating that changes tend to go unnoticed, partly because what matters is the picture, and partly because of the transient nature of the text, Little voices her concern about the potential impact on students' punctuation of a medium they spend such a large amount of time watching. She sees television as contributing to a change in punctuation practices that may come to impact the standard edited English of tomorrow. Minimalist punctuation is also mentioned by Crystal (2006: 95), this time in relation to Netspeak, where it is combined with the use of symbols like # that are outside the traditional punctuation system, and with the exaggerated use of other symbols, for instance a series of exclamation marks. For Baron (2000: 188–9), changes in punctuation practices form part of the growing interchangeablility of speech and writing, with punctuation facilitating access to the meaning of messages that are intended to be viewed quickly, or being used to capture prosodic features of speech, as they would have been used had the words been spoken, a kind of writer's inner voice. Once again, we are confronted with effects that vary with the medium and with production circumstances, and reflect human beings' ability to adjust to different conditions. Overall, there appears to be a stronger link between ICT and spelling and punctuation than between ICT and pronunciation. This is presumably because spelling and punctuation are aspects of language that are learnt rather than acquired, and are therefore intrinsically more open to change.

Register

Register is variety according to use as opposed to user (Halliday, McIntosh and Strevens, 1964: 77), i.e. functional variation. As Halliday (1989: 45) points out, functional variation has always existed, and unwritten languages have been shown to vary in register. Nevertheless, the invention of writing brought in new production conditions that had a major impact on this kind of variation. After studying the patterns of historical register variation in English, Biber (1995: 300) hypothesizes three separate stages in the evolution of written registers:

1. genesis
2. early development
3. split between popular and specialized registers.

In stage 1, written registers start to diverge from typical spoken language in line with their different primary purposes and production circumstances. Over the course of stage 2, considered to have taken 100–200 years in the case of English, all written registers evolve to become even more sharply distinguished from spoken registers in ways that extend the range of register variation. Stage 3 sees the development of two sharply distinct trends. Some registers reverse their earlier course towards more literate styles to cater for the needs of a widening public. Others, on the other hand, become more specialized in response to the development of academic, scientific and institutional fields and their need to report current research findings, and more sharply distinguished from spoken registers.

Unsurprisingly, the history of register variation reflects and is intricately intertwined with the evolution of ICT. Hughes (1988: 93) notes that from the very beginning 'printing encouraged diverse publishing ventures and accentuated different kinds of language'. One of these kinds of language was an educational, ostensibly neutral, mode. Another was promotional language, which in Caxton's case, was employed to market his books. There was also the authoritative statement, usually on religious or political matters, as well as polemical controversy, commonly deriving from these same religious issues. In the case of English, Biber's stage 2 corresponds to the seventeenth and eighteenth centuries, when we observe a certain amount of diversification in line with the growth of printing and the rise of the middle classes. But it is in the nineteenth century, with the invention of the steam press and the rotary press, that printing output takes off, and with it the proliferation of texts and development of new registers.

It is a trend that has continued unabated ever since. It is currently in evidence on the Internet, with the emergence of new kinds of register or subregister that selectively and adaptively display properties of both speech and writing (Ferrara, Brunner and Whittenmore, 1991). The pace of change is thrown into relief by the differences between the first and second edition of a book by Crystal on Internet language. The first edition recognizes four varieties: emails, synchronous and asynchronous chatgroups, virtual worlds and the World Wide Web, each of which is said to have 'characteristics closely related to the properties of its technological context as well as to the intentions, activities, and (to some extent) personalities of the users' (Crystal, 2001: 224–5). The second, published five years later, has two more: blogging (the publication of online journals displaying entries in a reverse chronological order) and instant messaging. Crystal (2006) comments that, while he had expected some evolution to take place, he had not anticipated that further varieties would develop so soon. It certainly took much longer for radio and television to evolve subvarieties even if they are now provided with many different types, from newsreading and weather reports, to sports commentary and programme announcements.

In the case of the press, centrifugal tendencies have resulted in a hierarchical separation of registers in the British press, with the popular newspapers exhibiting a shift towards informality similar to the one noted with reference to broadcast media in the last chapter. Fowler (1991: 57) accounts for this phenomenon as follows: 'The reasons for adopting a conversational style [in the press] have partly to do with the construction of an illusion of informality, familiarity, friendliness. But there is a more important ideological reason. [...] Conversation implies a commonly held view of the world, a shared subjective reality that is taken for granted and does not have to be proved.' Having described the illusion of orality as 'cued by devices like slang words, syntactic contractions and fragmented layout', Fowler (1991: 61–4) proceeds to discuss various ways of producing 'the illusion of a "person" with voice and opinions', including the use of different typefaces to suggest variations of stress, tone and pace, simplifications of spelling in line with pronunciation, short, incomplete sentences, the use of first names and nicknames, deictic markers such as 'you', 'here', 'now', and modal expressions which enhance subjectivity.

One of the most striking features of newspaper language, and one which not only spans the divide between the tabloids and other papers but crosses national boundaries, is what is sometimes referred to as headlinese. One of the characteristics of headlinese is to give currency to short and emotive words and make them flexible in grammatical function. For example, it has spread the use of 'axe' as a verb, the first recorded use being in a quotation from the *Glasgow Herald* in 1922 (Hughes, 1988: 133). It also makes much use of metaphors, referring to agreements as 'pacts' and 'deals', and to disagreements as 'clashes', 'rows' and 'battles'. Although it is full of innovations, these seldom propagate beyond journalism. One of the reasons why they do not result in language change is that the syntax of headlinese does not conform to that of common speech. As Hughes (1988: 141–2) observes, 'one can hardly imagine two people in a bus queue using verbatim in a conversation such phrases as "new Kissinger peace dash" or "glory day for Tottenham" '. For L2 users and language learners, the idiosyncratic syntax of headlinese can present a problem, so that, where objectives include being able to understand newspapers, it is essential for the language syllabus to cover the lexical items, collocations (e.g. 'hawks' and 'doves') and special structures which headlinese is so fond of.

Unlike headlinese, the language of advertising is to be found outside the mass media, but it is mostly through the mass media that we are exposed to it. Among the most noticeable features of this variety is a predilection for unreserved and laudatory language, including recourse to adjectives like 'new', 'revolutionary' and a high incidence of intensifiers (e.g. 'extremely', 'highly'), standardless comparatives ('Brand X washes whiter') and superlatives ('best',' finest', etc.) (Hermerén, 1999: 184). Another important aspect of advertising discourse is its creative tendencies, which can be seen in the use of verbal strategies such as metaphor and metonymy, alliteration and rhyme, and in the occurrence of deliberate misspellings, as in the slogan 'Beanz meanz Heinz'. In addition, advertising discourse uses personal pronouns, questions and imperatives to make the message appear more interactive and to give the impression that it is addressed to an individual rather than a mass of people. The language is informal and conversational in tone. In this it echoes the merging of private and public spheres epitomized by the use of first names in television interviews, but found in other domains such as the conversationalization of interactions between professionals and their publics or clients (Fairclough, 1995: 11).

Language spread

In the section above, I outlined some of the ways in which ICT alters the world's linguistic landscape through its effect on the make-up of individual languages. In this section, I turn to a very different kind of impact and discuss the role of ICT in language spread.

Scholars agree that, contrary to popular notions that some languages are better than others, or more capable of expressing a wide range of meanings, languages do not spread or attain international status because of some inherent qualities that make them intrinsically superior. Whatever the French may claim, clarity is not the preserve of the French language, and the fact that the French lay much store by the ability to produce cogent arguments does not entitle the French language to have an international role. If French has an international role, it is largely as a result of past glories on battlefields. For centuries, military might has been the main reason behind the rise and decline of languages. Provided it lasted, military conquest expanded the territory over which the victor's language was spoken. Defeat, on the other hand, tended to lead to the demise of the loser's language. Military superiority often went hand in hand, and contributed to, economic strength, and the two in turn helped raise the status of the languages of powerful countries, adding new motives for learning these languages. In recent times, economic and prestige factors have grown in importance. If English has overtaken French on the international scene, it is not because it is uniquely equipped for the role of a global language. It is because English has repeatedly found itself in the right place at the right time, that is to say at the centre of major social, economic, political and technological developments (Fennell, 2001: 244). Like French, English initially spread as a result of colonialism. But it went on to spread as the language of British leadership in the Industrial Revolution, as the language of American economic superiority and political leadership, and more recently, as a consequence of American technological domination.

English was in the right place at the right time when Caxton set up the first printing press in Westminster in 1476. By this time English was becoming established as the language of the nation, whereas 100 years earlier, it was still in competition with French, which remained the official language of government in London, while in the previous century, Latin reigned unchallenged as the official language of Europe. Had printing spread before it did, the fate of English, French and Latin would undoubtedly have been different from what they have been. But in Caxton's time, although Latin was the mark of a properly educated person and the language in which many of the earliest books were published, and while French was still an accomplishment for people with ambitions, the problem was not in which language to publish, but which variety of English to select. Caxton's dilemma is epitomized by the famous anecdote of the merchant who failed to get understood when he asked for eggs using the word eggys/egges instead of eyren (Caxton, 1490).

Although Caxton did not set out to bring uniformity, he was instrumental in resolving the problem of linguistic diversity of which he was so acutely aware: 'By deciding, for better or for worse, to adopt the dialect of London and the South-East as the English for his books, Caxton took a decisive step forward in establishing that particular variety as "the English language"' (Harris and Taylor, 1997: 91–2). Although most books were initially in Latin, works in English soon started to appear, including an English translation of the Bible in the mid sixteenth century, the publication of which is deemed to have been a decisive moment for Standard English (Leith and Graddol, 1996: 138). In a similar way, the survival of Welsh is said to have sometimes been attributed to the publication of a Welsh Bible during the Reformation (Leith, 1996: 193). Thanks to printing, other European vernaculars too began to fructify and grow. For instance, the proportion of books published in French in Paris rose from under 10 per cent in 1501 to 21 per cent in 1549 and over 50 per cent in 1575 (Febvre and Martin, 1976: 321). In addition, printing endowed scholarship with new powers by providing access to languages that had been unavailable. Eisenstein (1979: 224) describes how the number of languages in polyglot Bibles went up with each new edition, to the point where 'no less than nine (including Persian and Ethiopic) had to be mastered by the compositors and correctors of the London edition of 1657'.

English was again fortunate in being the language in which the telegraph system was developed. Following the building of the first railway telegraph in Britain in 1837 and the patenting of the Morse code in the same year, the first public telegraph line was opened in the United States in 1844. It ran from Baltimore to Washington. Fennell (2001: 256) notes that 'the development of technology in the age of steam often quite literally went side by side with the spread of English: when railway tracks were laid, telegraph cables were laid along with them'. In 1864, Britain's desire to communicate by telegraph with India led to the signing of the Indo-Ottoman Telegraphic Convention that allowed the erection of a landline through Turkey and stipulated that 'the Turkish administration would employ clerks "possessing a knowledge of the English language sufficient for the perfect performance of that service" and that the Constantinople office would have officials "thoroughly conversant with the English language"' (Headrick, 1991: 21).This was a somewhat ambitious goal and reality turned out rather less rosy, with messages taking several days to arrive and reaching their destination in a garbled form. But it laid the foundations for the use of English as the international language of the majority of telegraph operators and paved the way for its role as a lingua franca in telecommunications and trade. By 1870, Britain had links with North America, Europe, the Middle East and India, and was well ahead of France, Germany, Russia and the United States, which were still busy developing their domestic networks. It would remain the control centre of telegraphy until the next century, when the USA, another English-speaking country, took over.

By contrast, telegraphy did not come at the right time for France. The enthusiasm of the French for the aerial telegraph, a system of semaphores introduced by Chappe in 1793 that gave the government a feeling of control, led them to overlook the superior potential of the telegraph. In effect, France failed to recognize and seize an opportunity. It is ironical that France appears to have failed to learn from this lesson and that history recently repeated itself when, after developing an excellent national telecommunication system in the form of the Minitel, France rested on its laurels and failed to join other countries and invest in the Internet. Once again it found itself lagging behind, not only in terms of investment in and access to a technology with a promising future, but also from a linguistic point of view, letting English dominate the Internet. In the early years, the presence of French on the Internet relied almost entirely on French Canadian sites, although France has since woken up to the need to try and make up for lost ground.

The advantages that accrued to English as Britain became the hub of a global telegraph network were compounded by the country's position at the forefront of the Industrial Revolution. As a result, English, in the nineteenth century, became the passport to industrial knowledge, before being once more at the centre of technological progress when the first telephone patents were filed in 1876. Although Britain was relatively slow to adopt the telephone, the new technology was embraced with remarkable speed in the United States, which seized the opportunity to develop a technology which used techniques and equipment similar to the telegraph and could be made to work over many of the existing lines. The rapid spread of the telephone in an English-speaking country that was eventually to come to dominate telephone technology combined with the precedent offered by the telegraph to give English a head start when international calls became possible. At that time calls still had to be set up manually by operators, and English was one of the three languages chosen as lingua franca by international agreement (alongside French and German).

Although the advent of automatic dialling has taken away the benefits of this particular choice, English continues to gain from the dominance of the United States in other areas. For example, because of the important role played by the United States in aircraft production, English is used throughout the world in communications between planes and control towers. In the second half of the twentieth century English profited from the success of American films, satellite television and computer technology, with entertainment becoming 'America's second largest net export, racking up a trade surplus in the billions' (Dominick, 1996: 55). American films prevail in the box office of many countries, while a programme like *Baywatch* is deemed to have had a total weekly audience of about 1 billion people spread across 140 different countries. Although the impact on other languages is sometimes reduced by using dubbing rather than subtitles (as was the case with *Baywatch* in France), fear of cultural and linguistic domination has led certain countries to place quotas on the broadcasting of foreign materials. The threat looms large in countries like Sweden that are economically and culturally aligned with the English-speaking world and where there is widespread competence in English. Noting the amount of exposure to English that Swedish children and youth get via satellite television, Findahl (1989) expresses concerns that the Swedes may not be speaking Swedish in 100 years' time. Other Scandinavian countries too experience a high influx of English material, so much so that many Icelandic children are said to have gained considerable knowledge of English before they start learning it at school (Kvaran and Svavarsdóttir, 2002: 88). Even where the national language is not felt to be in such danger, there is concern that bilingualism in English may adversely affect bilingualism with other languages. This is one of the factors behind France's change of heart with regard to the place and importance of minority languages, as it sees the popularity of French as a second language slipping down, whereas English goes from strength to strength. One can only speculate whether France's reluctance to embrace the Internet contributed to this loss of popularity, but it can hardly have been an incentive to learn French.

In recent years, it is again English that has been the main beneficiary of computer technology. Just as the Morse code was developed for English, and originally only allowed combinations of up to four symbols that did not cover accented characters, ASCII, the code used by computers to represent characters, was based on the English alphabet. Changes were later introduced that made it feasible to write software based on other languages, although software development in less widely spoken languages that do not offer a sizeable market remains constrained by financial considerations. This raises important social inclusion issues as well as posing a serious risk to these languages. However, there are signs that companies are becoming more aware of the importance of local languages. Protests at the absence of certain languages from some software programs led to an announcement by Microsoft in March 2004 that it was going to support linguistic diversity by translating Windows software into another set of 40 languages. Called 'The Local Language Program', this new initiative is said to be 'designed to provide people with access to technology in a language that is familiar to them and which honors their cultural distinctions' (Microsoft, 2004). The threat posed by the ubiquity of a language like English is nonetheless a real one, and was increased by English becoming entrenched for a while as the language of the Internet. Again, although English remains the main medium, the presence of other languages has been rising and the Internet is becoming much more multilingual.

Fennell (2001: 267) claims that 'if English is to be seen as a "killer" language, communication technology must be interpreted as one of its major weapons'. What we have seen certainly corroborates that ICT has altered the status of, and balance between, languages. It has favoured some languages, most of all English, while working to the detriment of others, its effect depending on non-linguistic factors, including wise or unwise political and economic decisions. It is undeniable that by making large quantities of English available, modern media, notably the Internet and other electronic resources, amplify the importance of English internationally (Chapelle, 2003: xi). But with the conjunction of so many factors, it is not possible to assess the exact significance of the media as an influential source of language contact. How can one separate out, for instance, the effect of international television programmes in English, from the growing place of the language in the educational provision of other countries? The picture that emerges is one of unprecedented complexity, in which the popularity of English stems from the 'synergy between top-down and bottom-up processes' (Phillipson, 2003: 89), as pressures in professional life, education and the workplace combine with personal interest in activities connected with fields such as music, dance, sport and computers where English predominates.

In so far as it has the potential of transforming social network patterns, the Internet poses challenges for many languages. But it can also assist endangered languages through the possibility it gives to people of staying in touch with their family and community wherever they are, thereby fulfilling home-community intimacy functions similar to the telephone. As for the mass media, their impact has so far tended to benefit languages that are well established rather than those under threat: 'Not only are mass-media efforts in threatened languages few and far between (and infinitely weaker than those associated with the Big Brother rival), but even the few that do obtain are often not consciously and conscientiously linked to reinforcing home or school language functions' (Fishman, 2001: 15). Nevertheless, it is possible for the media to be harnessed as part of a well-thought-out language maintenance programme and help save minority languages. If so, English may not turn out to be a killer language. Apart from the fact that it may splinter as it spreads, it may come to coexist with other languages rather than replace them.

Conclusion

The focus, in this chapter, has so far been on language rather than language users and learners. It is time now to consider the implications of the phenomena discussed above for L2 users and language learners. The first observation to be made is that by virtue of their distinctive affordances, new media offer new environments for using language which constitute pressures for change. As such, new media can be regarded as inherently centrifugal. But their effect on language, both globally and in any given case, will depend on the broader context, and in particular on whether they are used to support standardization or diversification. It will also vary with the type of media. As the 'dominating presenters of language in our society at large' (Bell, 1991: 1), the mass media can help new forms of expression cross the boundaries of their original context to enter other domains, thereby serving a centripetal function. In general, centripetal forces will work to the advantage of L2 users and language learners in promoting sameness and stability, and in so doing limiting the number and range of forms that might be encountered or need to be produced. In contrast, because they lead to the proliferation of divergent forms, centrifugal forces would seem to have a negative impact on L2 users. But, by giving respectability to deviant language, centrifugal forces create a more accommodating environment for the production of language. It is possible, therefore, for L2 users to find a technological context that tolerates or even encourages linguistic innovations (e.g. IM, Internet Chat) less forbidding than a traditional medium, even if unconventionality on the part of others creates additional difficulties.

It can be seen from the description above that ICT has been instrumental in various ways in the development of many new forms of expression. Expansion faces language users with a huge and complex task, both in terms of the sheer volume of forms competing for attention, and the difficulty of matching them with the appropriate context. This is particularly challenging for L2 users and language learners, who find themselves at a disadvantage compared to a monolingual speaker because of the limited exposure they get to L2 forms (in the course of their lives, if not within a given period). Clearly the significance of changes will vary with that of the area affected. Alternative punctuation conventions, for example, are unlikely to be problematical because of the marginal importance of punctuation itself. Of the ICT-related changes discussed above, vocabulary growth and the emergence of new registers probably represent the main challenges. However, while there is no doubt as to the ultimate importance of the effects of ICT, the consequences of change are best considered with reference to specific media. Focusing on a particular media, as is done in the case study at the end of this book, allows the impact of the introduction of and evolution of a particular artefact to be pinpointed more accurately. This makes it is easier to analyse and identify what difference it has made to the linguistic environment in which L2 users and language learners operate, and, consequentially, to their experiences and likely objectives. Another, complementary approach is to focus on genres and compare communication that functions similarly in a range of media (e.g. news stories) to try and determine the effect of the media on the nature of communication (Herring, 2003: 4). Ultimately, what is of interest to language users and learners is not the issue of whether ICT causes or induces change, and if so, how, but the outcomes of evolutionary processes, including the existence of correlations between certain media and particular forms of language. Like everyone else, L2 users and learners are free to flout conventions deliberately, but need to know what these are.

Unlike internal changes, language spread is a phenomenon that necessarily arises out of contact between members of different speech communities. As such, it is directly associated with some form of language acquisition or learning. It also has more far-reaching consequences, since it affects the relative positions of languages to the point where some may cease to be taught or even die. In addition, language spread impacts on motivation, as students tend to be more favourably disposed towards learning a language that is spreading than towards learning a language that is not. As a vehicle for language, ICT has always played a role in language spread. With the advent of globalization and global communication systems, its influence on the linguistic landscape has intensified and acquired greater visibility. Whereas the spread of satellite television and the Internet have benefited certain languages by making them accessible all over the world and by strengthening their associations with certain domains of use, other languages remain largely confined to conventional means of communication. This has major consequences for language learning and language professionals which will be returned to in Chapter 5.

4
ICT and Education

Introduction

This chapter brings a change of perspective. Up to this point, reference has been made to the implications of technological progress for L2 users and language learners in general. In this chapter and the next, teaching and learning take centre stage. Unlike language acquisition, which occurs spontaneously without being deliberately fostered, and in common with the learning of other subjects, language learning presupposes an intervention of the kind ordinarily subsumed under the terms 'education' or 'instruction'. It is the influence of ICT on this intervention that forms the subject of these two chapters. The present chapter is concerned with the broader picture and examines relevant effects of the impact of ICT on education. In other words, it asks the question: to what extent have approaches to education changed in response to technological advances and, subsidiarily, how has this affected language learning and language teaching? The next chapter has a narrower focus and discusses subject-specific effects that derive from the nature and characteristics of language learning.

It is not possible within the scope of a single book, and a fortiori of a single chapter, to cover all the aspects of the relationship between ICT and education. All that can be done is to offer some informed reflections on issues of special interest. The chapter therefore begins with a discussion of the purpose of education before considering the impact of ICT on models of educational organization and on the teacher's role. Attention then turns to the relationship between ICT and educational content, and to the reconceptualization of literacy in the light of recent technological advances. The chapter concludes with an assessment of the strengths and weaknesses of current media and an appraisal of the current situation.

ICT and the purpose of education

There is a widespread tendency in many parts of the world, especially those countries that have seen the development of mass state education, to equate education with schooling. But schools and institutions such as colleges and universities are only one of a range of providers of education: 'Education is a ubiquitous activity that can take place anywhere, anytime when someone wants to learn how to solve some kind of problem' (Tiffin and Rajasingham, 1995: 49). Who the providers are is secondary at this point. What matters, because it differentiates education from the incidental learning that is part and parcel of everyone's daily experience, is the notion implicit in the term 'education' of a systematic process. In this respect, it is noteworthy that the expression 'lifelong learning', which, strictly speaking, refers to a natural phenomenon, has acquired in recent years a specialized meaning that turns it into an educational process. It has thereby been brought under the umbrella of what we are considering here: the impact of ICT on undertakings deliberately aimed at imparting knowledge and skills and/or at building up capacities and character.

Within this broad area, it is usual to differentiate between formal and non-formal (or informal) education. 'Formal' takes us back to schooling and official, prescribed and recognized systems of education, whereas 'non-formal' and 'informal' evoke a less top-down, less rigid approach. Fleshing out this binary distinction, Pattanayak (1981: 114–15) describes formal and non-formal education as distinguished by three main characteristics. The first is that formal education expects all learners to reach a given goal within a single timescale, irrespective of their educational and social background. By contrast, non-formal education is flexible enough to allow the learner to move at their own pace, and is able to cater for the specialized needs of particular groups. The second difference between formal and informal education is that formal education works on the basis of a prescribed syllabus and textbooks aimed at the mass of average students, whereas the syllabus and materials in non-formal education are fluid and needs based. Finally, formal education works towards the achievement of qualifications, whereas qualifications are incidental to non-formal education. Pattanayak acknowledges, however, that formality is a matter of degree, and that every kind of education has some degree of formality and some degree of informality.

Formal and non-formal education can thus be seen as contrasting on two primary dimensions, both of them pertinent to all subjects. The first relates to learner centredness and autonomy. The second is the purpose of education, as expressed, above all, in the relative importance of preparation for work versus personal development. These two primary dimensions have framed the introduction and use of educational technology. Since the 1970s, when the use of computers for educational purposes began to attract attention, individualization and greater learner control have repeatedly been put forward as major advantages of ICT, and have been presented as features that opened the way to individual education provision and self-managed learning on a scale that had been unimaginable in the past. The following statement encapsulates this point of view: 'New information technologies will make it possible for students to learn what they want, when they want, and how they want, without schools' (Lemke, 1998: 295). However, as Illich (1971: 77) observes, technology can develop independence and learning but can also serve to reinforce someone else's agenda and be used to develop bureaucracy and teaching. Illich gives the example of poor countries faced with two alternatives: to spend money on TV installations that broadcast institutionally produced programmes and benefit a minority, or to supply a significant percentage of the population with tape recorders permitting both literate and illiterate to listen to prerecorded tapes and do their own recordings. Educational software design provides another illustration, from the possibility of locking learners into a fixed, predetermined sequence, as done in the very first computer language programs, to software offering a mix of choices, feedback and support that allows students to increasingly take charge of their learning.

Illich is well known for his opposition to obligatory schooling, which he regards as both economically unfeasible and intellectually emasculating: 'Equal educational opportunity is, indeed, both a desirable and a feasible goal, but to equate this with obligatory schooling is to confuse salvation with the Church' (Illich, 1971: 10). While acknowledging that teaching may sometimes contribute to learning, Illich claims that most knowledge is acquired outside school. That much is learnt outside school is borne out by common experience, and is confirmed by research like Smith and Curtin's study of children, computers and life online, which found that children 'determine what and when they need to know, in conjunction with knowledgeable specialists such as "Dad", and they find learning satisfying' (Smith and Curtin, 1998: 227). This is likely to happen even more with the diffusion of the World Wide Web, which opens the door to vast amounts of information for those with access to computers.

According to Illich, a good educational system has three purposes: 'It should provide all who want to learn with access to available resources at any time in their lives; empower all who want to share what they know to find those who want to learn it from them; and, finally, furnish all who want to present an issue to the public with the opportunity to make their challenge known' (Illich, 1971: 75). What Illich advocates is, in effect, something akin to Lemke's 'interactive learning paradigm', one of two competing paradigms of learning and education. The interactive paradigm is not as widespread as its rival, the 'curricular learning paradigm', which dominates many educational institutions, and in which other parties determine what people need to know, and fix the order and schedule of what is to be learnt. In the interactive paradigm, which is typically found in institutions like libraries and research centres, decisions as to what to learn are taken by the learners themselves in consultation with knowledgeable experts. It is also the learners who decide the order and pace of learning, so that learning can take place just in time for people to make use of what they have learnt. The two paradigms are inspired by, and embody, philosophical approaches to learning that are radically different. According to Lemke (1998: 294), the curricular learning paradigm, which developed with industrial capitalism and factory-based mass production, 'feeds into their wider networks of employment and careers, and resembles them in its authoritarianism, top-down planning, rigidity, economies of scale, and general unsuitability to the new information-based fast capitalist world'. The interactive learning paradigm, by contrast, is 'the learning paradigm of the people who created the Internet and cyberspace' and 'the paradigm of access to information, rather than imposition of learning'. In terms of the distinction referred to earlier between formal and non-formal education, the curricular learning paradigm is typical of formal education, whereas the interactive learning paradigm is associated with informal education.

Notwithstanding their associations with different developments, the curricular and the interactive learning paradigms have long coexisted, at least embryonically: 'This tension between the purpose of education in drawing out the intellectual and personal potential of children and its role in preparing a workforce for the industrial needs of society has characterized debates on schooling since the beginnings of mass formal education' (Cummins and Sayers, 1995: 84). What has happened is that, by tilting the balance in favour of the interactive learning paradigm, recent advances in ICT have fuelled the controversy, and turned it into a topic with a high profile, both within and outside the field of education. Not only have recent technological developments challenged conventional education by opening up the range of time, space and all the other parameters that combine to create a system of education. They have been instrumental in creating a world in which skills rapidly become obsolete, and have made the view of education as the transmission of knowledge hard to defend. Might it be possible, however, to reorganize and deliver education in a way that acknowledges the merits of each paradigm and exploits what each has to offer?

ICT and paradigms of educational organization

If there is one domain over which ICT seems to have had an impact, it is the organization of education. Once again, ICT did not cause obsolescence. One type of organization did not suddenly replace another. What ICT did was open new avenues and add new paradigms. The models that were in place remained in use and have, in fact, endured to this day. But as the world changed, so did the favoured model of educational organization. As might be expected, the first turning point came with the printing press. Three organizational models could be found before print. The most widespread paradigm was learning through one-to-one modelling. As continues to be the case in some parts of the world, and as is the case throughout the world during infancy, people learnt by watching and doing, by observing and imitating. Transmission of knowledge and skills from one generation to another relied on the everyday participation of children in adult life, either within the family or tribe, or through a more formal type of apprenticeship to a master. Children were not sent away to a special environment. They learnt through contacts with adults: 'Everyday life constantly brought together children and adults in trade and craft, as in the case of the little apprentice mixing the painter's colours' (Ariès, 1979: 356). The more affluent had access to an alternative paradigm: going away to an expert. This paradigm too involved learning by imitation and the direct use of tools, but mostly resorted to the voice as the technology of instruction, and entailed a great deal of listening and remembering. The third possibility came from the spreading of knowledge beyond temporal and geographical proximity through writing. However, knowledge dissemination was restricted by the scarcity of reading skills, and depended on the availability of secondary experts able to read and interpret the expert's words. There were schools, which taught reading, but they were relatively few in numbers, and, in early Europe, were mostly intended for future clerics.

This state of affairs was dramatically altered by the invention of the printing press, which, by permitting fast text reproduction, helped emancipate learning. Teaching and knowledge moved out of the hands of priests and the wealthy. From the fifteenth century, education increasingly became a matter for the school. The extension of school education had initially little effect on the majority of the child population, as girls were not affected until the eighteenth and nineteenth centuries, and schooling for boys only made inroads into the middle classes: 'the great families of the nobility and the artisan class remained faithful to the old system of apprenticeship, providing pages for grandees and apprentices for artisans' (Ariès, 1979: 358). However, schooling grew in the seventeenth and eighteenth centuries under the auspices of the Church, before passing into the hands of the state and becoming subjected to the kind of standardization that ruled industry. The establishment of mass education was a long-drawn-out process, that, even in the more developed countries of Europe, took most of the nineteenth century. In England, for example, 'the state began to subsidize the church schools in 1833 and inspect them in 1846, but elementary education only became universal in 1870, compulsory in 1880, and free in 1886' (Vincent, 2000: 31).

Print had a threefold impact on schools and the expansion of schooling. It opened up the teaching profession, making the ability to read the key requirement for instructing others. It helped disseminate ideas about the importance of, and need for, schooling. Lastly, it raised the profile of literacy, making it the lynchpin of formal education. Ironically, through the publication and proliferation of self-help and self-improvement books, print was also used, from the sixteenth century onwards, to provide an alternative to the very institution it was helping to set up. Prior to the sixteenth century, the inability of master craftsmen to provide detailed comprehensive descriptions of what they did had combined with dialectal differences and lack of knowledge and interest on the part of others to hamper the writing of study manuals (Ong, 1967: 234). Suddenly, there was what Eisenstein (1979: 243) refers to as an 'avalanche' of books setting out the steps involved in a host of tasks, from drawing a picture, mixing paints and keeping accounts, to handling various tools and designing buildings. The effect of these 'how to' publications was to encourage independence by enabling people to learn by themselves via print: 'Even though the new so-called "silent instructors" did no more than duplicate lessons already being taught in classrooms and shops, they did cut the bonds of subordination which kept pupils and apprentices under the tutelage of a given master' (Eisenstein, 1979: 244). They were the means and the embodiment of a transformation of the approach to knowledge: 'Knowledge, and especially knowledge associated with the various professions, callings and trades, was no longer a secret, something to be guarded and passed on only to those chosen few who were members of the "mysterie"' (Charlton, 1965: 298). In addition to expanding opportunities for book writing, 'do it yourself' manuals vindicated the idea that knowledge should be shared, while the potential benefits that would accrue from reading them promoted literacy and self-help. They also presented an implicit and incipient challenge to formal education that dimly foreshadowed that of the World Wide Web and other contemporary forms of ICT.

Since the invention of the printing press, education has come under the influence of several other technological innovations, starting with the introduction of correspondence education in the wake of the development of postal services, and some early attempts at telephone teaching. Although, as Laurillard (2002: 83) observes, 'none of the media was developed as a response to a pedagogical imperative', all the major developments of the twentieth century have spurred educational applications. However, technological tools have been primarily used until now as teaching aids, or for additional activities that did not alter the basic character of education.

According to Collis, following the development of the WWW, education stands poised on the brink of a paradigm shift. Collis names the new paradigm 'interconnectiveness' and characterizes it as 'being able to connect to human experts, to customized resources, beyond one's own local possibilities' (Collis, 1996: 582). Interconnectiveness is, in effect, the realization of what Illich described as 'the most radical alternative to school', namely 'a network or service which gave each man the same opportunity to share his current concern with others motivated by the same concern' (Illich, 1971: 19). Before the globalization of communication, personal direct contact with originators of ideas could only be provided on a token basis, if at all. But it is becoming increasingly feasible. This paves the way for starting to plan education, as Illich advocated, by asking the question: 'What kinds of things and people might learners want to be in contact with in order to learn?' We have in the Internet, among other things, the means of implementing the four complementary approaches that he outlines:

1. provide access to things or processes used for formal learning
2. set up skill exchanges enabling people to list and demonstrate their skills for credits or money, i.e. act as skill models
3. establish a peer-matching network allowing people to find others interested in a particular topic
4. set up reference services to educational administrators, pedagogical counsellors and intellectual leaders.

ICT and the teacher's role

It is widely anticipated that, like print, computer technology will have significant implications for the teaching profession. At the very least, technological advances will bring operational changes at the chalk face. As in the past, teachers will have to update their skills and learn to integrate new tools into the way they teach. But, if Collis's prediction of an imminent paradigm shift is correct, the teacher's role is set to undergo a much more fundamental transformation. This may include the scenario evoked by Squires (2000) in which peripatetic electronic teachers (PETs) with multiple telepresences – pedagogical, professional, commercial and managerial – appear alternately as teachers, members of the teaching profession, freelance workers and administrators. But, while the way in which support is delivered may change, the need to support learning will continue. It is therefore helpful to examine the various facets of a teacher's role and then consider the relationship between communication characteristics and the provision of support.

Education has been described by Dilts and DeLozier (2000) as involving the provision of four different kinds of support for learning: guiding, coaching/training, teaching and mentoring. Guiding is the process of directing another person along a path. It involves attending to the external context and supporting learning by providing maps for people to follow when faced by a changed or new environment. Coaching and training are concerned with the improvement of behaviour based on some analysis of current performance. Teaching, on the other hand, focuses on the acquisition of general cognitive abilities, on learning and understanding, rather than on what the person can do. Lastly, mentoring involves drawing out and validating a person's unconscious competences. Thus, while guiding operates more at the level of the environment, coaching and training relate to behaviour, teaching is concerned with capability, and mentoring takes us into the area of beliefs about oneself, and ultimately into values. Teachers act as guides when they issue reading lists and give advice on resources. They act as coaches when they give exam practice. They spend a lot of time presenting and explaining new material, i.e. teaching, and they are involved in mentoring when supervising original work. However, what is given priority in any particular instance is liable to vary with the teacher's personal style, and will also depend on the prevailing orthodoxies and the kind of learning environment available.

As far as language teaching is concerned, the place of the four forms of support will depend on the purposes of language learning and the relative importance of individual aspects (grammatical accuracy, fluency, pronunciation and so on). For instance, giving a high priority to an area like pronunciation, which requires intensive practice and precise feedback, will automatically heighten the role of the teacher as coach, although thanks to the availability of audio technologies, part of this role may be delegated to ICT. It hardly needs stating that equipment capable of taking over some of the teacher's functions are a double-edged sword liable to mesmerize educators and policy makers into making ill-conceived changes. What happened with the language laboratory in the 1970s is an obvious example. Instead of relieving teachers from attending to the more mechanical aspects of language teaching, as they were supposed to, language laboratory facilities actually resulted in teachers sitting at a console spending time on coaching tasks.

Which form of support a media can best assist with clearly depends on its properties and the characteristics of the communications it is used for. In Chapter 2, I looked at communication characteristics from the point of view of their impact on language users. In what follows, I consider communication characteristics from a different standpoint, that is to say in terms of their ability to enhance or impede the delivery of particular forms of support. As in Chapter 2, I take each parameter in turn, beginning with space coordinates, followed by time coordinates, range of symbolic cues, interactivity (i.e. reciprocity and feedback potential) and action orientation, and examine its relationship with specific forms of support.

As can be inferred from the discussion above, space coordinates impact on education by shaping access to sources of support. Without the ability to span space, support can only be given by those within the same physical environment as the learner. Without mediated communication of any kind, support will be given by human beings out of the knowledge they have accumulated. As we saw, this very limiting constraint was overcome by writing, but the breakthrough that writing represented only affected a significant proportion of the population after the invention of the printing press. Access to external sources of input is a major asset for education. Its enhancing effects have long been recognized, and were an argument used by Reith in his defence of the BBC's decision to depart from its stated function, entertainment, and broadcast lectures to schools. After asserting that the lectures 'are in no way intended to replace anything in existing curricula; they are supplementary to them', Reith describes the purpose of the lectures as follows: 'the general object may be stated as that of bringing, to a very large number of schools in each area, *that which no one school could expect to obtain*, namely lectures on subjects allied to the curricula by the outstanding exponents of them' (Reith, 1924: 157, italics added). The ability to break out of the immediate circle is, in principle, liable to benefit all forms of support, and, again in principle, the greater the reach, the wider the pool of experts that can be drawn on.

The situation regarding time disjunction is somewhat more complex. Leaving aside issues of relevance and linguistic evolution, the importance of the duration of the time gap between production and reception lies mainly in how crucial it is for support to be delivered at a specific point in time. How precisely timed support needs to be depends on the form of support. Typically, in order to be effective, coaching support must follow closely on performance, or even be virtually simultaneous. This gives a very small window of opportunity which makes time coordinates a much more important parameter than in, say, mentoring, where short delays are unlikely to affect effectiveness. Whether mediated support meets requirements will depend on the properties of the technology and its reliability. There is a risk that accidental mismatches may occur. It is true that this can also happen in face-to-face, since, for a variety of reasons, a shared temporal context does not guarantee that support will be appropriately timed. But it is technically feasible, at least theoretically, whereas this may not be the case with mediated support.

As far as range of symbolic cues is concerned, it can be surmised from Chapter 2 that, in general, the presence of properly handled multiple cues will enhance support and increase its effectiveness. How important the number of cues is, and their relative importance, will vary with the form of support being given, and the activities involved. Typically, guiding (e.g. guiding students through resources) will benefit from recourse to standard navigation and orientation aids such as drawings and diagrams, which will put a premium on access to the visual channel, as well as entail the use of particular modes of meaning. Teachers are well aware of this, and are used to resorting to different means of conveying meaning. What is new is the multiple, varied affordances of modern media, which allow certain techniques to be manipulated in ways that have been shown to have a positive effect on the mastery of cognitive skills, for instance the use of zooming to overtly model the process of singling out details (Salomon, 1979: 139–40).

The notion of an exchange of roles that lies at the core of reciprocity may appear at first sight to have egalitarian overtones somewhat inconsistent with traditional classroom hierarchies and the notion of support. It will be recalled, however, that reciprocity does not require the roles to be equally shared. Reciprocity is a descriptive term referring to a communication feature that arises from a right to speak that is socially determined, but does not in any way entail social equality. Classroom discourse provides many illustrations of this. Moreover, learning is increasingly conceived in educational circles as the result of collaborative actions that often involve gaining support from peers as well as from teachers. From such a perspective, support is something negotiated that easily accommodates reciprocity. It enables the learner to intervene to ask questions and to comment on and shape the support they receive. In other words, reciprocity permits two-way explicit feedback. It is useful for all forms of support, but is particularly useful for teaching and mentoring, which depend heavily on verbal interaction. In this respect, teaching and mentoring are better served by face-to-face and other kinds of dialogical communication than by one-way communication. With regard to the other component of interactivity, we saw in Chapter 2 that simultaneous feedback allows the source to take self-corrective action. This makes feedback a valuable asset in an educational context, since it allows teachers to monitor learners' reactions to the input they are receiving and calibrate the delivery of support accordingly. Again the effect is enhanced by multiple cues. Where feedback is multichannel so that the learner is both auditorially and visually present, it will be easier for the teacher to fine-tune the support given to the learner, irrespective of whether or not the latter subsequently takes over as source.

By enabling support to be better tailored to the recipient, interactivity links up with action orientation, which is specifically concerned with the issue of personalization. A high degree of interpersonal specificity is clearly a major asset in education, since it allows support to be customized in the light of what is known of the recipient's needs. It is often indicative of an ongoing relationship and is essential in mentoring. As a dynamic characteristic that is helped by interaction, it is more likely to be found in face-to-face and mediated, point-to-point interactions than in mass communication, where the source cannot monitor the effect of the support they are providing. By implication, action orientation will also benefit from the presence of multiple cues. This is one more reminder that we are dealing with interacting parameters.

Looking back at recent developments, it seems to be the scope and need for guiding that has most grown with technological progress. This is not only true with respect to learning. Rebillard (2000) has drawn attention to a parallel development in journalism, where the journalist is becoming a link node, someone who sifts and acts as portal rather than as commentator. As the number of alternative ways to learn increases, so does the need for someone with an overview of the learning landscape, someone who knows the various resources and experts, and their degree of fit with certain types of needs:

> The more there is to choose from, the more we will occasionally crave someone to help us with decisions. The more we move to self-choice and personal decision making about learning, the more we will occasionally desire external reward and feedback for our work and achievements. The more we talk to anyone, the more we will crave having a special person to talk to that really knows us and our history and our needs. (Collis, 1996: 583)

This should be a comforting thought for any teacher fearing that change will make them redundant. They might also consider that far from replacing teachers, printed books called for an increase in their number: 'A consequence of the improved availability of printed matter was that many more of those engaged in government, commerce, medicine, law and even agriculture had to be literate to cope with the explosion of ideas and knowledge that followed. So teachers retained their importance in the educational process' (Bates, 2005: 41).

In fact, the needs were so great as to make it necessary to organize schools in a more economical manner. Despite this reassuring precedent, teachers have tended to feel threatened by new media. The use of the media for educational purposes has repeatedly met with resistance and been greeted with prophecies of doom. Writing in 1933, Matheson records how, after the introduction of broadcast lessons, 'newspapers indulged in visions of robot schools staffed entirely by loudspeakers' (Matheson, 1933: 179). A decade later, fears had subsided, and it had become generally accepted that broadcasting was not a substitute for teachers. It is well known that the computer provoked similar qualms and equally gloomy predictions, that, again, have proved overly pessimistic. But the parallel can be taken further. Just as print ultimately benefited the teaching profession by raising the profile of literacy, so the importance of good navigation, processing and analytical skills may turn out to work to the advantage of teachers:

> I would argue that one important task which now faces teachers at all levels of education is to help pupils towards a full realization of what is now on offer and how they might access it. As we know, the content of the information available is likely to change rapidly,

> so that increasingly it may be the case that there is little point in learning the facts of a topic. What is more important is to learn how to access them efficiently, how to interpret what is found, and to have well-developed strategies for coping with the new problems which are likely to emerge as new knowledge is synthesized. (Fisher, 1993: 75)

This implies a change in the teacher's role, but not that teachers will become superfluous. What may happen is a kind of cross-over between the functions of teachers and those of librarians. As institutions that cater for the reading and learning aspirations of those below or beyond the standard age for education, and as organizers of reading sessions for school-age children, libraries, as Kempster (2000: 25) reminds us, 'have always been in the education business'. British libraries now routinely provide public terminals, CDs and DVDs as well as books and cassettes, and librarians have been upskilling to use and offer guidance on ICT. Since the Internet allows schools to be connected with libraries and museums, we can envisage the two professions growing closer, and a concomitant move from a curricular to an interactive learning paradigm.

In all this it is imperative not to lose sight of the fact that education is not all about cognitive development, but includes areas in which it may be inappropriate to use technology. There remain qualitative differences between face-to-face and mediated interaction that militate against a total switch-over. Even where the focus of attention is not on the social skills associated with face-to-face, the intrinsically social quality of most learning argues for retaining some form of direct contact. What the particular mix, and the role of teachers and other learners in it should be, will depend on the emphasis placed on interdependence by the psychological underpinning of education. Where, following Piaget, mental development is regarded as a process that is largely determined by maturation and direct experience, and that goes through certain phases and stages more or less regardless of the social environment, one can expect the social dimension to be played down. The teacher's main function will be to provide suitable materials and learning opportunities, and co-learners will play a subsidiary role. Where, on the other hand, learning is conceived as a social activity which 'awakens a variety of internal developmental processes that are able to operate only when the child is interacting with people in his environment and in cooperation with his peers' (Vygotsky, 1978: 90), the teacher will act as 'an active, communicative participant in learning' (Jones and Mercer, 1993: 22) who utilizes the learner's zone of proximal development to enable them to reach levels of development they could not achieve by themselves. This calls for educational software promoting awareness and collaboration rather than the kind of individualistic, behaviourist or cognitive programs that dominated the early days of computer-assisted instruction. In language teaching, the development of simulations and games took a step in the right direction, but, in order to be successful, they demanded the provision of conditions conducive to communication that were sometimes overlooked (Kenning and Kenning, 1990: 78–9). I return to the issue of the contribution of technology to collaborative activities in Chapter 5.

ICT and educational content

Perhaps the most visible evidence that ICT affects educational content is the expansion of the curriculum to accommodate ICT-related subjects. In order to stop the curriculum becoming overcrowded, the integration of new subjects is often achieved at the expense of those already established, which find themselves with a reduced time allocation, or, in extreme cases, removed altogether. IT, media studies and electronics are all examples of relatively recent additions to the school curriculum which have undermined the position of other subjects. In Britain, the introduction of new subjects has been particularly detrimental to languages. The way in which option blocks are organized often makes taking two languages difficult and even learning one language beyond the age of 14 has become optional.

These changes raise the question of who decides the curriculum and revive the vexed issue of prescribed curricula and syllabuses. It may be that, as argued by Lemke (1998: 294) with reference to the USA, national curricula are no longer appropriate given the variability and unpredictability of future needs. Whether or not curricula remain tightly controlled at a national level, the issue of which cultures are to constitute the curriculum must be given serious consideration. Evidence shows that it is still common for formal education in the West to have a middle-class bias that favours high culture. As a result of this, school culture frequently finds itself at odds with what the majority of pupils are used to, and like. McFarlane captures the mismatch as follows:

> The current school culture is one which attaches great importance to neat handwriting and spelling, reading 'good' books and poetry and

> generally valuing the work of dead white men. The current home culture is one where all children watch TV and video and use the telephone and an increasing number access the Internet and use e-mail. And some children may read books. (McFarlane, 2000: 22)

School culture and home culture are out of step on several fronts. They make use of different technologies. They draw on and develop different skills. And they lay store by different types of knowledge. As underscored by the adjective 'dead' in the quote above, cultures are subject to change. It is easy for schools, with their attachment to the past, to lag behind the rest of society. Such a situation may be defensible if education is conceptualized as a complement to home culture. However, if the intention is that education should enhance people's ability to participate in society, then educational content and activities need to take culture change on board:

> Participation in the 'popular' cultural forms of radio, television and video and computer games far outweighs attendance at the theatre and so on – an argument not for the abolition or exclusion of those forms from attention in school, but for the wider bases of cultural participation and the need for school curricula to incorporate wider definitions of culture. (Beavis, 1998: 241)

It would be a mistake to jettison cultural heritage, but, equally, it is unwise not to take account of the context of people's lives and the various cultures found in the contemporary world. Both cultural plurality and inclusivity, and what Beavis describes as 'the old pedagogical priority of "starting from where the students are at" ' (Beavis, 1998: 241), call for a response to cultural and technological change that encompasses making room for popular culture texts in the curriculum. This might include using the kind of good video games examined by Gee (2003), on the grounds that, far from being a waste of time (as they are often thought to be), such games can be shown to promote situated and embodied thinking and doing, and entice children to put in lots of effort leading to the achievement of some meaningful success. At the level of language syllabuses, it means ensuring that pupils on exchange visits are able to ask their partners where they bought their clothes, a subject of much greater interest to them than whether their partner has blue eyes (which they can ascertain for themselves), or what their parents do. By implication, this reorientation entails reconsidering what we mean by literacy.

ICT and literacy

As shown by the entries in the *OED* (*Oxford English Dictionary*) Online for 'literate' and 'literacy', literacy is traditionally taken to refer to the ability to read and write. As such, it is bound up with the invention of writing, though its spread undoubtedly received considerable impetus from the invention of the printing press and subsequent improvements in printing methods. Significantly, in the early stages, literacy spread outside formal education, making the impact of ICT on the acquisition of knowledge and skills a bottom-up, rather than a top-down, process. Using Rogers's terminology (1983: 37) as quoted in Chapter 1, we may describe the spread of literacy as resulting originally from optional innovation decisions rather than authority innovation decisions. The former situation still obtains in some parts of the world, but in the majority of countries, literacy has become intertwined with state intervention, so that the association between mass education and literacy tends to be taken for granted.

It is often assumed, for instance, that literacy grew in Europe as a consequence of mass education, whereas, in reality, widespread literacy often preceded the expansion of formal education. This is not to deny that the state has been a dominant force in the provision of literacy, but simply to underline that the growth of the reading public did not wait for the setting up of mass education. There is some disagreement among scholars as to the extent of literacy prior to the nineteenth century. Eisenstein's (1979: 62) opinion is that, given the persistence of local dialects, many rural areas probably remained untouched until after the coming of the railway age. Others think that a fairly wide social spectrum may have been affected quite rapidly. Thus, according to Fennell (2001: 156), 'by Shakespeare's time up to half the population of London was literate. And during the seventeenth and eighteenth centuries the rise of the middle class brought with it an increase in leisure time for reading and a general interest in education and learning.'

That a tradition of reading became established relatively quickly is supported by statistics concerning the ownership of books between 1474 and 1630 in Valencia, Amiens and Canterbury. In Valencia, for instance, one-third of estate inventories between 1474 and 1550 mention books, including 14 per cent of the inventories of textile workers, and 10 per cent of those of other manual workers (Chartier, 1999: 270). Chartier concludes: 'Throughout Europe in the cities of the Renaissance, books were not foreign objects in popular circles. Admittedly, only a minority owned books, but that minority was never negligible, and at times it included a sizeable proportion of the population studied.' It stands to reason that printers would not have produced increasing numbers of publications, had there not been a demand for books and a public to purchase them. Of course, book ownership does not guarantee that books were actually read, but this is a plausible assumption. It is supported by evidence such as the Paston Letters, a collection of private and business correspondence from the fifteenth century, and is consistent with the role of printing in promoting and diffusing a standard uniform language. In some cases, whole populations learnt to read before the beginning of the nineteenth century:

> Prior to 1800, a handful of countries in the north and the north-west [of Europe] had achieved something like mass literacy in terms of reading skills. Sweden, Denmark, Finland, Iceland, Scotland and Geneva had disseminated the capacity to decode a text across most of their population, and parts of France, Germany and England were nearing that level of competence. (Vincent, 2000: 8)

The advances of literacy were partly due to the efforts of church schools, and partly to individual enterprise. They were consolidated in the nineteenth century with the advent of mass state education:

> In the nineteenth century, the reading public of the Western world achieved mass literacy. The advances made towards general literacy in the age of Enlightenment were continued, to create a rapidly expanding number of new readers, especially for newspapers and cheap fiction. [...] In Britain [...] male literacy was about 70 per cent in 1850, and 55 per cent of females could read. The German Reich was 88 per cent literate in 1871. (Lyons, 1999: 313)

It should not be assumed that the existence of books and school texts guaranteed their availability in school. School equipment in the nineteenth century was rudimentary. There were often no tables, and in order to save money, children learned to read from cards rather than books (Lyons, 1999: 324–6).

Why did literacy become popular? What prompted people to learn to read? One can only presume that it was the perception that literacy conferred benefits that were worth having. This must have been particularly obvious to the illiterate ready to pay six sous to listen to the latest news being read aloud in one of the public reading places to be found in Paris at the beginning of the eighteenth century (Smith, 1979).

More recently, the motivating power of conspicuous pay-offs has been corroborated by the experience of the Brazilian educator Paulo Freire, who reports that people can learn to read very quickly, if they are taught words that matter to them, because they relate to current important issues in their lives (Illich, 1971). In a similar vein, Kempster (2000: 28) argues that 'children learn in schools because they have to – they learn in libraries because they want to. The urge to know, understand and enjoy is the real stimulus for literacy.' The same applies to computer skills, with many people becoming what has been called 'computer literate' of their own free will, because they perceive the acquisition of computer literacy skills to be advantageous.

Debates over literacy fall into two types. In the first type, discussion centres on the purpose of literacy as traditionally understood, and only involves ICT to the extent that it provides tools for implementing certain ideas. In the second type, ICT lies at the root of the matter, as the debates revolve around the implications of technological progress for our understanding of literacy. Both types ask the question: 'What is literacy?', but the second calls for a broader evolutionary definition and interpretation of literacy that acknowledges explicitly that the culture we live in is not entirely print-based and verbal. Hence the use of the plural 'multiliteracies', a word designed to encapsulate 'the multiplicity of communications channels and media, and the increasing saliency of cultural and linguistic diversity' (New London Group, 1996: 63).

One of the best known and most innovative ways of teaching reading and writing is the method devised by Célestin Freinet, the founder of the Modern School Movement, in the 1920s. Freinet, who taught in southern France, developed a three-stage approach to the development of literacy. He would get his pupils to write spontaneously about familiar subjects, often after taking them for a walk through their town to gather information. They would then produce copies of their texts using a printing press. Finally the copies would be sent by post to a partner class in another part of France. In this way Freinet gave reading and writing a real, authentic purpose, and avoided the demotivating effect of sterile writing tasks undertaken solely for practice and assessment purposes. This encouraged his pupils to master the mechanics of reading and writing, the printing technology they had access to providing a further incentive. In language teaching, concern for authenticity has been prominent in discussions of pedagogy, and underlies the fostering of penfriend and tandem learning links. As it happens, the potential of Freinet's ideas for foreign language learning and bilingual education was demonstrated when, during the Spanish civil war, the school came to include both local French children and refugees from Spain. The pupils corresponded with a class in Barcelona. After taking a walk together, they collectively dictated a text. One day the text was written in Spanish by students from Spain. The next day it was drafted in French by French pupils. This scheme created a motivating context for the French children to collaborate with their Spanish classmates in writing letters of support to the children in Spain and comparing the two communities. Many reportedly became able to dictate texts with equal facility in French or Spanish (Cummins and Sayers, 1995: 349–50).

Freinet's pedagogy of intercultural learning partnership was adopted and adapted by, among others, Mario Lodi, who taught in Italy in the 1960s. Lodi updated the technology used by Freinet, replacing Freinet's movable-type press with typewriters, mimeograph machines and audiotape recording. This shift was partly motivated by a desire to harness the most current educational technologies available, but it also suited Lodi's aim to use the students' local dialects as a basis for fluency in the standard variety. It is worth noting that we find an intimation of the second type of debate over literacy in Lodi's presentation of the exploitation of audiotapes as a stepping stone towards traditional literacy. This is how Cummins and Sayers describe Lodi's position:

> Lodi felt that the exchange of tape recordings, while squarely based on existing oral language skills, placed demands on students that were similar to those of written compositions:
>
> a) to communicate with someone who isn't present, to whom it is necessary to be explicit and explain everything
> b) to plan the speech, anticipating its parts and assigning them to different speakers;
> c) the impossibility of using gestures, facial expressions, and other indicative movements that simplify the understanding of oral language so much; and
> d) not receiving an immediate reply and having to wait for one. (Cummins and Sayers, 1995: 133–4)

From this extract, it is clear that Lodi's approach was broader than that of many of his contemporaries and has affinities with the standpoint of the advocates of functional literacy, which is discussed below.

Freinet's work foreshadows the emergence of computer-based learning networks such as I*EARN (the International Education and Resource Network) and Orillas, which facilitate the creation of communities of learning across the globe. As well as turning reading and writing into genuine, meaningful communicative acts, participation in these communities enables students to compare their experiences and ideas with those of students in other countries. This promotes reflection and questioning, and can lead to social action, just as Freinet's learning walks induced his pupils to improve the living conditions in their local community. Thus, like Freinet's pedagogy, I*EARN and Orillas foster critical literacy as well as functional and cultural literacy. In addition to developing the skills necessary to operate effectively at work and in daily life (functional literacy), and imparting the particular content or knowledge required to understand texts or social situations (cultural literacy), learning networks help develop the ability to analyse, to grasp the subtext and purpose of a particular communication, and the ideology it serves to propagate. As with Freinet's printing press and Lodi's audiotapes, technology supports and enhances collaborative and intercultural learning, but is ultimately dispensable and secondary, since, as Heppell observes, 'literacy is, of course, always a product of some technology in the very real sense that whatever transmission and representational form we adopt as a vehicle for our narratives will depend entirely on the technology of the moment, from prehistoric cave painting, through Babylonian cuniform to algebra or the notation of modern dance' (Heppell, 2000: xii).

By contrast, technology is central to the second type of debate, which, in the main, adopts a functional approach to literacy based on the evolution of means of communication. In their discussion of functional literacy, Cummins and Sayers (1995: 88) point out that the definition of functional literacy is relative to changing social demands. This can be illustrated by the high level of literacy skills required of a car mechanic today in order to cope with the complex technical manuals consulted during the repair process by comparison with what was needed 30 years ago. The case for broadening our conception of literacy simply extends this line of argument to encompass media other than print, on the grounds that the ability to resort to these new technologies has become part and parcel of our ability to function adequately in employment and social situations typical of industrialized societies at the beginning of the twenty-first century. This bias towards functional literacy is apparent, for instance, in Mikulecky and Kirkley (1998), who argue that intertwined economic, organizational and technological forces comprising participation in the global marketplace, democratization of workplace decision-making, synchronous production, and multiple roles on most jobs, as well as new technology, have brought about transformations of literacy in the workplace. Regarding the impact of new technology, they write: 'New technology permeates the work activities of nearly half the adult population and creates new literacy demands for communication, gathering information, solving daily work-related problems, and monitoring performance' (Mikulecky and Kirkley, 1998: 304).

More than a century has gone by since what Lyons (1999) portrays as the golden age of the book in the West, a short-lived affair confined to the end of the nineteenth century: 'The first generation which acceded to mass literacy was also the last to see the book unchallenged as a communications medium, by either the radio or the electronic media of the twentieth century' (Lyons, 1999: 313). Although it is many years since print was dislodged from its secure position, it is only relatively recently that the evolution of ICT has come to be regarded as a problem for traditional views of literacy. Concurrently, it has become commonplace to apply the term 'text' to communicative artefacts that are not made up, or wholly made up, of written words, contrary to traditional practice. TV adverts, for example, are described as 'media texts'. It is therefore logical to construe literacy as 'the ability to produce, understand and use texts in culturally appropriate ways' (Graddol, 1994: 50), or, given the slant of this book, as the ability to extract and convey meaning in contemporary media. Hence studies on media literacy (e.g. Meinhof, 1998).

The adoption of a wider definition of literacy that acknowledges that even print literacy is multiple, rather than unitary, raises fundamental pedagogical issues which have yet to be properly addressed. Among these is the need for exposure to a wider range of materials than the narrative or expository printed prose that still forms the staple diet for many school pupils. As argued by Mikulecky and Kirkley (1998: 304), appreciating narrative fiction and following cogently argued texts do not prepare pupils well for the literacy demands of the workplace, which entail gathering and evaluating information from a variety of print and other sources. Consequently, 'even students who have mastered traditional school literacy face challenges'. The issue is not so much what texts to include but what skills to develop, in the face of multiple possibilities:

> Using a computer children can represent their creativity with text, graphics, speech, video, animation and more, they can do it at school or away from school, singly and in private or collaboratively and en masse, synchronously or spread across a long time period. But which subset of those choices would we regard as necessary for base literacy? (Heppell, 2000: xiii)

Mikulecky and Kirkley's (1998: 313) recommendation is that decisions should be made with reference to four goals:

- the development of critical thinking
- familiarity with technologies for processing information
- the provision of diverse materials
- laying the foundations for lifelong learning.

It is clear that the adoption of such an approach to literacy has a raft of implications, including the development of new kinds of tasks, new assessment strategies, and agreed scales of competence.

One of the casualties of an enlarged concept of literacy that embraces multiple media and hypermedia is likely to be expository writing. The discursive presentation of an argument, an account, or a story, that forms the cornerstone of the essay in its various guises, has been under siege for some time. Described by Bolter (1998: 7) as arguably 'a product of the age of print', the essay has been undermined by inventions inclined towards the oral and the pictorial. The forms of persuasion used by radio and television provide few opportunities for sustained arguments and it is safe to say that, whatever its merits, articulating a coherent thesis has little to do with the way in which most people engage with texts once they leave formal education. Another blow to discursive prose has been the development of technologies that allow texts to be put together through a cut and paste process that is increasingly blurring the boundaries between reception and production. To be sure, not all printed texts contain discursive prose designed to be read linearly from beginning to end. Newspapers, magazines, reference works, telephone directories are dipped into and perused in a piecemeal, interrupted fashion. But like the zapping of remote-control devices, this does not amount to the full-blown pick and mix approach characteristic of reading and writing with a word processor, hypertext and the World Wide Web.

The impact of word processors on writing soon attracted attention when personal microcomputers became available in schools. Turkle (1984) cites the case of Tanya, a pupil who, from never writing anything, grew to see herself as a writer. Tanya, who had previously been put off writing by the poor aesthetic appearance of her handwriting, was seduced by 'a product that looked "so clean and neat" that it was unquestionably right' (Turkle, 1984: 125). Watson (1984: 34) describes how 'pupils became motivated to write and continually re-draft their work, not just because of the speed of the process compared with the laborious task of hand-writing, but also because they themselves rather than through the mediation of the teacher, were encouraged to re-draft the material'.

A number of scholars (e.g. Hawisher, 1988; Haas, 1989; Pennington, 1993) have drawn attention to the fact that word processing promotes different mental processes from pen and paper, encouraging an organic approach to composition in which conception and execution often take place together rather than sequentially. Because cut and paste facilities make text easy to edit and malleable, there is a tendency to try things out, to experiment with alternative wordings and sequences, to let the text grow and develop, rather than follow a pre-established plan: 'In on-screen composition, thought processes are in a sense "enacted" and developed on-screen, in the form of deletions, substitutions, revisions, and editing' (Mishan, 2004: 135). Haas (1996) reports that people plan more when using pen and paper than when they use computers, and that the use of computers is associated with planning at the local rather than conceptual level. Mishan points out that composing online can have negative repercussions, as the editing process can interrupt and curtail the train of thought.

Haas (1996: 138) also found that, as well as altering the composing process, the use of different material tools and artefacts affected the effectiveness with which people carried out writing-related tasks such as recalling and retrieving information and reading to revise. As far as reception is concerned, reading from a computer screen is markedly different from reading out of a book, both perceptually and pragmatically. However, from the recipient's point of view, basic word processing during text production leaves the end product fundamentally unchanged: a document to be gone through in a particular order determined by the author. By contrast, the multiple paths offered by hypertext turn text construction into a collaborative venture in which the author proposes possible moves and the reader decides which of these moves to make. In so doing, hypertext magnifies the active, participatory nature of the reading process (which always requires bringing in personal knowledge in order to make sense of the text), to the point where cooperation turns into collaboration. Intentionally or inadvertently, the presence of links alters the way in which materials are read and interpreted, if only because of the implied connection that a link expresses (Burbules, 1998: 105). Reading becomes a journey in which meaning is co-constructed through the choices made by the user (Lamizet, 2000).

Hypertext alters writing in various ways. To begin with, by multiplying the number of sources of information that can be gained access to in the course of text production, the availability of hyperlinks privileges skimming, scanning and rapid value judgements. As a result, the effective combination of interesting finds may be on the way to supplanting independent thinking and logical coherence as the hallmark of quality and originality. Bolter (1998: 10) is not alone in thinking that hypertext 'undermines the rhetorical foundations for the teaching of writing – that is, the need for a unified point of view and a coherent thesis'. Second, as stated by Pickering (1996: 48), hypertext induces pedagogy to shift from instruction and memory to discovery and search skills. Consequentially, 'competence which used to be assessed by the capacity for recall and critical analysis shifts towards performance and ironic collage as the essay becomes the composition'. Of course, where the product is a hypertext, the act of embedding links also draws on the author's ability to see connections and make appropriate assumptions about the kind of threads readers might wish to follow. Finally, modern facilities allow writing to be a joint, collaborative undertaking in which participants interact to create, revise and edit documents. Wikis are a clear example of this.

In so far as learning a foreign language encompasses becoming literate in that language, modern language teaching is bound to be affected by changing views of literacy. As in other subjects, word processors and the Internet are now routinely used in language classrooms. But, in education as elsewhere, the latest fruits of technological progress find themselves in competition with older innovations. Continuing with the distinctive broader perspective of the present chapter, the next section takes stock of the current situation in educational technology and asks: what is the pedagogic potential of the individual media at our disposal, and how has it been exploited?

Educational technology: strengths and weaknesses of individual media

Although the term itself is relatively recent, educational technology actually goes back to the beginnings of ICT. The media have served two functions in education: to enhance instruction and to remove the shackles of time and space, thereby ushering in distance learning. For a variety of reasons, some technologies have made more of an impression than others, but all major advances have been experimented with. Print, the oldest of the technologies discussed in this book, has been exploited for educational purposes for over 500 years. The telephone entered the educational world towards the end of the nineteenth century, while radio has been in use in education for some 80 years. Film made its appearance in the classroom in the 1930s, but declined with the advent of television in the 1950s. Experiments involving mainframe computers started soon after, although it is the microcomputer which, in the 1980s, brought computer technology into schools.

In most situations, media selection is a complex matter subject to the influence of strategic, economic and instructional considerations. These considerations include the size, characteristics and location of the target group, capital expenditure (e.g. development and production costs, purchase price) and recurrent costs (e.g. maintenance), as well as the strengths and weaknesses of the medium and its applications. Inevitably, the particular mix will depend on circumstances, as some factors will weigh more heavily in certain situations or contexts than in others. Interactivity, for instance, is bound to be more significant where the only alternative is for teachers and learners to correspond with one another by post, and two-way technologies have therefore been embraced much more wholeheartedly by distance education than by classroom instruction. Different categories of stakeholders will also have different perspectives, as demonstrated by the contrast between the attitude of policy makers and that of the teaching profession towards computer technology. Attracted by the appealing prospect of dealing with increasing numbers of students and widening participation in education without commensurate increases in teachers and resources, policy makers have often promoted computer technology verbally, backing their speeches up with a moderate amount of financial investment. Understandably, the teaching profession's reaction has been much more wary. The outcome is that computer applications currently often fall short of expectations, due to what Kirkup and Jones (2000: 215) describe as 'a complex interaction of predictable factors such as access, training, and resources and the culture and infrastructure of the institution', together with the fact that 'teachers will make their own cost-benefit analyses and decide whether an investment in ICTs will help deliver their particular curriculum objectives'. This is substantiated by Sasseville's (2004) research, which shows that teachers are not opposed to the integration of ICT, but adopt a pragmatic approach in which technology is evaluated cautiously in terms of its effectiveness as a learning tool.

The distinctive priorities of politicians also lie behind the installation of computer terminals in libraries. Rogers (1983: 392) observes that until the 1970s, 'most diffusion programs simply ignored the equality issue, generally trusting in the "trickle-down theory" to cancel out the gap-widening tendencies of innovation diffusion in the long run'. Since then, there has been growing awareness that a decrease of equality in a social system is a common consequence of the diffusion of innovations. Like the lending of books, the implantation of computer technology in libraries stems from a desire to try and mitigate the negative effects of socio-economic boundaries. Faced with the task of reducing educational inequalities, those in authority have chosen an institution that, from the founding of the great library of Alexandria about 300 BC, has been associated with learning. An institution which, unlike school, is said to represent 'a place and space that is unfettered by judgements, where you make the choice to spend time, waste time, dip into the difficult and the different, where you can extend and deepen your learning and extend your educational success' (Kempster, 2000: 27).

As far as instructional criteria are concerned, effectiveness tends to rank high among learners and teachers' desiderata. Unfortunately, media effectiveness does not lend itself well to objective unambiguous measurements. Even when improvements or deteriorations in learner performance are recorded, one cannot usually be sure that the change is attributable to the medium itself. Media are more or less suited to different types of use, and their effective exploitation requires different treatments and skills. Furthermore, studies suggest that a given medium may only be superior to another for certain groups of students. Thus less able students, who often have trouble with understanding printed or electronic texts, appear to gain more than successful readers from audiotapes and television (Johnston, 1987).

One important instructional variable is the senses that the learning experience appeals to, in other words the communication channel. Audio technologies are best suited to subjects that can be taught aurally, like music and language. They can be used for other subjects, but have the drawback of presenting information linearly and more slowly than print or computer screens. On the other hand, they preserve suprasegmentals and are therefore particularly useful for emotive texts, drama, etc. Visual technologies can be divided into static and dynamic and come into their own whenever information is best presented to the eye. Static media can display verbal text, numbers, musical notation, diagrams and pictures, but, unlike dynamic media, cannot show movement directly. Dynamic media, on the other hand, are useful for demonstrating gestures and change, and can be helpful for the development of motor skills. To the degree of subject–channel fit must be added the effect of the learner's learning style orientation (visual, auditory or kinaesthetic).

Many technologies combine both aural and visual elements. This, however, does not produce a simple amalgamation of the advantages of monochannel media. As mentioned earlier, hybrid media such as television tend to be regarded as primarily visual. This is borne out by the lexis surrounding their use. Television and film are 'seen' or 'watched', not 'listened to' by audiences that are said to be made up of 'viewers', not 'listeners'. While hybrid media are as good as their silent equivalents where visuals are concerned, they do not match monochannel audio when verbal discourse really matters. Several factors come together to make audio superior in these cases. They include the fact that many concepts cannot be expressed visually, the distracting effect of extraneous pictorial elements, viewers' expectations, and viewers' dislike of programmes with a smaller visual component than they are used to. Consequently, hybrid media are best at showing non-silent events, processes or images that are enhanced by a commentary.

Another major instructional variable is the degree of individualization of the learning experience. There are two facets to individualization, according to whether the tailoring of the experience is carried out by the teacher or by the learner. From a technological point of view, individualization by the teacher is largely a function of the affordances of the media with regard to interpersonal specificity and interactivity. Just as customizing tuition in face-to face is easier when dealing with an individual than with a group, so point-to-point media are more capable of delivering experiences that meet the learner's needs than broadcast media. First, because the norm is for a single learner to be catered for, which means that they are given undivided attention. Second, because it is possible for the teacher to adapt what is said or done in the light of the learner's reactions. Individualization by the learner usually goes by the name of learner control and takes two forms. The learner may participate in the decision-making process and negotiate a different instructional pace or content. In so far as this negotiation presupposes dialogical, personal interactions, it too requires a point-to-point media. Alternatively, the learner may individualize the experience through direct intervention, by selecting what to focus on, or by deciding what constitutes a manageable chunk. Translated into technological features, this assumes the various facilities or opportunities for storing, retrieving and manipulating content provided by print, by audio and video recording and playback devices, and by computers.

Because of their distinctive attributes, the media differ in the kinds of learning they are best suited to promote. The kind of learning experience that a media supports is used by Laurillard (2002) as the basis for a division into five types of media: narrative, interactive, adaptive, communicative and productive. Narrative media support the presentation of a linear narrative by providing a structure creating global coherence. They include print, audio and video cassettes and television. Interactive media are also essentially linear presentational media, but offer more scope for learner control. However, unlike adaptive media, they remain unchanged by the user's actions. Nevertheless, interactive media 'do allow the user to be responsive to what they find, even if the medium is not responsive to their actions' (Laurillard, 2002: 103). Hypermedia and Web resources are examples of interactive media, while adaptive media include simulations, virtual environments and tutorial programs. Communicative media such as audio and video conferencing bring people together to discuss issues, while productive media such as modelling programs facilitate the student's own production of material. Within each type, different media will support different kinds of teaching. This is how Bates summarizes the potential of print and television:

> In general, print is best for teaching in a condensed way, dealing with abstract principles, where knowledge of detailed facts or principles is important, and where knowledge is clearly defined. Television on the other hand is much better for presenting complex or ambiguous 'real-world' events, for providing concrete examples to illustrate abstract ideas or principles, and for encouraging students to make their own interpretations and to apply to new situations what they have learned in an abstract way. (Bates, 2005: 104)

Although education continued to be predominantly oral long after the invention of the printing press due to the relative dearth of books, and remains so in some parts of the world, print has been, and continues to be, the most widespread instructional medium. Print has many advantages. Generally speaking, print is appropriate in circumstances that require the presentation of large bodies of facts, abstract principles, intricate arguments, or complex algorithms. It has the drawback of not catering for learner variability, but some allowance for differences can be made through targeted guidance within the text (e.g. 'if you already know that... then you might like to skip to...'), while its relative permanence makes for good learner control by allowing texts to be read and reread. Print is also relatively cheap, and more convenient than digitized text, since it does not require special equipment for the text to be displayed. However, it is not easy to update. Last but not least, print can easily be combined with other media (e.g. it can be used in conjunction with audio cassettes), and this offsets some of its limitations.

For reasons that are not hard to guess, educational uses of the telephone have been largely confined to reaching scattered learners prevented by geography or some other obstacle from attending ordinary classes. It may involve one-to-one tutor–student interactions, link a tutor to one or more remote groups on split campuses, or provide a link between a tutor and several geographically dispersed students (audio conferencing). The pedagogic exploitation of telephones in language learning is considered in Chapter 6.

Other audio technologies have made more of an impact on education, although their potential remains underexploited (Laurillard, 2002; Bates, 2005). Audio technologies, especially radio, audio cassettes and CDs, have several features to recommend them. They are cheap, score high on access, and are easy to use. Bates (2005: 115) makes the point that 'radio is accessible to more people that any other single technology. Millions of people around the world who cannot read or do not have access to television have a radio set.' This is confirmed by recent world statistics on ownership of household goods showing that the number of radio broadcasting receivers per 1000 inhabitants rose from 245 to 418 between 1970 and 1997, compared to a rise from 81 to 240 in television sets. This makes the availability of radio nearly double that of television, the difference, in the case of Africa, approaching one to four (UNESCO, 1999). This means that radio is considerably better at reaching certain target groups, e.g. the poor and the illiterate, than other technologies. And, over the course of the last 60 years, it has been used in various ways for teaching and training purposes. It is particularly useful in conjunction with cassette recorders, which lessen the need for repeat broadcasts. In an age of plentiful recording devices, it is easy to forget that the evanescence of speech once imposed serious constraints on radio schedules, as shown by the following excerpt from an article on 'English by Radio':

> It will be remembered that [...] we broadcast each programme several times during the course of the day. The primary object of these repeat broadcasts, which are on various combinations of wavelengths, is to provide a wide choice of listening-times, and to serve different areas of Europe in turn; but they also have the secondary object of making it possible for many of our listeners to hear the items twice or more, with all the advantages for ear-training that that connotes. (Quinault, 1947: 124)

It is regrettable that radio cassette recorders, unlike video recorders, do not usually come with a timer, as this makes radio less easy to record remotely than television. However, digitization and the development of devices such as MP3 players may give radio a boost.

Education in countries like the United Kingdom has made much more use of television, which has the advantage of combining a wider range of symbolic cues. Television can be used, among other things, to demonstrate experiments and processes, to show cultural scenes, and to present case studies. Its use has been boosted by the invention of the video recorder and, more recently, of DVDs, which enable broadcasts to be recorded for playing back at a more convenient time. Among other things, time-shift recording has increased opportunities for broadcasting educational programmes at night, with many instructional broadcasts going out between 2 and 5 a.m. Recordings have the advantage over live broadcasts that they can be stopped and resumed, and played more than once. This is very useful for closer analysis or for comparing different sections. It also allows the user to pause and consult external materials. This versatility makes for better learner control, albeit not on a par with what computers are able to offer.

Computers have been used for teaching and testing for over 30 years, and have been described as having a wide range of educational assets, including interactivity, individualization, learner control, motivational power and privacy. The last decade of the twentieth century saw two significant developments in the way in which computer technology is used in education: the move to multimedia and the introduction of the Internet. Multimedia enhanced and expanded the scope of computer programs, while the Internet initiated a shift from computers as teaching tools (i.e. interacting with computers) to computers as communication devices (interacting through computers). It introduced unique opportunities for collaborative learning, and gave access to a cornucopia of documents. As a source of information, the Internet has several invaluable advantages over print. It 'represents a way of offering up ideas that textbooks cannot match: It is current, it invites us to use information selectively, and it presents multiple interpretations of events and phenomena' (Garner and Gillingham, 1998: 227). While the amount of information available can be overwhelming, the Internet can be used to teach learners to search rather than surf and can be helpful for developing critical literacy.

In recent years, the diffusion of technologies for accessing, downloading and/or uploading files onto small wireless portable devices (e.g. mobile phones, MP3 players) has brought a further development:

the emergence of mobile learning (or m-learning). Although still in its infancy, m-learning is held by some as heralding a major change in social and educational practices: 'With constant connectivity and the volume of information new mobile devices can deliver, mobile learning will shape the new landscape for organizational training and life-long learning as well as impromptu information gathering for problem solving' (IJMLO, 2006). Some applications of mobile learning to language learning are considered in Chapter 6.

Conclusion

This chapter has shown that the extent to which education has been influenced by technological advances varies according to the aspect of education under consideration. In some areas, technological progress has been followed by significant changes. In others, it has had much less of an impact. Overall, where there have been radical transformations, e.g. the introduction of mass education, these have been ideologically motivated, not technologically induced, although ICT may have facilitated change. Crucially, an overview of current media shows that 'none of the current learning media covers the full iteration between reflective and adaptive discussion and interaction in the way that a teacher in a practical session could. However, they cover the majority of learning activities, and in combination, they cover all the essential activities in the learning process' (Laurillard, 2002: 173).

Does this mean that we are facing a new situation? As we have seen, a number of scholars think so. But similar statements have been made before without predictions coming true. At the same time, factors such as the capabilities of today's computers, the accelerating pace of technological innovation, technological convergence, and the mismatch between home culture and school culture create a pressure for change that seems to be gathering momentum. The forces for change are not necessarily new. Technological advances are not a novel phenomenon. Neither is the existence of a gap between home and school cultures. What is new is the speed at which changes are taking place. There is also a greater reluctance to impose middle-class standards than in less democratic, egalitarian eras, together with a developing consensus that, rather than deplore the demise of the old ways, we should acknowledge the epistemological implications of contemporary social trends. For unless we recognize and integrate the skills of the 'digital natives', we risk destabilizing education by encouraging autonomous learning to develop not simply parallel to, but antagonistically with, formal education, with all the deleterious consequences this may have.

It may be that, as suggested by Tiffin and Rajasingham (1995: 78), the way forward lies in blending virtual and conventional classes so as to exploit their complementary potentials: 'Telelearning offers the possibility of classes of common interest and compatible range of competence which is attractive for cognitive learning while conventional classrooms offer the possibility of developing social skills and communities ties and values.' It is arguable that a judicious mix would go some way towards resolving the many profound tensions facing educational systems. Tensions between competing paradigms, between modernity and cultural heritage, and between the appeal and power of technology and our yearning for face-to-face interaction.

5
ICT and Language Learning

Introduction

As my general exploration of the intersection between ICT and language learning comes to a close, the discussion turns ever more towards language learning rather than language use. Accordingly, in this chapter, I examine how the role assigned to language teaching and the nature of language learning have changed along with, or possibly in response to, technological progress. I start with the observation that it is easy, unless you have school-age children engaged in learning languages, and perhaps even then, to underestimate the extent to which language pedagogy, like any other human activity, is subject to the influence of societal developments and trends. The technological side, the fact that we now have a whole new set of communication tools likely to be of help, is fairly obvious. But other aspects are not. When you stop to think about it, the changing face of language learning across the ages is a fascinating multifaceted issue. How widespread was language learning three, four centuries ago? What languages did people learn and how? What was regarded as a high priority, both in terms of languages and skills? And what role, if any, was assigned to technology?

Such questions are not just a matter of historical interest. Looking at technology-related aspects of the evolution of language learning can lead to a better understanding of issues in applied linguistics and thereby help shape the future. It makes it possible to discern trends and patterns and reveals insights of relevance to the current situation and to current debates. As Levy (1997: 13) emphasizes, the identification of key themes and issues in past developments can serve to build on what has gone before, despite the increasing speed with which technology advances. From this point of view, it is worthwhile to go back in time and take a long view of language education in its interrelationship with ICT.

I begin the exploration of the specific ways in which ICT has impacted on language learning by examining why people learn languages and whether and how this is influenced by technological progress. I ask: what evidence is there that advances in ICT stimulate, discourage or have a variable effect on the take-up of language learning as an activity? How does this affect the popularity of individual languages? Another dimension of the changing face of language learning across the ages is the way in which language learning is conceptualized and language teaching approached. This is the subject of the next section, in which I investigate the relationship between ICT and methodological changes. The last three sections are devoted to the use of ICT in language learning. After providing a historical overview of the place of ICT in language learning, I outline possible rationales for the exploitation of ICT, before turning to the contribution, both actual and potential, of current technology.

Motivation and goals

There is little information on the value placed on language learning in former times, on what prompted people to study foreign languages and what they did with their newly acquired language. Motives and goals must be inferred from people's behaviour and what is known of the overall context. Here, one fact immediately stands out: the absence of overt prescriptions. For centuries, language learning was a private undertaking, confined to certain parts of society and largely the prerogative of boys and young men. In contrast, language learning in modern society mostly takes place in educational institutions, and is heavily regulated, as well as being more popular among girls than boys. There are official directives on the place of language learning in the curriculum, the age at which it should start, how long it should last, and how many foreign languages should be studied. Reform proposals stimulate public debate on whether or not language learning should form part of the core curriculum, which languages should be taught, and the benefits of an activity that requires a substantial investment in time and money. There is therefore no shortage of public documents, to which can be added the results of research into people's perceptions regarding the usefulness of learning a language or how difficult it is.

It hardly needs stating that student motivation does not necessarily coincide with official rationales and will rarely have much to do with the intellectual, cognitive and social benefits put forward by academics and by professional and official bodies. Personal motivation may be lacking altogether. Or it may be linked to the study of a specific language, such as English, just as it is not uncommon at policy level for non-linguistic considerations to weigh on the selection of foreign language on offer. Geographical proximity, economic ties and political alliances, whether historical or desired, religion, perceived cultural importance, as well as tradition and teacher supply all work to promote or protect certain languages at the expense of others, and will often prevail over educational arguments (e.g. in terms of the relative difficulty of certain languages) in support of diversification and change. The influence of these external pressures is demonstrated by the recent history of foreign language teaching in Britain, where attempts to introduce alternatives to French have tended to be unsuccessful. It is epitomized by the two-tier arrangements of the initial set of National Curriculum proposals, which obliged schools wishing to teach a language such as Chinese, Russian or Gujarati to also offer an EC language (Phillips and Filmer-Sankey, 1993). Following the rise of English as an international language, and with other pressures on the curriculum, the study of a modern language has recently been demoted in England, losing its status of core subject after age 14 in complete disregard of the interrelatedness of language learning and citizenship in a multilingual Europe. Many English native speakers believe that the recent spread of English throughout the world makes it unnecessary for them to learn other languages and show little interest in doing so. This is not true of everyone and never has been. But it is an attitude, which, in so far as it derives from the current dominance of the English language, testifies to the importance of the social matrix.

A related, possibly more striking example of the influence of social trends is the snowball effect of the popularity of English and English language classes in other countries. It is hardly an exaggeration to say that in today's world, virtually everyone, everywhere, seems to have a smattering of English and to be eager to improve their command of the English language. This is not the first time that a language has come to hold sway over others. Greek, Latin, French, to name but three examples, have all at some time enjoyed great prestige. But their popularity was restricted to certain circles, whereas the high status of English is a world-wide phenomenon. It is also a recent development. Four hundred years ago, English was a low-prestige language restricted to some parts of the British Isles and ignored by the rest of the world. Howatt (2004: 14) relates how it was not until the early sixteenth century that 'the polyglot dictionaries and phrasebooks, which were a popular device for acquiring a "survival knowledge" of foreign languages in Renaissance times, began to include English alongside the more widely-known languages like

French, Italian, and Latin'. This slow start is corroborated by Ariès (1979: 371), who states that, despite the publication in England at the end of the fifteenth century of a couple of double manuals to teach English and French, the text of the manuals of etiquette from which French children learnt to read and write in the sixteenth and seventeenth centuries 'was sometimes printed in several languages, in vertical columns, each column in a different type: French and Latin of course, but also Italian, Spanish and German (*never English*, a language which at that time had a limited audience and no cultural value)' (italics added). From these inauspicious beginnings, English has risen spectacularly, overtaking all its rivals to become a lingua franca and *the* language that everyone wants to learn.

Britain is not alone in bowing down to social pressure. In the rest of Europe too, 'national education policies have generally followed voters' wishes that their children learn one of the languages of wider diffusion rather than trying to impose or encourage diversity [...]. The citizens of Europe are not in large numbers, choosing to learn languages for other reasons: proximity, culture, solidarity' (Wright, 2000: 3). Throughout the world, people are opting to learn English because it promises greater returns in terms of access to knowledge domains and contacts with others. English allows communication not only with a large number of native speakers, but also with a larger and increasing number of second language users. It enables you to be understood almost wherever you go, in real life or on the Internet. English language materials are plentiful, and soaring numbers of learners add to the incentive to master English, rather than some other language, increasing further the dominance of English and fuelling macro-acquisition on an unprecedented scale (Brutt-Griffler, 2002). As noted in an earlier chapter, the growing ascendancy of English has been consolidated by its connection with industrial and technological developments. Although English now seems to have acquired a momentum of its own by virtue of its lingua franca status, it continues to benefit from its association with high-prestige media such as satellite television and the Internet. This shows that technological advances are liable to affect both the uptake of language learning and the popularity of a language.

In all this, learner motivation would seem to be instrumental rather than integrative, to use Gardner and Lambert's (1972) classic distinction between motives centred round practical, utilitarian advantages, and those stemming from a genuine interest in the culture and language of the other speech community. But the matter is far from clear-cut. We may safely label the motivation of the English merchants of the fifteenth century to learn foreign languages as instrumental, since the ability to speak a foreign language was an essential requirement of their trade. Similarly, it was a professional aim that led young nobles to learn languages from private tutors, who would accompany them in their travels abroad. They knew that foreign languages, and the manners and customs they became acquainted with during their travels, would be of service to them in some public capacity later on. This practical orientation is reflected in the contents of the double manuals produced by the information and communication technology of the time, bilingual works that typically contained lists of customary greetings, crafts and trades, and simple texts introducing vocabulary for food items and household utensils, together with phrases useful to travellers or in commerce.

With the exception of specialized courses, and perhaps even there, the motivation of today's learners, or rather of those who willingly undertake to learn a foreign language, is less clearly instrumental. It is true that linguistic proficiency in other languages enhances career prospects. But it also facilitates travel and contacts in an age in which mobility is on the increase and highly prized. In the case of English, the distinction between instrumental and integrative is further blurred by the fact that learning English opens the door to a culture that enjoys high prestige. If you want to make it on the international pop scene, it is an advantage to sing in English, as shown by the career of the Swedish pop group Abba, and more recently by that of the French Canadian singer Céline Dion. But, more importantly, learning English allows you to join an international community of English users, which is particularly appealing to young people eager to communicate across frontiers. In many countries, English is cool. There is thus often an integrative element to people's motivation, with the difference that the community they wish to enter is a surrogate community not exclusively made up of native speakers. It is spurious, in any case, to discuss motivation as if it was fixed once and for all. Motivation can change over time and what started as wholly or predominantly instrumental may change into integrative (or vice versa).

National curricula are not the only reason why language learning has become more widespread than it used to be in previous centuries. We are surrounded with incentives to learn languages which people simply did not use to have. Members of certain classes would undertake to study a foreign language out of professional need or, later on, because speaking a foreign language was regarded as a social accomplishment, as was the case with French in England. But for the majority of the population, who would not come into contact with foreigners or foreign texts in their daily lives, learning a foreign language was neither feasible nor an attractive proposition. For language learning to take off, there had to be more opportunities to learn a foreign language, together with obvious benefits. In this respect, it is instructive that in England, 'the teaching of French received a great stimulus with the influx of French Huguenot refugees in the second half of the sixteenth century' (Charlton, 1965: 230), but that learning French would appear to have gone into decline in the seventeenth century following the departure of the refugees (Howatt, 2004: 34). Similarly, the expansion of travelling in the nineteenth century that followed the developments of the railways, was paralleled by both an increase in the number of people learning foreign languages and a growing demand for travellers' phrasebooks. Yet, although noticeable, such developments, again, only touched a small proportion of the population. In this, they contrast with the present situation. At the source of the difference are two phenomena: the lack of stability of modern communities of communication, and the severing of the link between contact and mobility. The fact is that as a result of advances in ICT and globalization, and whether we travel or not, daily life not only calls for a much wider range of linguistic competences than used to be the case, but also provides the wherewithal.

As mentioned above, this situation currently works to the advantage of English. Because vast quantities of films, pop songs and television programmes flood out of the US and give speakers of other languages some familiarity with the sound of English and certain basic recurrent terms, English has become 'both the vector and the beneficiary of globalizing tendencies' (Wright, 2000: 80). This state of affairs will not necessarily last. Lemke (1998: 292–3) and Crystal (2006: 230–7) are among the scholars who anticipate that the dominance of cyberspace by English and Western culture will be short-lived. Several factors are liable to counteract the position of English as the language of the Internet, although perhaps not its use as a global lingua franca. They include progress in automatic translation, which reduces the need to understand or produce English; the usefulness of the Internet for linguistic diasporas, which spurs people to use their native tongue; interest on the part of small businesses and individuals in using the Web for local communication, which will normally entail the use of the local language; the ease with which content can be posted; and the fact that limiting searches to a language other than English is likely to turn up a sufficient number of hits (Nunberg, 2000). There are undoubtedly signs that the stranglehold of English over the Internet is loosening. At the same time a strong presence on the Internet and automatic translation are only commercially viable for a small number of languages, so that for many people keeping abreast of research and developments will continue to require competence in more widely spoken languages.

This does not prevent advances in multilingual information retrieval translation from raising the awful spectre of a world in which people might simply stop learning languages and certain language professionals become redundant. However, similar concerns have been expressed in the past, notably in relation to the setting up of language laboratories, without the prophecies of doom coming to pass. Nor is there persuasive evidence that this bleak scenario is about to unfold. On the contrary, 'current MT {machine translation] systems remain imperfect, and there are still many social, business and political situations in which being able to communicate directly in a shared language is greatly preferable to computer-mediated communication' (Atwell, 1999: 24). In addition, the machine translation services of Internet companies do not compete directly with professional translators but tap a different market. As Atwell (1999: 55) goes on to point out, machine translation services do no more than extend the readership of documents that would otherwise only be accessed by those fluent in the language they were written in. It has even been argued that, rather than jeopardizing the livelihood of professional translators, machine translation raises their profile and may bring them further business (as well as useful tools): 'people using the crude output of MT systems will come to realize the added value (i.e. higher quality) of professionally produced translations. As a result the demand for human produced translation will rise' (Hutchins, 1998: 13). Anyone who has made use of the free translation services available on the World Wide Web is likely to be inclined to agree.

Will people still want to learn languages? It is clear that irrespective of advances in ICT and machine translation, language is likely to continue as a barrier to communication, at least in the short to medium term. In the light of this, is it too optimistic to think that the increased social contacts arising from the use of ICT and from mobility will stimulate our natural curiosity in other speech communities and incite us to learn the languages they speak? After all, the dual role of language, for identification and/or communication, acts to protect languages from being displaced by English in their mother tongue role, and has been instrumental in the maintenance and/or revival of a range of regional languages. What we learn and how this is learnt may well be different. It may be, for instance, that speech recognition will re-emphasize oral skills and demote written competence. Nevertheless, it is to be hoped that even speakers of world languages will continue to engage in language learning activities, and acquire both the cross-linguistic and intercultural competence that provide the stepping stone for real communication and mutual understanding.

ICT and methodological changes

Turning to how languages were taught and learnt, this section considers the evolution of theories and methods of language learning and teaching against the backdrop of technological progress. It seeks to answer the following questions: what part has ICT played in the development of ideas about language learning and language pedagogy? Were the major turning points in the history of language pedagogy in any way influenced by technological progress, or were they unrelated to technological matters? Do the works of seminal writers refer to technological innovations? Is there any evidence that technological developments influenced thinking and approaches, and, if so, how significant was their impact?

Although interest in language goes back many centuries to antiquity, the emergence of linguistics and foreign language pedagogy as independent fields is a comparatively recent phenomenon. As a discipline, linguistics is a creation of the twentieth century. As far as foreign language pedagogy is concerned, influential figures can be found from around the 1650s, but the field only came of age with the efforts of the academic scholars and language teachers involved in the Reform movement of the late nineteenth and early twentieth centuries (1880–1914). There is some information on how language study was approached before that time, but little attempt at theorizing. One is therefore unlikely to come across discussions of technology. All that can be done is draw inferences from the contents of textbooks and any accompanying statements (e.g. prefaces).

The slow emergence of language pedagogy as a separate subject is partly accounted for by the fact that in many countries modern language teaching remained a private enterprise outside the school system. There were some exceptions. For instance, in the 1560s and 1570s, Huguenot refugees such as Holyband opened schools in England where classical and vernacular languages were taught side by side. It is also known that at the beginning of the seventeenth century, some Scottish burghs paid certain Frenchmen to act as masters in the town. Nevertheless, foreign languages were usually learnt from private tutors, and were not a major educational concern. In addition, the humble status of vernaculars had not made them objects worthy of attention. Consequently, there was a dearth of grammatical and other descriptions.

As a long-established subject, Latin was bound to influence the teaching of vernaculars. All the more so as Latin was also the language of religion, the normal medium of instruction, and the European lingua franca. Although it had become a relic, its status and functions were not far removed from the current status and role of English in certain parts of the globe. And in the same way that English as a foreign language has come to influence the teaching of other languages, so the methods used to teach Latin formed the backdrop against which other tongues were taught, serving both as a model and as a foil. Not only do we find in the foreign language manuals of the time echoes of Latin textbooks, as we will see, the history of Latin teaching itself exemplifies the controversies that have surrounded and continue to surround modern language teaching, including the place to be given to grammar, and the occasional ban on the use of the native language in the classroom. In earlier times, matters were further confused by the blurring of the distinction between native and foreign language teaching. Bilingual manuals were addressed to speakers of both languages and were supposed to work both ways, while monolingual mother tongue grammars were often optimistically described as suitable for foreigners with a basic knowledge of the language (Howatt, 2004: 3–4).

When, following the invention of the printing press, manuals began to appear in large numbers, there was little choice but to rely on the traditional method for teaching spoken Latin in the Middle Ages, namely the use of dialogues. These 'manières de langage', as the manuals were called, consisted of printed questions and answers relating to topics of everyday life and included lists of items for sale, that were meant to be memorized. If nothing else, such works were at least suited to the practical objectives of the learners. Among the procedures borrowed from Latin teaching was the technique of double translation, which consisted in translating from the foreign text into the native language and then recreating the original text from its translation. The seminal work here was Ascham's *Schoolmaster*, published posthumously in 1570, from which Holyband drew inspiration for a French manual with a similar title (*The French Schoolmaster*). Written double translation exercises constituted the culmination of the lesson, which started with the pupils hearing the dialogues read aloud and repeating them until they had a good grasp of the pronunciation and could produce sentences fluently (Howatt, 2004: 28). Unlike most of his contemporaries, Holyband used an inductive approach in the teaching of grammar, only introducing a discussion of rules after the students had become familiar with the texts. Elsewhere, pupils generally learnt grammar deductively, from rules set out in works like *A Short Introduction of Grammar*, published in 1540 and generally credited to William Lily (1468–1522), the first headmaster of St Paul's School. Described by Howatt (2004: 37) as 'the best-selling language teaching textbook ever written', *A Short Introduction of Grammar* enjoyed royal backing, selling around 10,000 copies a year against a usual run of 1250 copies, and remained unrivalled in England for some 200 years. Throughout the history of language teaching, inductive and deductive methodologies have coexisted. Their use predates the invention of printing, and their popularity has fluctuated as a result of factors that had little to do with ICT, inductive approaches being preferred during the late Renaissance and early twentieth century, and deductive methods during the late Middle Ages and the eighteenth century (Kelly, 1969: 34). All we can note from the above is a general compatibility between the emphasis placed on translation and grammar teaching and a technology involving the printed word. By compatibility, I mean that translation and grammar exercises were activities that print lent itself to more readily than purely oral communication would have done, as is evident when one compares the relative difficulty of translation and interpreting. It was a convenient, but dissolvable, partnership, which may well have been dissolved at times, since, as mentioned in the last chapter, it cannot be presumed that books were necessarily available. They remained expensive, and not all teachers looked favourably on their use by pupils.

One of the few times in the early history of language teaching when technological advances seem to have played a part in a significant methodological development is the publication of Comenius' *Orbis sensualium pictus* (The Visible World in Pictures), the first fully fledged scheme of teaching vocabulary with pictures. Comenius' pioneering work, which first appeared in 1658, required a technology capable of combining sufficiently detailed woodcut illustrations with informative material. Comenius is reported to have had difficulty finding the necessary woodcuts and had to send his manuscript to Nuremberg (Germany), where the cuts were made (Pioneers of Psychology, 2001). What made Comenius' approach truly innovative was not the inclusion of pictures as such, but their systematic use and their purpose. Unusually, for books were generally aimed at adults, *Orbis* was written with children in mind. As the title suggests, the use of illustrations was intended to bring the outside world into the classroom in order to create, both pictorially and verbally through the use of sentences, the meaningful context that Comenius believed to be necessary for the study of language, and, in particular, the acquisition of vocabulary, by children. *Orbis* was translated into several languages, the English translation by Charles Hoole appearing in 1659. It continued to be reprinted for over 100 years, but, although now held as a precursor of the Audiovisual Method, it failed to make a lasting impact. Even contemporaries familiar with Comenius' work appear to have been reluctant to adopt his unconventional ideas (Loonen, 1994). This may have been because it was technologically ahead of its time and the high cost of producing illustrations restricted its circulation. Hoole is said to have deplored its prohibitive cost (Kelly, 1969: 219). But part of the problem seems to have been due to the low regard in which illustrations were held in educational circles: 'pictures were not considered serious, and while they might be used with infants or to amuse the semi-literate working classes, they were not appropriate in the schoolroom' (Howatt, 2004: 54).

While part of the modern resonance of Comenius' work lies in the emphasis that was placed on vocabulary, the key issue in the case of the reforms introduced by the famous Port-Royal school was the medium of instruction. It was the norm in the seventeenth century to teach Latin via the direct method. Pupils were taught in Latin and were forbidden to communicate in the vernacular. Again the impetus for breaking with tradition was ideological, not technological, being rooted in a desire to hasten clear thinking, which was seen as an essential goal of education. Promoting clear thinking required the adoption of efficient methods. This included removing the obstacle that the prohibition of the use of the native tongue in the classroom put in students' way. Lancelot, one of the main Port-Royal educators and the author of *Nouvelle Méthode pour apprendre facilement et en peu de temps la langue latine* (A New Method of learning the Latin tongue quickly and easily), published in 1644, regarded a good grounding in the vernacular as an essential preliminary step to learning other languages and provided explanations in French. He made use of what contemporary technology afforded, employing a different typeface for French and Latin and putting comments in smaller print. However, this strategy was no more than a judicious application of procedures that had been in use for some time. Here again, the contribution of ICT was marginal.

The same applies to the evolution of language teaching over the next 300 years, including the vehement pedagogical debates of the Great Reform. In his overview of English language teaching in Europe in the nineteenth century, Howatt (2004) identifies three major developments. The first was the gradual integration of foreign language teaching into a modernized secondary school curriculum, and was associated with the development of the grammar–translation method, which set great store by the translation of sentences into and out of the foreign language. Inasmuch as translation required constant reference to the printed text, the method can be said to have been supported by ICT. But the aim was to endow language learning with academic respectability, and the role of ICT was confined to providing a convenient tool for delivering techniques that it had not inspired. The second development was the relatively unchronicled expansion of the market for utilitarian language learning as commercial contacts between nations increased, and had roots that were not directly connected with ICT. The third development was the emergence of individual reformers with new ideas on how languages could be taught more easily and efficiently.

It might be supposed that since the rise to prominence of the mastery of the spoken language followed in the wake of the invention of the telephone (1876) and the phonograph (1877), the thinking of the reformers of the late nineteenth century was shaped by contemporary developments in the field of ICT. However, while it is true that the Great Reform (1880–1914) involved a swing to learning languages by ear and a move away from Grammar–Translation, signs of discontent regarding the prevailing method go back much earlier, to motivations unrelated to technological progress. Gouin's dissatisfaction with Grammar–Translation, for example, stemmed from the contrast he observed between the progress made by his three-year-old nephew in acquiring his native tongue and his own fruitless attempt to learn German. Hence his assessment that 'the classical method, with its grammar, its dictionary, and its translations, is a delusion – nothing but a delusion' (Gouin, 1896: 35). For Gouin (1896: 301–2), to present language study as a solitary individual affair to be undertaken with the help of a grammar and dictionary is like saying: 'Here is a hammer, a square, and a chisel, and there lies a block of marble, [. . .] You have here everything that is needed for carving any statue you please. You will now set to work and carve from this block the statue of the Emperor of China, whom you do not know, and it must be a good likeness.' The only difference is that, in this case, the grammar is the hammer, chisel and square; the dictionary, the block of marble; and the statue of the unknown Emperor of the Celestial Empire represents the language to be constructed. And so Gouin proceeded to devise his own method, arguing that the receptive organ of language is the ear and that language is best learnt through the spoken words of a teacher.

The primacy of the spoken language was something that Viëtor, Passy, Sweet and Jespersen were equally adamant about. Without banning reading, Passy (1899: 21) declares unequivocally: 'c'est par l'enseignement oral qu'il faut commencer' (one must start by teaching the oral language). Passy's aim is to get pupils to think in the target language as swiftly as possible through the creation of an environment that calls for reusing the teacher's utterances. This includes the use of physical actions (e.g. getting up) and their verbal descriptions in a way that brings to mind Asher's (1969) Total Physical Response Approach and is derived from Gouin. All the proponents of the Direct Method, as it is usually known, played much stress on the value of phonetics. Sweet (1964: 5 (1899)) explains how phonetics can help pronunciation by confirming auditory impressions, arguing against the 'popular fallacy' that imitation is enough: 'This is as if fencing could be learnt by looking on at other people fencing.' While acknowledging the value of grammatical analysis, Sweet (1964: 163 (1899)) maintains that detached sentences should not be substituted for connected texts, as happens with methods which make grammar, rather than the text, the centre of instruction: 'It is only in connected texts that the language itself can be given with each word in a natural and adequate context.' The use of disconnected sentences is also criticized by Jespersen (1904: 48) on the grounds that, in addition to making language learning monotonous and lifeless, it brings about an overemphasis on translation and grammar rules: 'Now is it right to say that the *purpose* of instruction in a foreign language is that the pupils may learn to *translate* fluently and exactly (from and into the language)? The answer must be an emphatic No.' Deploring the poor pronunciation of learners taught by traditional methods, Jespersen (1904: 176) describes phonetic transcription as 'one of the most important advances in modern pedagogy, because it ensures both considerable facilitation and an exceedingly large gain in exactness'.

Like the great teaching reformists that preceded them, the principal figures of the Reform Movement were above all reacting to the poor results obtained by the Grammar–Translation method. Their interest in phonetics clearly chimed with the contemporary interest in science and technological innovations, but the latter did not exert much influence on their thinking. In assuming that they did, we overlook the fact that technologies improve. We project into the past a state of affairs that was still to come. Although remarkable inventions, the machines available to Sweet and Jespersen were very primitive and, as the following excerpt makes plain, were a long way from what would eventually be achieved by later models, let alone the quality of sound reproduction that digitization has put at our disposal:

> I shall add a few words on the use of the phonograph. The apparatus has been very much perfected of late years and renders beautifully

> most vowels and all the general features of stress, intonation, etc. But the rendering of most consonants is still far from perfect; you cannot always tell whether you hear a *p* or an *f*, etc., and it is impossible to rely on a phonographic record for minute shades of *s*-sounds and the like. (Jespersen, 1904: 177)

Sweet (1964: 46 (1899)) makes similar comments, in addition to pointing out that speaking into the funnel of a phonograph without either becoming inaudible or unnatural requires practice.

Nevertheless, both Sweet and Jespersen foresee some role for the phonograph:

> In the hands of an able teacher I have no doubt that it will prove a valuable help: it is patient and will repeat the same sentences scores of times, if required, without tiring or changing a single sound or intonation; you may also have different records of the same short piece as pronounced by one man from Berlin, another man from Hanover, a third from Munich, and a fourth from Vienna, which may be very useful for comparisons, even if, as a matter of course, in your ordinary teaching you stick to one particular standard of pronunciation – and in various other ways phonographic records may be used to stimulate the pupils. (Jespersen, 1904: 177)

However, Sweet and Jespersen lay stress on the fact that the role of the phonograph can only be a modest one. In fact, for Sweet (1964: 45 (1899)), 'whenever we have access to native speakers, the phonograph is superfluous, for at the best, it cannot speak better than a native', while Jespersen (1904: 177) states explicitly: 'Even if the apparatus were nearer the ideal than it is now, it could not replace the teacher.'

In short, while the language teaching theorists of the late nineteenth century were aware of technological progress and its potential benefits for language learning, the changes they advocated had their roots elsewhere, in linguistics and in psychology. This is also true of subsequent methodological changes. Even the Audiolingual Method, despite its close association with the tape recorder and the language laboratory, had a declared linguistic and psychological basis. There is no doubt that the move to teaching techniques relying heavily on memorization, imitation, and pattern drills promoted by the audiolingual method was greatly facilitated by the new equipment. But its origins were ideological and lay in the adoption of principles consonant with the dominant linguistic and psychological paradigms of the time:

structuralism and behaviourism. Teaching aids, and in particular the language laboratory, feature prominently in the works of the advocates of the method. Brooks (1960) devotes a whole chapter to the language laboratory, and Lado (1964) includes a third part entitled 'technological aids' with three chapters discussing in turn the language laboratory, visual aids, and teaching machines and programmed learning. But the focus is very much on practical issues, and great emphasis is put on the fact that the language laboratory is only a useful adjunct:

> Language laboratories can be simple and inexpensive as well as luxurious and costly. Regardless of the investment, the return depends essentially on the integration of work in the classroom with activity in the laboratory. At best, laboratory work can be only peripheral to authentic talk. Its virtue is to provide the repetitions for overlearning that are absolutely essential to the student but tedious and taxing to the teacher. (Brooks, 1960: 148)

Far from being a panacea, technology is put at the service of a pre-existing methodology whose credentials are taken as already established. Lado, for his part, presents the contemporary changes in language teaching as the work of four main forces: advances in linguistics, new techniques of teaching, the invention and mass production of recording and viewing equipment, and a growing interest in learning foreign languages. In his view, language and language learning are too complex for machines to replace teachers. Again, modern forms of ICT are seen as delivering greater efficiency, rather than as being essential: 'The same teaching effect is achieved without a teaching machine, though less automatically, by a two-ply answer sheet with easy cut-out peepholes for the choices' (Lado, 1964: 205).

Much the same applies to the other main approach of the 1960s, the Audiovisual Method. In a survey of developments in language teaching, Jerman (1965) outlines how filmstrips were first introduced into NATO courses to complement taped lessons, before being adopted systematically in a number of courses developed by the French Research Centre, CREDIF (Centre de Recherches et d'Etudes pour la Diffusion du Français). Again we note the impact of military developments and the primacy of oral fluency, together with an emphasis on conditioning, albeit with some toning down owing to the motivational effect of pictorial stimuli that contextualize the sentences and turn the lingual drill into 'an exercise loaded with meaning' (Jerman, 1965: 45).

In the light of the current interest in the application of computer-mediated communication to language learning, it comes as a surprise to discover how little impact ICT has had on ideas about language learning and language teaching. If ICT has shaped thinking, this has left relatively few traces. That this should be the case might be anticipated with respect to the earlier part of the time span we are interested in, when technological progress took place at a fairly slow pace, but is more surprising when we reach periods closer to the present. Even over the past 50 years, the contribution of ICT to the conceptualization of language learning and teaching (as distinct from classroom exploitation) can be said to have been fairly modest.

The thrust of the evidence is therefore that ICT did not instigate change, but occasionally acted as a catalyst or, on the contrary, as guardian of the status quo. The main drive for change came from changed views on the purposes of language learning, related, in turn, to changed circumstances, such as the opening of new markets (the first Berlitz school was founded in the USA in 1878), changes in intellectual climate and/or dissatisfaction with current methods. Since the 1960s, there has been a general move away from single methods towards an eclectic approach set within a broad conceptual framework. The main goal of language teaching has been to prepare learners to use their second language successfully in authentic situations. This shift in orientation from the learning of grammar rules and/or the production of totally correct forms to the appropriate use of language in the real world has been coupled with the study of communicative needs and the development of syllabuses based on behavioural targets, in other words on what learners should be able to do at the end of a unit or course: ask for directions, write a postcard to a friend, etc. This reorientation fits in well with the modular view of communicative competence taken by Canale (1983), according to which communicative competence extends beyond grammatical competence (mastery of the language code), to encompass sociolinguistic competence (appropriateness of meaning and form), discourse competence (cohesion and coherence) and strategic competence (use of devices that compensate for breakdowns in communication or enhance effectiveness). It is a view of communication as actively interactional. Communication is understood as 'the exchange and negotiation of information between at least two individuals through the use of verbal and non-verbal symbols, oral and written/visual modes, and production and comprehension processes' (Canale, 1983: 4). In the classroom, the accent has been on skill-oriented activities using information gap techniques, simulations, etc. Some of these have involved ICT, but again, generally speaking, ICT has simply provided the means of implementing pre-existing ideas. Nonetheless this period has seen the blossoming of the field of educational technology, both in education as a whole, and in language teaching.

Educational technology in language learning: historical overview

'Educational technology' is a relatively new expression, which seems to designate a particular and distinct type of equipment, but in fact refers to the appropriation by education of a subset of technologies designed for general use. In the UK the term gained acceptance in official circles with the establishment of the National Council for Educational Technology (NCET) in 1967. Educational technology, or instructional technology as it is sometimes called, is a fuzzy concept, defined by bodies and organizations such as the NCET, and the US Commission on Instructional Technology in terms that suggest a concern with efficiency gains that was not found in previous expressions referring to the use of media in education. For example, the definition of the Commission on Instructional Technology (1970: 199) reads: 'A systematic way of designing, carrying out, and evaluating the total process of learning and teaching in terms of specific objectives, based on research in human learning and communication and employing a combination of human and non-human resources to bring about more effective instruction.' This special emphasis, with its implication of improved cost-effectiveness, poses a particular problem for language pedagogy due to our imperfect understanding of the learning process. Fundamental questions such as the relationship between first and second language learning, and the extent to which the latter proceeds differently from other forms of cognitive development, remain the subject of fierce debates. It is a state of affairs that presents the profession with a fundamental obstacle in deciding how to use technology, since the more unique second language learning is, the more likely it is to call for types of applications that differ from other subjects.

Faced with such difficulties it is tempting to concentrate on financial matters and reduce efficiency and effectiveness to a cost issue. This was the route taken in the early days of computer-assisted language teaching, when claims were made about the ability of computers to provide tuition more cheaply than human beings. Even on such limited grounds the case for technology proved to be less convincing than originally thought. First, because initial calculations tended to focus on delivery costs and leave out items such as materials development time, hardware and training, which form part and parcel of full economic costs. When these aspects were factored in, technology-enhanced teaching appeared much less likely to achieve higher levels of cost-effectiveness than other modes of delivery. Second, the items that had been left out were hard to measure precisely. They could only be estimated, which further weakened the basis of any comparison. Cost-effectiveness no longer dominates discussion agendas. However, falling computer costs continue to exert pressure on educational decisions and are still used as an argument from moving from face-to face to machine-assisted teaching, irrespective of the effectiveness side of the equation.

According to Ellington, Percival and Race (1993), since its emergence as a separate discipline after the Second World War, the field of educational technology has gone through three overlapping phases, as the emphasis moved from mass instruction, through individualized learning, to group learning. This evolution reflected changes in its theoretical basis, from industrial technology, to behavioural and then humanistic psychology, and was manifested through the use of different media as broadcasting and video were joined, and to some extent eclipsed, first by computer-assisted learning exercises, followed by computer games and simulations. The rise of web-based applications is a further development favourable to group learning, yet one that is also capable of accommodating previous paradigms.

The same three-stage evolution can be found in language pedagogy and its use of ICT. As early as 1924, Reith (1924: 158) was drawing attention to the potential of broadcasting for language learning: 'In connection with schools or otherwise, the teaching of foreign languages may be greatly simplified and improved by means of wireless.' Reith (1924: 160) portrays the radio as offering the advantage that 'perfect pronunciation, often the greatest difficulty, is guaranteed through the talks being given by a native of the country'. The second stage in the evolution of language pedagogy began in the late 1940s when the advantages of individualized learning were highlighted by those experimenting with language laboratories. Kiddle, one of these early adopters, describes a laboratory established in September 1949 at the University of Michigan, the third he had planned and supervised. This laboratory had six listening positions equipped with machines consisting of a dual speed turntable ($33\frac{1}{3}$ and 78 rpm) and a wire-recorder. Kiddle (1949: 127) reports great enthusiasm on the part of the students before concluding: 'The language laboratory, by providing an efficient way to supplement the work of the classroom and by giving the highly-motivated learner a means to advance at his own pace, offers language teachers an important new medium for achieving our goal: the steady improvement of modern language teaching.' Benefits such as individualization and privacy (presupposing individual use) were also put forward in early discussions of computer-assisted language learning. However, since the 1980s, the focus has shifted to applications supporting group activities, in which the computer acts as a stimulus for exchanges between participants. Early experiments in this area (Piper, 1986; Jones, B., 1986; Jones, G., 1986) that used a range of materials, particularly simulations and adventure games, revealed the need to develop a special methodology that preserved the key technique of creating an information gap. A common formula at the time was to allocate participants distinct roles, to move most of them away from the screen, and to appoint the others as intermediaries with the computer program, but the development of more sophisticated programs and virtual reality has opened up new possibilities. In a similar way, video technology introduced a degree of potential individualization that television was unable to afford, although neither media can compare with computer technology with regard to versatility.

It has been claimed that one of the main reasons why the language laboratory failed was the lack of research on how it could best be used to enhance language learning (Pederson, 1987: 102). Most media, in fact, appear with hindsight to have been introduced with little systematic research, except on their engineering aspects. This may be because of the fascination that technology exerts on some people. But it is also due to the rapid pace of technological progress. Kelly (1969: 269) writes: 'The great Renaissance grammars were still being published in 1780; but [...] the life of a modern text is not much more than twenty years.' Since this statement was made, the pace of life has speeded up, leaving little time for reflection on how to make the most of technology. As a result, reliance has often been placed on the results of experiments that may not be replicable without the special funding they attract and the feeling of participating in developments at the cutting edge.

One field which stands to benefit greatly from computer technology is second language acquisition (SLA) research, where one of the main obstacles has always been the difficulty of observation. It has long been recognized that one of the main assets of the computer for SLA research was that it becomes possible 'to probe into aspects of study habits and learning patterns which are not readily amenable to direct enquiry, either because they are intrinsically difficult to get at, or because the fact that the subjects know themselves to be under observation is liable to distort the results' (Kenning and Kenning,

1983: 163). Computers may be used on their own, or in conjunction with human observers and/or other devices such as audio and video recorders. Among their many advantages are 'more control over the collection, examination and manipulation of data, as well as convenience (and speed) of data recording, storage, and computation within an appropriate experimental design' (Doughty, 1987: 134–5). Another significant advantage of computer technology is the availability of increasingly sophisticated record-keeping routines. Tracking learners' moves makes it possible to test hypotheses and provides insights into processing and into learner needs and preferences, which can be used to inform pedagogy. For instance, Robinson (1989) reports the findings of a comparative CALL (computer-assisted language learning) study in which an experimental and a control group were given instructional materials sharing the same basic content, but embodying different pedagogical principles and applying different answer-judging strategies for error feedback. The materials of the experimental group referred to people they knew (e.g. the name of the learner's favourite singer was inserted in texts), used narratives as opposed to unconnected sentences, were humorous, etc.; they also gave implicit feedback rather than overt error correction (I eated bananas would be replied to with: oh, you ate bananas, what else did you eat), and gave students more control over error correction. This group was found to perform better, confirming that meaningfulness and discovery strategies are useful ingredients.

Chapelle (2001) summarizes a number of studies that have used computers to manipulate instructional conditions in order to compare explicit and implicit learning. The results are said to be overwhelmingly in favour of explicit types of instruction, a finding corroborated by Norris and Ortega (2000). However, as Chapelle underlines, some results were obtained in laboratory settings and may not be generalizable to classroom settings. One use that computers are particularly suited to is the measurement of reaction times in word and sentence recognition tasks. Computers are also useful for monitoring the use of help facilities in strategy research (Hulstijn, 1993; Hulstijn and Trompetter, 1998; Pujolà, 2002). They have had a significant impact on the study of language acquisition and use, but, as Hulstijn (2000: 39) notes in a survey of computer-assisted SLA research, they remain a minority interest. This is to be regretted. Admittedly computers do not explain phenomena, but they provide 'the means to get closer to the *processes* of language acquisition and use', and in so doing, stimulate fresh thinking. This means that for the first time in the history of language pedagogy, we are witnessing real interaction between technology, methodology and theories.

Development of a new rationale

How might one approach building a rationale for the exploitation of technology? One possible starting point is the conventional distinction between language learning and language use. Like many such oppositions, the distinction between learning and use can be criticized as implying a dichotomy that does not correspond to reality. There is a sense in which language learning and language use are inextricably interlocked, since you cannot learn a language without making some use of it, and since proficiency improves through use. There is nevertheless an essential difference between the two constructs. The first refers to a preparatory stage involving procedures that entail some use of the language but are aimed at meeting eventual needs that currently lie in the future. In other words, language learning is forward looking. Language use, by contrast, is an everyday activity that arises out of the need, or desire, to communicate in the here and now. To the extent that language learning begins before language use, it can be said to be chronologically prior, although the two soon become intertwined. The fact that language learning precedes language use creates pedagogical problems, and much of the thrust of language teaching in the past decades has been to try and bridge the gap between learning and use through activities promoting more authentic use of the foreign language, such as simulations, role plays and school exchanges. In recent years, ICT has come to make an increasing contribution to these attempts, thanks to the opportunities offered by CMC (e.g. chatrooms, virtual reality games from MUD (Multi-User-Dungeon) and MOO (MUD Object Oriented) sites). While it remains the case that the main use of ICT in formal language learning settings has been as an instruction platform, one can expect the versatility of modern technology to be instrumental in a further erosion of the distinction.

Although much remains unclear about how second languages are learnt, and although no consensus exists about what promotes and hinders SLA, there is considerable empirical evidence that instruction can help language learning. In a landmark publication, Larsen-Freeman and Long summarize the results of research on the effect of instruction on second language development as follows:

> Formal SL instruction does not seem able to alter acquisition sequences, except temporarily and in trivial ways which may even hinder subsequent development. On the other hand, instruction has what are possibly positive effects on SLA *processes*, clearly

> positive effects on the *rate* at which learners acquire the language, and probably beneficial effects on their *ultimate level of attainment*. (Larsen-Freeman and Long, 1991: 321)

Over the past 15 years much work has gone into verifying and documenting these conclusions through fine-grained studies. SLA has been repeatedly found to be at once highly systematic and highly variable. Highly systematic with respect to the route of development, which has been shown to be largely independent of the learner's native language and the way in which L2 competence develops (i.e. whether competence develops through instruction or through natural acquisition). Highly variable with regard to the rate and outcome of the learning process. There are important implications for syllabus design and classroom practice in such findings, both generally, and with respect to the exploitation of ICT. Little (1998) is right in stressing that, however understandable it may be to want immediate answers, the question of how a particular technology might be used to facilitate language learning must first be answered theoretically, in the light of our understanding of the language learning process. This is not a question that can be addressed satisfactorily on a purely practical level, but requires that language teachers and language teaching institutions 'reflect carefully on the nature of the language learning process and the role that should be played in it by media technologies' (Little, 1998: 79).

Inevitably, the use made of ICT will vary with the second language learning theories that underpin the teaching, whether such theories are fully articulated or remain implicit. I have shown elsewhere (Kenning, 1999) how approaches built round the distinction between declarative knowledge and procedural knowledge and the conversion of the former into the latter provide a clear set of pointers for the use of ICT. By its very nature, the development of declarative knowledge (knowing that, as opposed to knowing how) calls for features such as data accessibility and retrievability that allow learners to go over the same ground as much as they need to. Consequently, declarative knowledge development is likely to be better served by media used to record language (books, videos, CD-ROMs), that provide this kind of opportunities, than by transmission devices with an ephemeral output (radio, television), that do not. To use Jung's (1994) terminology, declarative knowledge has greater affinity with product media than with process media. The situation is reversed in the case of procedural knowledge, when process media, which require language to be processed in real time under normal conditions, have the advantage, especially in the later stages of language learning. This is the point at which contemporary ICT truly comes into its own. For, thanks to advances in computer technology, it is now possible to interlace different media, and to exercise quite sophisticated control over operating conditions, instead of facing learners with raw materials that make no allowance for their as yet imperfect competence. A host of variables can be manipulated: speed, pace, access to additional information, etc. This offers unprecedented opportunities for implementing Johnson's strategy of gradually increasing task complexity. It becomes possible to create intermediate steps and put learners 'in a position where they have less attention available...than they actually need to perform a task with comfort' (Johnson, 1996: 139) without causing panic and despondency, and then crank things up a bit more, as and when appropriate.

Following Myles (2002), theories of SLA can be divided into three groups, each with distinctive implications for teaching methodology: universal grammar (UG) models, cognitive models, interactional and sociocultural models. In UG models, L2 development is seen as driven and constrained by an innate mental language faculty that makes intervention beyond the provision of sufficient linguistic input largely futile. Cognitive models claim that learning a language entails a shift from controlled to automatized processes, with, in the case of connectionist models, an emphasis on pattern building. As illustrated by the application discussed in the last paragraph, they see practice as crucial for the development of fluency and control. As with UG models, the focus is on explaining learner-internal mechanisms but, contrary to UG, language learning is seen as similar to other types of learning. In addition, cognitive models place more stress on how the input is decoded by learners, emphasizing the role of noticing and attention. In contrast to the other two types of model, interactional and sociocultural models focus on the role of interaction, with varying degrees of attention to the social and cultural context.

The implications of an interactional perspective for CALL activities are discussed at some length by Chapelle (1997), who identifies two critical questions for CALL: what kind of language does the learner engage in, and how good is the experience for L2 learning? From an interactional perspective, the main requirement is that in common with classroom discourse, linguistic exchanges involving computers, whether in the form of oral discussion around computers, CMC, or learner–computer interactions, should contain repetitions, recasts and expansions of previous utterances, which are held to aid learning. Calling for more discourse analysis research to be conducted, Chapelle

(1997: 10) writes: 'Ideally, then, we would want to observe interaction displaying learners' moves in which the normal structure of interaction was disrupted to request modification of the input they had received.'

Research within the sociocultural framework has a somewhat different slant, and has highlighted 'the ability of CALL to provide an arena for natural, meaningful, and realistic language production and reception between and among native and nonnative speakers of the target language' (LeLoup and Ponterio, 2003). In an early analysis of the distinctive features of CMC from a sociocultural perspective, Warschauer (1997: 477) reaches the conclusion that 'when viewed in the context of sociocultural learning theory, which emphasizes the educational value of creating cross-cultural communities of practice and critical inquiry, these features appear to make online learning a potentially powerful tool for collaborative language learning'. Research shows that CMC leads to increases in the quantity of language output compared to face-to-face discussions and a more equal distribution of talk among participants, including a greater ratio of learner talk to teacher talk (LeLoup and Ponterio, 2003; Liu et al., 2003). Particular interest has been shown in tandem language learning by email, which is predicated on interaction and collaboration between peers learning each other's native language, and offers learners a comparatively safe environment in which to try things out (Appel, 1999: 17). However, as discussed below, evaluation studies have shown that telecollaboration is not straightforward and that a successful outcome cannot be guaranteed.

From a language use point of view, the case for integrating ICT into language education rests on the pivotal role of ICT in everyday communication. This is not the same as supporting the deployment of ICT on the grounds that learners need to be equipped with the skills necessary for handling modern technology. What people have in mind when such an argument is made, is global, transferable skills like electronic literacy. The focus is on technology, not on language. What is at stake here is something much more specific pertaining to the fact that language, in today's world, tends to be experienced as mediated communication. CMC is not a stepping stone to grander types of communication. As argued by Warschauer and Healey (1998: 64), it can safely be assumed that in the networked society described by Castells (1996), 'the ability to read, write, and communicate effectively over computer networks will be essential for success in almost every sphere of life'. This ability will sometimes involve the mother tongue and sometimes second languages. Like other subjects, language learning needs to be properly embedded in social practices, not just to enhance the relevance of classroom activities and learner motivation, but also in order to capitalize on student experience in the world outside.

Two factors in particular must be borne in mind. The first is that exposure to, and communication in, a foreign language no longer entail travelling to the extent that they used to do. Satellite television, the Internet, telephones, bring foreign languages to us without any need for travel, while globalization makes contacts with speakers of other languages more likely. The other factor is, paradoxically, the high mobility of an increasing proportion of the population. Mobility is no longer confined to certain professions or social strata and extends beyond the occasional holiday to include extended periods of residence abroad for young and old alike. Unless you only interact with expatriates, residence abroad calls for linguistic expertise and intercultural competence, including the ability to carry out ordinary tasks and activities involving mediated communication, such as phoning a plumber or watching the local news. Such facts of life have a part to play in the definition of objectives and call for more research to be conducted into spontaneous L2 use both at home and abroad. There is a parallel here with the need to reconceptualize literacy in the light of the evolution of society and the impact of advances in ICT on communication. Given that communication practices and media consumption have an idiosyncratic component in that they are known to vary from person to person and situation and situation, findings are bound to have limited predictive value, but they would allow pedagogy to be better informed than is currently the case as to the relative importance of listening, speaking, reading and writing skills in day-to-day living, and the kind of vocabulary and grammar necessary. Obvious needs such as greetings, forms of address and familiarity with the vocabulary of recorded instructions, for instance numbers and the names of keys, do not provide a full enough picture.

This does not mean that the classroom should mirror the outside world. Not only will there be practical obstacles, like lack of accessibility or cost, but in most cases the range of expertise required for effective communication will be better fostered through other media. It would be absurd to set up telephone links for students at an early stage of development, when the ability to handle telephone conversations can be promoted through other means, such as computer simulations and simple exercises in which learners sit back to back. It is a different proposition later on, when telephoning a real call centre with a plausible enquiry might be good practice. To try and model the outside world would actually be inconsistent with the facilitative nature of language teaching and the notion of progression. Language teaching is not about recreating the outside world and facing learners with situations that they are evidently still incapable of coping with, but about selecting and manipulating the target environment in appropriate ways. What is important is to determine what kind of intervention is required, by assessing what learners can reasonably be expected to pick up, what they need to be told explicitly, and how much repetition is desirable, if any.

A proper rationale for technologically based learning cannot be built without concrete evidence from empirical studies with sound theoretical underpinnings. Despite an explosion of interest in technologically supported environments, there is still a shortage of studies demonstrating that the use of ICT actually enhances language learning and produces qualitative as well quantitative changes, i.e. more than the increased output referred to earlier in connection with CMC. Evidence is patchy and there is widespread concern that research is overly interested in technological capabilities and efficiency (savings in time and money) rather than teaching/learning effectiveness, and is insufficiently grounded in language learning theories and design principles: 'Rather than focusing on the benefits and potentials of computer technology, research needs to move towards explaining how computers can be used to support second language learning (i.e. the kinds of tasks or activities that should be used and in what kinds of settings)' (Liu et al., 2003: 264). Until research changes in orientation, any rationale for ICT will continue to lack a secure foundation.

In search of a principled approach

We have seen in the course of this book that the consequences of communication characteristics vary with the lens through which they are observed. One of the distinctive features of language education is the dual status of language as both the object of study and its main vehicle. This duality, which has aroused one of the main ongoing controversies in language teaching circles – whether or not the learners' native language should be used in the classroom – means that communication characteristics have a twofold effect on language activities, which are impacted on as both communicative and pedagogical events. Awareness of broad effects of the kind that have been sketched out in the preceding chapters forms part of the background knowledge that is brought to bear in the construction of an informed approach to materials design and to tactical classroom decisions. But the point of departure needs to be the purpose that the activities or tasks are intended to accomplish. The first step and priority is to establish clear pedagogical objectives, and then look for means of implementation. This will require the adoption of a dialectical stance and an iterative process in which one travels back and forth between pedagogical and technological considerations. Much stress has been laid on closeness of fit (Levy, 1997). This is without doubt an important criterion. But it is important to bear in mind that, in a hierarchical decision network involving a complex system, what appears a good match at a particular level will have pedagogical implications further down the line that may not all be advantageous. Evidence of closeness of fit at an early stage should be interpreted as no more than indicative of potential, and needs to be checked against the opportunities and constraints that occur at other points of the development and implementation process. Salaberry (2000) usefully underscores the value of undertaking a cost trade-offs assessment, showing how technological limitations can be compensated through the use of appropriate pedagogical procedures. It is worth pointing out that features like controllability that are commonly regarded as desirable are only assets when used advisedly. Facilities for manipulating materials, to slow them down, to replay them, to add subtitles or consult reference works, and so on, can promote learning or hinder it, depending on how they are used in relation to the learner's ability to cope with the input (or, in Vygotskian terms, in relation to the learner's zone of proximal development). Badly used, they may make the task too easy, just as overzealous, overprotective parents can stunt their children's development.

Medium selection and use, whether at a strategic, institutional level involving investment in certain technologies, or at a tactical, course or classroom level constrained by availability, needs to be guided by knowledge of the unique characteristics of individual media and their relevance to the objectives to be achieved. If informed decisions are to be taken, note must be taken of what a medium has to offer, whether the same effect might be obtained through some other media or constellation of media, and so on. A summary of the main strengths and limitations of current media is given in Table 5.1.

The information displayed in Table 5.1 is expanded in Table 5.2, which provides a more comprehensive picture of the potential contribution of each media to a number of areas, using one, two or three asterisks according to the strength of the link and the degree of compatibility or probability. It must be stressed that asterisks refer to the direct support that a media is liable to give. They take account of the five communication parameters discussed in detail in Chapter 2, but are not altogether

Table 5.1 Summary of main strengths and weaknesses of individual media

Media	*Main strengths*	*Main weaknesses*
Print	Presentation of information, development of reading skills, self-pacing activities	Static; of little use for listening and speaking skills; no interaction
Radio	Development of listening skills, exposure to different spoken varieties and accents	Sound/listening only; constraints of broadcasting schedule; no interaction
Audio cassettes	Like radio but scope for learner control. Recording facilities can be used to improve speaking skills	Sound/listening only; no interaction
TV	Development of listening skills; access to cultural knowledge	Constraints of broadcasting schedule; no interaction
Video cassettes	Like TV but scope for learner control	No interaction
Telephone	Development of listening and speaking skills; scope for more genuine activities	Sound only
Computer program	Can be used to develop any of the four skills; scope for learner control	Weaknesses depend on application
WWW	Development of reading skills and listening skills; access to cultural knowledge; scope for learner control	Weaknesses depend on application
CMC	Development of any of the skills depending on form of CMC; more genuine activities	Weaknesses depend on application

free of a certain amount of subjectivity. It is taken for granted that skills are not wholly discrete and that gains from one domain may affect another, but this is ignored by Table 5.2.

The first area considered is the presentation of knowledge: the use of media as transmitters of information (including sets of answers to questions). The second aspect of competence covers the four traditional skills (listening (L), speaking (S), reading (R), writing (W)), as well as the development of intercultural competence (IC) through the presentation of illustrative examples or experiential learning. Interaction with learning materials refers to the provision of feedback on responses, while learner control refers to the ability to modify input. The table also

Table 5.2 Assessment of individual media

Media	*Presentation of knowledge*	*Aspects of competence*					*Interaction with materials*	*Learner control*	*Function*
		L	S	R	W	IC			
Print	***			***		*		***	Any
Radio	**	***				*			L, F
Cassettes	**	***	*			*		**	I
TV	**	**		*		**			L, F
Video	**	**		*		**		**	I
Telephone	*	**	***			*		***	F
Computer program	**	**	*	**	***	*	**	Variable	I
WWW	***	**		***	*	*		**	Any
CMC	*	*	*	**	***	**		**	F

includes my assessment of most likely functions based on Stevenson's (1991) distinction between three types of learning resources: leaders (L, resources that lead you to further learning by stimulating your desire to learn), integers (I, resources which form an integral part of your studies, i.e. learning materials), and followers (F, additional support material that represent the icing on the cake).

A number of caveats are in order. First, technology evolves. As has been repeatedly emphasized throughout this book, technological artefacts are not invariant entities, with immutable strengths and weaknesses. History has shown how the limitations of a medium identified as having nothing to offer to listening skills, as was the case with computers in early analyses (e.g. Ariew, 1987), may diminish or even disappear. As Warschauer and Healey (1998: 61) put it: 'Zeroing in on whether and in what ways computers can be used to enhance learning has been aiming at a moving target.' The tables only purport to capture some key aspects of the present situation. Second, the significance of a particular strength or weakness depends on the context of use. As a rule of thumb, judicious exploitation of ICT consists in delegating to ICT what it can do equally well as, or better than, the teacher. What has claims to being judicious in one case because of, say, geographical dispersion or physical isolation, may be unjustifiable or ill-conceived in others. Thus what is true for distance learning may not apply to other situations. Finally, pedagogical interventions are multi-layered processes involving a more intricate balancing act than suggested by simple descriptions in terms of nested binary choices: whether or not to have recourse to technology, one-way versus two-way technologies, authentic versus educational materials, genuine activities versus simulations, and so on. It is possible, consequently, for divergent inter-media affordances to be of lesser importance than differences between the possible applications of a given media.

Although speech synthesis and speech recognition systems still have a way to go before they sound natural or can deal with the challenges of deviant speech, and notwithstanding an acknowledged imbalance in the literature favouring reading and writing over other language skills, all aspects of language learning nowadays can be supported through technology. Whether, and to what extent, a specific language area or language skill is viewed as likely to be enhanced by ICT is obviously influenced by the affordances of technological artefacts. But it also depends on beliefs about the ways in which languages are learnt and the perceived significance of the particular area or skill. Taking issue with the view that it is enough for learners to master the major phonemes of a language, some linguists argue that pronunciation is critical to language processing and learning: 'If we cannot say the sounds quickly, our short-term memory span will be very restricted and consequently we will face severe difficulties with the processing of language and with storing the language in our long-term memory' (Cook, 2001: 86). This leads to the speculative conclusion that we should try to get learners to speak faster and the possibility of harnessing computers: 'I [...] once wrote a computer program called *Speedup* with this aim: students' L2 span and reading speed were measured; then they had to read sentences aloud from the screen, starting below their normal speed and getting faster and faster; finally they were tested to see whether their span had improved' (Cook, 2001: 86).

Similarly, recognizing that comprehensible input is not enough, Garrett (1987: 183) proposes that foreign language education should conceive of grammar in psycholinguistic rather than linguistic terms, and should use computers to implement such an approach. Garrett argues that an understanding of processing rules is more useful than a knowledge of linguistic rules, and that learners need some organizing principle for their learning, before suggesting an implementation framework covering '(1) consciousness raising, (2) major grammatical topics in the TL [target language], (3) particular structures, and (4) the surface structure'. In recent years, objections to grammar teaching have softened, giving way to the adoption of an eclectic approach in which grammar instruction is said to be 'a means to enhance and refine input by inducing noticing and consciousness-raising and, thus, to help language become intake in readiness for eventual acquisition'

(Klapper, 2005). Much of this can be done via technology, which provides a variety of means of making certain features salient. Computer-based courses routinely include applications aimed at the enhancement of grammar and vocabulary learning, and ready-made templates for creating a range of quizzes, games, gap-fill exercises, vocabulary cards, are readily available on the Web (e.g. Hot Potatoes, 2006). New subfields such as corpus CALL (the exploitation of corpora and concordancing software for language learning and teaching purposes) have emerged, with applications liable to contribute to several aspects of language education (Johns and King, 1991; Sinclair, 2004).

In the last decade or so, the development of intercultural competence has joined the four traditional language skills as a candidate for technological support. There has always been a cultural element to language learning, usually delivered, in part at least, through media. But it is only recently that the critical importance of intercultural competence has come to the fore (e.g. Hinkel, 1999; Rose and Kasper, 2001; Bardovi-Harlig and Mahan-Taylor, 2003), with scholars presenting cultural awareness as inextricably intertwined with language proficiency: 'Culture in language learning is not an expendable fifth skill tacked on, so to speak, to the teaching of speaking, listening, reading and writing' (Kramsch, 1993: 1). Approaching language as social practice entails that cultural awareness 'be viewed both as enabling language proficiency and as being the outcome of reflection on language proficiency' (Kramsch, 1993: 8). Intercultural competence involves five elements: attitudes (e.g. curiosity and openness), knowledge, skills of interpreting and relating, skills of discovery and interaction, and critical cultural awareness (Byram, 1997). It includes pragmatic competence, which in turn has two components: awareness of the appropriateness of a given speech act (e.g. apology, compliment) in a particular context (sociopragmatic competence), and use of appropriate linguistic forms to perform a speech act (pragmalinguistic competence).

As a means of gaining access to historical and literary texts and to up-to-date evidence on cultural conventions, modern media have much to offer to the development of pragmatic competence. The World Wide Web is an unparalleled resource for filling the gap left by the restricted opportunities for intercultural learning provided by teacher–learner interactions, while films and videos for the entertainment market routinely illustrate the use and form of thanks and apologies, telephone openings, etc. in different societies. Visual media are also useful in displaying key variables of non-verbal communication, notably what Sebeok (1994: 115) refers to as 'the indissolubly parallel foreign gesticulatory skills'. However, recent research shows that making contextualized, pragmatically appropriate input available to learners is not always sufficient, and that explicit teaching can be more effective. Areas which learners are believed to need help with include the interpretation of conversational implicature (the implied meaning of an utterance) and the social use of speech acts (Bardovi-Harlig, 2001: 31).

Due to intra-language variation, interactional norms can also prove problematical for speakers of a language who belong to different speech communities. Though fictitious, the following extract is a good example:

> The waitress, whose name, Darlette, was displayed on a badge pinned to the front of her apron, put a jug of iced water on the table and said brightly, 'How are you this evening, sir?'
> 'Oh, bearing up,' said Bernard wondering if the stress of the day's events had marked him so obviously that even total strangers were concerned for his wellbeing. But he inferred from Darlette's puzzled expression that her enquiry had been entirely phatic. 'Fine, thank you,' he said, and her countenance cleared. (Lodge, 1991: 104)

Mey (2001: 143) comments upon the incident as follows: 'the problem lies in the nature of the greeting, "How are you this evening, sir?". For Bernard, a British tourist in Hawaii, this is a question about his wellbeing, to be answered in some sort of (admittedly perfunctory) manner. For Darlette, his answer is baffling. Her question had not been a real question, but an instance of "phatic communication".' Any aspect of interactions can prove challenging for a newcomer to a culture. Thus Morsbach (1988: 192) reports that, due to the Japanese custom of using bowing as a mode of greeting, 'Japanese must learn how to shake hands properly before venturing to Western countries. Japanese etiquette books (sometimes illustrated with humorous cartoons) show them how to do this correctly: how much to squeeze so as not to present the other person with a "limp rag", to look their partner in the eye, so as not to appear "shifty", etc.' Conversely, Westerners need to learn to bow correctly and gracefully, bowing with the head and neck only, not from the waist. This is a type of problem that technological progress can help resolve. Visual media that display appropriate behaviour dynamically clearly have much to offer here, as have advances in virtual reality involving touch-sensitive devices that provide kinaesthetic experiences.

What has received most scholarly attention to date is the potential of telecollaboration for developing intercultural competence. Much has been written about the unique opportunities presented by international partnerships for improving knowledge of target culture norms, for enhancing appreciation of your own culture, for developing awareness of the link between language and culture, in addition to increasing motivation and enhancing linguistic competence. However, recent research shows that telecollaboration across linguistic and cultural boundaries is not always successful. Not only are violations of cultural norms liable to lead to misunderstandings and breakdowns in communication, from which the partnership may not recover (O'Dowd, 2004: 145), but participants are likely to be operating from different, possibly clashing cultural bases. In an analysis of socio-institutional influences on a German–American telecollaborative partnership, Belz (2002) shows how target language status and valuation, technological access and know-how, and learning accreditation interact multidirectionally with individual psychobiography and aspects of the situated activity to shape language learning and use. While the study points to the clash of cultural fault lines, it also presents instances where individual agency managed to counter the negative impact of the socio-institutional factors. Belz (2002: 76) ends with suggestions for 'guided cultural sensitization on social patterns of communication and institutional conditions which may influence (but not determine) the execution of task-oriented electronic collaboration'. The aim is to provide virtual partners with information that may enable them to avoid the perpetuation or creation of cultural stereotypes when faced with behaviour that they do not understand. What this scaffolding may consist of is fleshed out by O'Dowd and Eberbach (2004), who outline the strategies that they used to raise learners' awareness of intercultural learning and train them to make effective contributions and move from monologues to dialogues.

Focusing on the cultural embeddedness of technological artefacts, Thorne (2003) examines how cultures of use affect the manner in which intercultural communication plays out in an institutional context, and the consequential impact on the processes and products of language learning and use. Thorne discusses three case studies. The first is an older instance of French–American telecollaboration. It illustrates how French and American partners approached telecollaboration with clashing expectations (information exchange versus relationship building), that reflected different material conditions associated with different levels of acculturation into digital communities, and undermined the success of the relationship. The second case study also involves French and American partners, but concentrates on a single pair, who successfully moved from an email course-based relationship to authentic communication via IM. This is perceived to have benefited the pragmatic deployment of address pronouns and the acquisition of prepositions of locations. Case study three is concerned with generational shifts in communication tool preference, and the ecological questionability of email applications in the light of student perceptions of email as 'a communication medium well suited for vertical communication across power and generation lines, but utterly inappropriate as a tool to mediate interpersonal age–peer relationship building' (Thorne, 2003: 57). From this evidence, Thorne concludes that 'the mediational means available (e.g. IM versus email) and its cultural–historical resonance for users, play a critical role in how and even if the communicative process and accompanying interpersonal relationships develop' and suggests that 'for Internet-mediated interpersonal or hyperpersonal relationships to develop, [...] certain minimum alignments of cultures-of-use are a necessary condition'. These are crucial observations for the development of a principled approach.

From humble beginnings, the use of technology in language learning and language teaching has grown to become a major subfield with its own journals (including *Language Learning and Technology, Computer Assisted Language Learning, ReCALL,* and *System*) and an ever-expanding specialist literature. It also regularly appears in works on other aspects of language education (e.g. Flowerdew and Miller, 2005; Chapelle, 2005), although concerns have been expressed about continuing marginalization of CALL research (Coleman, 2005). Despite the use made of print, audio and video cassettes in classroom-based and individual language learning, and the educational benefits to be gained from satellite television (Hill, 1991; Meinhof, 1998), the trend has been for discussions to be increasingly dominated by computers. The number of publications devoted to computer-based applications outstrips that of works dedicated to any other media, and computer-assisted is taken to be synonymous with technologically enhanced (Thompson, 2005: 148).

Some works concentrate on one type of application, e.g. MOO as a language learning tool (Shield, 2003), or a particular skill, e.g. second language writing in a computer environment (Broady, 2000). Others offer practical ideas, for instance, for using the Internet (e.g. Windeatt, Hardisty and Eastment, 2000). Yet others offer both explanatory accounts and practical ideas on a range of applications (Chambers, Conacher and Littlemore, 2004). Within this broad envelope, there is a developing interest in highly popular and nascent environments, such as mobile phones, IM and MP3 players, and Web authoring tools such as Blogs (Web journaling tools) and Wikis (a form of Web collaborative software). Relevant notable publications include Eisenstadt, Komzak and

Dzbor (2003); Godwin-Jones (2005); Purushotma (2005) and Thorne and Payne (2005). A particularly useful resource for language teachers is a set of online training materials obtainable from the ICT4 LT website. Developed under the auspices of the Socrates programme, it comprises frequently updated modules ranging from 'Introduction to new technologies and how they can contribute to language learning and teaching' and 'Introduction to Computer Assisted Language Learning (CALL)' to 'Exploiting World Wide Web resources online and offline' and 'Computer Aided Assessment (CAA) and language learning' (Davies, 1999–2006).

The need for a principled approach grounded in SLA theory has been highlighted by a number of researchers (e.g. Salaberry, 1996; Chapelle, 1997, 2001; Felix, 2005). So too has the specificity of technological artefacts. For instance, Lamy (2004) stresses that unlike telephone users, participants involved in synchronous voice-based CMC sit in front of a screen and click, type or drag a mouse. Increasingly, discussions of approaches to task design are acknowledging the importance of factoring in the specific materiality of technological artefacts: 'A synchronous audiographic environment like Lyceum, with its written, spoken and graphic modes might resemble a face-to-face setting more than an asynchronous written environment but the materiality of the resources and the affordances of the modes still have a significant impact on interaction and communication' (Hampel, 2006). At the same time, the expanding presence of multimedia is enabling and prompting researchers to carry out experimental and empirical investigations that promise to shed new light on processing issues. Thus in a study conducted by Brett (1997), multimedia were found to achieve higher success rates for comprehension and recall than when the materials were delivered via audio or video plus pen and paper. Brett hypothesizes that the instant feedback (ticks and crosses) received by students in the multimedia delivery helped them monitor their comprehension and identify key items. Of particular interest are studies concerned with range of symbolic cues examining the contribution made by visual cues and the related question of which mode has primacy in the decoding process (Bell, 2003). These focused studies offer valuable pedagogical insights, such as the usefulness of glossing formats and ongoing feedback, or the drawing up of a checklist of factors to help in the selection of appropriate TV news material. Above all, they offer the prospect of an improved understanding of how language is processed, that can be used to achieve gains in effectiveness. The last statement in Kenning and Kenning (1990) gives an idea of the technological distance travelled over the past 15 years:

> There is no doubt that the future, with its promise of: input and output of the spoken word; systems capable of comprehending and producing something approaching natural language; systems capable of translating to and from the target language; cheap and effective means of incorporating authentic audio and video materials; integrated expert pedagogical systems with user access to software tools such as word processors, database systems, and other dedicated packages; rapid online access to information currently stored mainly in book form; international networking of software, data and mail; is bound to be exciting. (Kenning and Kenning, 1990: 135)

Many of the developments envisaged above have become reality in the intervening period. The availability of Internet resources in a range of formats and delivery platform has grown to the point where it is possible in certain languages for teachers to outsource much of their teaching to the Web (Felix, 1999). There are no doubt further technological innovations in store. My hope is that they will be not simply matched, but surpassed, by progress made along the avenues that are opening up in the realm of pedagogy.

6
Case Study: the Telephone and Language Learning

Introduction

This chapter brings together the ideas expounded in the previous chapters by means of a case study of the telephone and language learning. After outlining the exemplary significance of the telephone, I review the main milestones in its evolution. Next I turn to the place of the telephone in everyday life. I start by considering the traditional role of the telephone as a means of interpersonal oral communication before discussing the changes brought by recent developments such as call centres and SMS. In the last part of the chapter I examine the use of the telephone in education and language learning. Again I focus first on conventional telephony before considering the rise of mobile learning.

The telephone is not a medium that springs readily to mind when considering the interface between technology and language learning. It has received comparatively little attention in the scholarly literature and has been similarly neglected in language education. But although it may seem a peculiar choice, there are several reasons for considering the telephone an object of interest particularly relevant to the present work.

The first is the ubiquity and pervasiveness of the telephone. We live in a phone-based culture in which having ready access to, and making use of, a phone has come to be one of the basic necessities of life. People are routinely expected to give a phone number through which they may be contacted, and the inability to make and manage telephone calls is a serious impediment in everyday life, and inconceivable in a business context. If one adds that international calls are commonplace, then there begins to be a case for an enquiry into what skills and knowledge making telephone calls entails, and the attendant implications for language learning.

The reason why the telephone has been under-researched is not that it lacks intrinsic interest. Rather, the telephone appears to have been a victim of its success. It has suffered the fate of those unobtrusive everyday objects and practices that get overlooked because of their ordinariness. But the fact that we have become used to its presence does not mean that it is not worthy of consideration. Indeed, because it affects the lives of so many people, it has arguably a powerful contribution to make to our understanding of communicative behaviour. It is not the only medium to have been ignored. Experts have similarly devoted scant attention to Citizens' Band radio, concentrating instead on the mass media and their effects, and, recently, computer technology. So much so that 'upon reading literature on communication technology, one might think that communication technology is a television or a personal computer linked to a network' (Katz and Aakhus, 2002: 10).

The phenomenal growth of digital mobile communication, not only in industrialized affluent countries but across the world, has given the telephone considerable prominence. There is a growing awareness of the potential impact of mobile telephony on education, together with signs of a rapidly developing interest in the role of mobile technologies in language learning. A case study of the telephone is therefore timely and opportune.

Finally, as a medium with a comparatively long and well-chronicled history stretching back over 100 years to the second half of the nineteenth century, the telephone provides ample illustrative evidence of the evolutionary dimension of media use. There is enough to look back on, not only to flesh out the ideas put forward in earlier chapters with examples pertaining to a specific technology and its uses, but also to gain insight into issues relevant to other media. By using the telephone as a lens and as a comparator, it is possible to illuminate major trends and commonalities as well as bring out specificities. Focusing on telephony gives a better appreciation of the path humanity has travelled and underscores the difficulty of attempting to approach ICT at the level of a technology or media, rather than in terms of particular applications or services. This is obvious when one considers mobile telephony, which represents the embodiment of convergence by incorporating within a single compact device what used to be separate modalities of mediated communication. But it also applies to traditional fixed telephony, due to the proliferation of appendages and systems of various kinds.

Milestones in telephone history

The telephone has come a long way since the time when 'telecommunications consisted of a transitory dialogue in real time between two persons' (G.T. Marx, 1994: 540). So much so that it is doubtful whether Alexander Graham Bell would recognize a mobile handset as a descendant of the machine he invented.

The telephone was first envisaged in the 1830s, with the first prototype being produced by a German, Philip Reiss, in 1861, and Bell and Gray eventually filing patents on the same day in 1876 (Winston, 1998). It was to spread rapidly and benefit from multiple enhancements over the course of the next 130 years, from the setting up of manual switchboards and their replacement with automatic telephone exchanges, the laying down of a submarine cable link between England and France in 1891, and the first two-way conversation across the Atlantic in 1926, through the development of a range of new affordances and accessories, to digital telephony and the mobile phone.

What is truly remarkable about the telephone and gives it 'a unique place in the history of humanity' (Katz and Aakhus, 2002: 2) is that it represented an 'unprecedented extension of ear and voice' (Briggs, 1977: 42). The telephone introduced a totally novel possibility: 'By far the most radical aspect of the telephone as a technology for communication is that its invention enabled people, for the first time ever, to talk to each other as if they were co-present when in fact they were not' (Hutchby, 2001: 6). Katz and Aakhus make the interesting observation that there was nothing in the natural world to prepare people for what the telephone would deliver. Whereas one might fantasize about flying at the sight of birds or imagine travelling faster than on a horse, there was no model in the world around of instant communication across hundreds of miles, no inducement to imagine such a possibility. This helps explain why the possibility of transmitting sound along telephone lines in both directions did not immediately make the telephone the person-to-person communication device that it is today. For a while, the opportunity it offered as an entertainment and information device for transmitting music and news outshone its two-way capabilities. Briggs (1977: 43) describes how people queued at the 1881 International Electrical Exhibition in Paris to listen to music transmitted by telephone from a distance of a mile. It was a type of use that Bell himself had fostered with his lecture circuits, sharing with his audiences his vision of a future in which telephones in diverse locations would be connected by means of a switch (Aronson, 1977: 21). As stressed in Chapter 1, what comes to appear inevitable in retrospect is often not apparent to the contemporaries of an invention in the same way. Bell was an exception, a visionary with incredible prophetic power.

Through the transformation of 'what previously seemed an eternal aspect of space and time' (Pool, 1977: 5), the telephone was to have a profound impact on human beings' perception of the world and on their relations with one another. At the same time, as Gumpert (1987: 132–3) points out, you are aware when talking on the phone that your interlocutor is not there: 'Traditionally, the miracle of telephone communication emphasizes the dimension that has been overcome – *space*.' Part of the appeal of the telephone, once its capabilities became appreciated, was what would now be called its user-friendliness: 'It was of such universal value and so simple to use (a contemporary advertisement remarked, "Its employment necessitated no skilled labour, no technical education...") that there can be very few inventions in history which came into everyday use so swiftly' (Clarke, 1992: 112). In this the telephone supports Rogers's (1983) analysis of the features influencing adoption, which, as reported, identifies complexity as having a negative effect on diffusion, and therefore, by implication, user-friendliness as helpful.

This is not to say that telephony was embraced with equal speed in all countries. The most receptive terrain was the United States, with the telephone spreading initially among the business community, until the advent of independent telephone companies brought it within the reach of the more affluent section of the population. Critically, telephone use, as distinct from ownership, was not restricted to the well-to-do, but was available to others through pay telephones. By the beginning of the twentieth century, most inhabited places had at least one public telephone, and larger cities and towns had many more. How far ahead the United States were is shown by a rate of penetration of one telephone for every 60 people by 1900, against one for every 215 in Sweden, the first European country (Briggs and Burke, 2005: 122). Another indication of the speed at which telephony spread in the US is that 'by 1909, the hundred largest hotels in New York City had 21,000 telephones – nearly as many as the continent of Africa and more than Spain – which were averaging six million calls annually' (Aronson, 1977: 30). As these statistics indicate, diffusion was much slower in Europe, although the reasons varied from country to country, reminding us that 'inventions, like ideas, seldom encounter a neutral environment' (Perry, 1977: 90). In France, for instance, growth was delayed by the reluctance of the government to abandon its monopoly on telecommunications, whereas the main obstacle in Britain was the existence of an excellent communications system in the postal services and the nationalized telegraph industry. Consequently, the telephone tended to be considered in Britain as something of a luxury rather than as a necessity. There was also a lack of consensus as to what the structure of the telephone industry should be. This leads Perry (1977: 90) to conclude: 'Preexisting conditions, outlooks, and prejudices had more to do with the impact of the telephone than its intrinsic features.'

The influence of the social matrix can also be seen in differences in the rate of adoption (or differences in usage) within countries. Research has revealed differences between men and women, between different age groups, and between towns and rural locations, as well as fluctuations in the impact of the telephone at different points in time (e.g. before and after the advent of automobile and radio). Again the national dimension is liable to come to the fore. For instance, while in Britain the telephone was not seen as relevant to rural areas, these were the areas where the telephone was most in demand in Canada, the United States and Australia (Briggs and Burke, 2005: 121). One is faced with a complex kaleidoscope derived from the interaction of multiple social variables that supports the rejection of a deterministic view of the role of technology. On the other hand, it seems reasonable to interpret the degree of prescience of people like Bell as a sign of intrinsic technological potentials, that admittedly require a particular type of prevailing conditions in order to be realized, but are nonetheless hard to deny. This suggests the adoption of a middle-ground position that views technology as a germ that introduces new, inherently constrained, possibilities, that may or may not materialize.

What happens when circumstances are unfavourable is illustrated by the history of the latest incarnation of the telephone, the mobile phone. Emblematic as it is of the new millennium, the mobile phone goes back to an idea described in 1947 that went on to gather dust for two decades. The reasons for the delay were partly technical, but they were also partly social inasmuch as the mobile phone did not fit in with the values of the hierarchical and paternalistic world of the mid-twentieth century (Agar, 2003: 23–4). This time Europe, especially Finland, was ahead of the United States, which had a plentiful supply of home phones, and where the use of mobile phones was restricted by the charging system. Owners had to pay for incoming calls, which made them reluctant to give out their number, and favoured the use of mobile phones for business and emergencies rather than chat (Agar, 2003: 42).

One of the most obvious benefits of adopting a historical perspective on telephony is a better appreciation of the constantly evolving nature of media. The evolution of telephony is something that anyone born before the spread of mobile phones is likely to be aware of. The older you are, the more changes you will have witnessed, from the time when telephones were located in post offices and special booths, through shared and then single landlines, to a world where phones are portable and everywhere. You may remember speculations about scenarios that never happened, of way stations every 100 metres or so in major streets that people would be able to connect their phone to. And you will be aware of what these changes have meant in terms of your movements and actions and how you communicate with others. To the point perhaps of sometimes hankering after a world in which phone calls did not occupy such a prominent position in life, when there was no compulsion to be in constant touch, and you did not have to continually adapt to new patterns of behaviour and new communication practices.

It is not necessary to go very far back in the literature to find descriptions and remarks that are now outdated. Taking Schegloff (1986: 112–18) as an example, it can no longer be taken for granted that visually accessible aspects of talk-in-interaction (e.g. posture, facial expression) are denied to participants in telephone conversation. Facilities such as caller display, which provide the answerer with cues as to the likely identity of the caller, reduce the asymmetry between the information available to the two parties as to the occasion's relevancies (what might be talked about), while the 'summons', nowadays, does not necessarily come as a mechanical standardized ring tone, but may take a variety of forms, from customized ring tones to vibrations. In a similar vein, Gumpert's (1987: 127) 'partial inventory of future developments', which outlines a number of what were then nascent developments, such as call screening, call forwarding to a different location, number storage, mobile phones, is a reminder of how things used to be and, like Schegloff's remarks, highlights the progress that has been made in telephony over the past two decades, as does Moyal's (1992: 51) description of the telephone as a pervasive, invisible connector. Invisibility ended with the advent of mobile telephony, which has literally brought telephony out in the open, to the point of obtrusiveness.

The telephone in everyday life

Interpersonal oral communication

Although widely perceived as an instrument of two-way interpersonal communication, the modern telephone can be found in a variety of configurations. It can be used monologically to leave or listen to a message. It can also be used to communicate with multiple parties in an audio-conference setting. Or it can be brought in as an additional participant in a face-to-face encounter. Typical examples include ringing someone while at a party, calling a third party to settle an issue that you and your interlocutor are unable to resolve by yourselves, or deciding to 'phone a friend' in a game show. Here, and even more so where communication relies on texting rather than speaking, dyadic interactions can expand into a collective undertaking, with close friends or experts invited to join in, or to proffer advice on a suitable response or wording (Kasesniemi and Rautiainen, 2002: 182). The practice of involving others, which replicates the editing procedures of newspapers, provides evidence of the complex realities hiding beneath the deceptively simple notions of sender and receiver. While collective reading and composing of messages is a recent phenomenon, the issue of participant roles in relation to addressees is not. From the early days of telephony, it has been possible for parties other than that or those known, ratified and addressed by the speaker to form part of the audience. This may be through eavesdropping, most notoriously wire-tapping, but also misuse of party lines, extension lines or switchboard systems. Or it may involve acting as auditor or as overhearer (phones with an extra earpiece/cordless handset, speakerphones). Interestingly, provided ethical issues are addressed, there is here a window of opportunity for language learning (albeit one that is not easy to exploit), since this gives learners a chance to listen in to telephone conversations.

Turning to communication characteristics, one comes across other kinds of variability that point to the telephone as a microcosm of ICT. As far as space coordinates are concerned, the telephone can be seen as demonstrating the importance of reach, with a progressive extension of the distance covered by telephone calls culminating, from a language use and language learning perspective, in the introduction of international calls in the last decade of the nineteenth century. In another major leap forward, telephone users have been freed from their dependence on equipment tied to specific places, first through the introduction of cordless phones, which provide a measure of mobility within a certain radius, followed by full-scale liberation with mobile telephony. People conversing over mobile phones may be virtually anywhere, or, indeed, on the move. Consequently, whereas in traditional telephony those engaged in a personal conversation normally have some idea of the spatial context of their interlocutor, mobile phone users do not know where the other person is. Among the effects of this 'spatial indeterminacy of the cellular phone user' (Licoppe and Heurtin, 2002: 100) is the not infrequent appearance in mobile phone conversations of references to the caller's or callee's location. What is noteworthy here is that utterances such as 'I am on the train' or 'We are just coming up to a roundabout' sound distinctly odd outside the context of mobile telephony. Sane people do not normally go around making such statements. However, their occurrence within mobile phone calls opens the way for some novel authentic language learning practice.

Whatever the parameter under consideration – space coordinates, time coordinates, range of symbolic cues, interactivity and action orientation – it is not possible to associate the modern telephone with a particular set of values. Not only is the distance between participants liable to vary within, as well as across, interactions (if, for example, one of the parties is using a mobile); with technological progress, what was once a synchronous, voice-based, interactive technology that offered different degrees of action orientation depending on the identity of the participants and their relationship has been transmogrified. As shown by Table 6.1, the variations are manifold: asynchrony (e.g. answerphones, voicemail, SMS) or synchrony, availability of the visual and/or aural channel, presence or absence of reciprocity and simultaneous feedback. Thus dial-it services (for instance, weather information), email and WAP (wireless application protocol) enabled phones have different sets of characteristics. Yet, in all its forms, the telephone remains indissociable from oral interactions. Notwithstanding its many uses, the product of the metamorphosis of the traditional telephone into a miniature powerful computer continues to be perceived as an artefact for conversing with absent others.

Telephone conversations depart from face-to-face on two dimensions: space coordinates and range of symbolic cues. Although it is possible for people to communicate by telephone within a shared physical environment, space separation remains the norm, and a fundamental characteristic of telephone calls (and mediated communication in general). In contrast, technological progress has begun to reduce the difference between telephone and face-to-face interactions with respect to symbolic cues. While tactile cues remain unavailable, the more sophisticated of today's mobile phones allow interlocutors to see each other, even if the array of visual cues does not match that of the canonical face-to-face situation.

Voice-only communication, a novel phenomenon at the time of the introduction of the telephone (if one excepts the few occasions in life when circumstances prevent interlocutors from seeing each other),

Table 6.1 Communication characteristics of different forms of telephone interaction

	Communication between fixed points	*Synchrony*	*Range of symbolic cues*	*Interactivity: reciprocity*	*Interactivity: simultaneous feedback*	*Degree of interpersonal specificity*
Landline telephones	√	√	Sound only (except for videophones)	√	√	Towards high end
Mobile phone conversation	No	√	Sound, sometimes with access to visual cues	√	No (see earlier discussion)	Usually high
Answering machines and voicemail	Device dependent	No but need to decode/encode in real time remains	Sound only	No but need to assume both roles remains	No	Low
Calls to call centres	Device dependent	√	Sound only	√	Line dependent	Towards low end
SMS	No	No	Written language	Not within single message	No	Usually high

presents challenges that affect interlocutors in two different ways: according to whether they are the source or the receiver of the message, and in their position as beneficiary or provider of feedback. Specifically, in voice-only communication, the source cannot make use of non-oral resources to convey or reinforce the meaning, and only receives feedback auditorially. Conversely, the receiver must interpret a purely oral message and the feedback they provide is also purely oral. This places particular emphasis on linguistic skills and tends to make telephone calls difficult to cope with for less expert speakers. The absence of visual cues also has socio-psychological effects, which have been explored by manipulating conditions experimentally, outside a telephone environment. For example, in order to pinpoint the impact of different factors, researchers have studied the consequences of placing a curtain between the subjects, so that they are physically together, but without visual contact. As argued by Rutter (1987: 38), 'If communicating by telephone is to be understood properly [...] cues which are present and those which are absent must *both* be considered.' Overall, the effect of the absence of visual cues has proved elusive, and has been shown to be intertwined with other factors. It can produce psychological distance, but, when it enables interlocutors to remain anonymous (e.g. in hotline counselling), it can also encourage psychological proximity and intimate content. What emerges from the research is not a simplistic cause and effect picture, but people's ability to circumvent difficulties and make the most of the telephone's communicative affordances. Aside from space and range of symbolic cues, telephone talk resembles face-to-face in involving synchronous communication in real time, albeit with occasional glitches, in implying reciprocity and allowing simultaneous feedback (depending on the type of connection), and in offering various degrees of action orientation.

Despite the constraints under which they are conducted, telephone conversations have been found to only differ from other kinds of conversation with respect to their openings and closings: 'The openings of telephone conversations generally do have a distinctive shape. We regularly find a sequence not often found in "face-to-face" conversation – a sequence where the parties identify and/or recognize one another' (Schegloff, 1977: 416). In face-to-face, identification/recognition is accomplished by visual appearance so that, unless they happen to be strangers, there is no reason for participants to state who they are. In addition, telephone openings sometimes use words in ways that do not coincide with face-to-face. Thus, instead of representing an informal version of 'hello', 'hi' is used in telephone conversations as a variant of 'yeah' when the answerer is confident about the identity of the caller. Typically, the caller will have promised to 'call right back' (Schegloff, 1986: 121). One suspects that the introduction of facilities such as caller identifier (caller ID) make the occurrence of items like 'hi' more frequent, since the answerer has some idea of who the person might be.

Although opening sequences may seem unimportant, they can be an obstacle to negotiating the initial moves in a telephone call successfully and cause friction. This typically happens where there is a mismatch in expectations between interlocutors: 'There are situations in which, as answerers, we can feel put out if someone we feel ought to treat us as not-called-but-talked-to (for instance, our in-laws) treats us merely as answerer-not-called' (Hutchby, 2001: 104). Since, as highlighted by Pavlidou (2000), opening and closing sections of telephone conversations between acquaintances, including who speaks first, how recognition is accomplished, how fast one gets to the reason for calling, are managed differently across countries/languages, telephone openings can be problematic for foreigners. For example, compared to their German counterparts, Greek openings and closings contain an interactional surplus of phatic utterances, so that a German caller who fails to produce the expected phatic utterances will tend to be perceived by a Greek answerer as attending to the reason for calling too quickly. This highlights how telephone conversation 'remains a sensitive area in intercultural encounters, even for those who have mastered the basics of a foreign language and culture' (Pavlidou, 2000: 121). This is true in a business as well as a domestic setting. Halmari (1993) documents several differences between Finnish and Anglo-American business-related talk conventions which may, cumulatively, have a negative outcome in an area where understanding is essential to success. They encompass the status of the 'how are you' sequence (a routine greeting for English speakers, but a prompt for a lengthy non-topical sequence for Finns) and the frequency and location of initiated overlaps.

How conventions are acquired by native speakers, given that one side of a conversation normally remains hidden to non-participants, is an intriguing question. As far as L2 speakers are concerned, there is a need for explicit teaching, not only of useful phrases and tips on how to use the phone (Townsend Hall, 2000; Flippo, 2006a), but also of culture-specific norms, unless learners are able and allowed to eavesdrop on conversations in the manner evoked above. An alternative, complementary approach is to foster telephone tandem learning by setting up telephone links between partners learning each other's language (Holtzer, 2003). Admittedly, the (usually) tightly controlled framework within which tandem interactions tend to take place, with sets of prescribed topics to discuss, does not strictly reproduce the conditions of casual telephone talk in everyday settings. Nevertheless, telephone contact with native speakers allows learners to familiarize themselves with the rituals and conventions of the L2, and with the techniques and language used to carry out communicative tasks, for instance the introduction of a new topic.

An examination of the developmental trajectory of the telephone and its uses reveals several recurrent themes in the literature. Among these, as already mentioned, is the different conduct of men and women. Women are said to talk more than men on the telephone, and to use it for chatting rather than instrumentally, a behaviour famously captured by Mark Twain in a one-sided humorous sketch of a lady on the telephone written in 1880 (Twain, 1996). That women and men's usage of the telephone is different is supported by recent studies. Smoreda and Licoppe (2000), which is based on French data but discusses findings that are unlikely to be culture specific, at least in Western civilization, identifies significant differences in intensity of domestic telephone use between men and women with regard to both frequency of use and duration of telephone calls. It is argued that the greatest effect on how the call is managed, and on its overall duration, is exerted by the receiver's gender, with calls in which the receiver is a woman lasting longer than those in which the interlocutor is male. Moyal's (1992) study of the gendered use of the telephone in an Australian context is of particular interest for this book because of the attention paid to non-native speakers. Moyal shows that the telephone often makes a substantial contribution to women's sense of autonomy and well-being. It is a means of overcoming isolation, used by women from migrant backgrounds to keep in touch with kin in their native country, as well as to seek information from agencies. In the latter case, communication may take place through intermediaries with better English-speaking skills, such as a woman's children. Crucially, Moyal notes how the telephone can arouse apprehension for those with less developed linguistic skills, who may shrink from answering incoming calls. This supports the claim made here that, as an indispensable element of contemporary life, the telephone needs to be given greater attention in language education. This implies acquainting learners with the special features of telephone talk and, through back-to-back activities or telephone simulations, getting them used to dispensing with visual cues.

Texts about the telephone reveal fascinating parallels between the concerns of contemporaries of early adopters of the telephone and the concerns expressed about modern developments like SMS, the mobile phone and Internet Chat. Thus, etiquette was hotly debated, not only at what time it was permissible to call, but also what kind of language should be used. The *Electrical Review* of 1889 complained about the relaxation of common courtesies of speech, writing: 'Who cannot remember when the telephone was put into commercial use, being sometimes addressed by an unseen, and often unknown speaker, in language such as a man would rarely use face to face with another man', while subscribers to an Ohio telephone company overheard by operators to be using language considered to be improper and vulgar had their telephone removed (Marvyn, 1988: 88–9). The telephone also prefigured developments such as Internet Chat in creating 'unprecedented opportunities not only for courting and infidelity, but for romancing unacceptable persons outside one's own class, and even one's own race, in circumstances that went unobserved by the regular community' (Marvyn, 1988: 70). It initiated the blurring of the distinction between the private and public spheres by allowing outsiders to invade domestic life. A century or so later, the distinction is being further eroded by the proliferation of mobile phones in public places, and the consequent disruption of established patterns of behaviour. Again, measures are being taken to minimize the disruption caused where it is found most obnoxious, with, for example, the designation of certain train carriages as 'mobile free' (an expression which, like other modern neologisms such as 'mobile number' and 'texting' would have greatly puzzled people in the days when 'mobile' was either an adjective denoting the ability to move or be moved, or a noun designating a device that you put above a cot to entertain a baby by its swinging in the breeze). In a similar move, people started to install answering machines, which are often not so much intended to provide information to callers as to screen calls. These machines, which present callers with a distinctly different environment, are the subject of the next section.

Answering machines and voicemail

There is little difference from the caller's point of view between answering machines and voicemail. With either, a recording device acts as a substitute for the answerer, transforming the interaction into a prompt–response process that lacks the dynamic to and fro of conventional telephone conversation. Liddicoat (1994) describes invitations to leave messages on answering machines as typically made up of three obligatory moves: identification ('this is X'), warrant ('I can't come to the phone right now') and instruction ('please leave your name and number'). There may also be a greeting ('hello'), an undertaking ('I will return your call as soon as possible') and an acknowledgement ('thank you'). In contrast, the default voicemail message of a system provider like British Telecom consists only of identification and instruction, with no phatic element: 'This is the BT voicemail service for [number]. Please leave a message after the tone. When you have finished, please hang up or press the hash key for more options.' Ultimately, the wording does not matter. Since the content is highly predictable, it is not strictly necessary for the caller to understand the words.

What may be necessary is the ability to leave a coherent and comprehensible message without the benefit of simultaneous or delayed feedback. Analysis of the caller's contribution shows that, although less highly routinized, it is typically made up of three elements: an opening phase with obligatory self-identification, due to the impossibility of establishing identity if the callee fails to recognize who the speaker is, a message phase, and a closing phase. More is required, however, than the ability to compose a message. The caller's contribution must begin on a signal given by the machine, and must not exceed a certain duration. Together, the rationing of time and the need to start promptly (since a delay may mislead the callee into thinking that no message has been left), but not before the signal (which would lead to part of the message not being recorded), put a premium on fluency and conciseness, and make leaving a message a challenging prospect for someone with imperfect language skills. It is something worth rehearsing, and even native speakers often hang up in order to do just that.

Call centres

A comparatively recent industry, call centres are organizations set up to deal with a large volume of calls relating to customer service, sales or enquiries. Call centres are used by many types of business, from banks and hotel chains to mail-order catalogue organizations and computer product help desks. They have a high penetration rate and L2 speakers are likely to have to phone a call centre at some point, at least when living among an L2 speech community.

When considering the issues that arise for telephone users, a distinction must be made between issues pertaining to the nature of call centres and those due to offshoring. One major problem within the first category is the likelihood of encountering a keypad automated menu or, less frequently, a voice recognition system. Automated menus offer the caller a menu of choices, deliver information or prompt for further input, and may allow a voice message to be left. Negotiating an automated menu requires data processing and navigation skills, and often leads to frustration. Thus, although over 65 per cent of the people in Katz, Aspden and Reich's (1997) sample reported accomplishing what they wanted, only 26 per cent liked the experience. They complained about having to listen to irrelevant options, and reported difficulties in describing their problems. Apart from knowing the name of keys, what is crucial, from a less fluent speaker's or a language learner's perspective, is that assessing the relevance or lack of relevance of options presupposes that you can make sense of what is being said. Inability to do this precludes the possibility of making an informed choice, and may prevent achieving a successful outcome (at least in the absence of an opportunity to speak to a human being or of alternative language options). Upon calling a British credit card helpline, for instance, you will typically hear the following pre-recorded message:

> Welcome to XXX credit card services. To help us improve our service to customers your call may be recorded. If you are an existing customer, please have your 16 digit account number to hand. For information on your XXX credit card, please press 1. To report your XXX credit card lost or stolen, please press 2. For information regarding other XXX products, please press 3. To repeat these options please press zero.

Much of what is said here is predictable if you are used to calling helplines, but figuring out in real time what each utterance refers to, and which key to press, without the possibility of obtaining clarifications is not unproblematic if you have a limited command of English. It hardly needs stating that the same applies to any other information supplied. Where there is an opportunity to leave a message, the challenge of having to enunciate a problem on one's own, without prompting, will be compounded by not having the necessary vocabulary or grammar. Lastly, the limited ability of voice recognition systems to understand human speech produced by a mother tongue speaker with a strong regional accent suggests that the words of a non-native caller are unlikely to be recognized.

Another problem with interactions with call centres, if and when the caller gets to speak to a human being, is the low level of interpersonal specificity of such interactions. Ringing a call centre involves speaking to strangers who know nothing of your personal situation. Even if you have already called with the same problem, the person you are routed to will probably be the first agent available rather than the person you spoke to previously, so that you will again face someone unfamiliar, a daunting prospect for anyone with an imperfect command of the language.

Problems intrinsic to phoning a call centre are often exacerbated by difficulties caused by offshoring, the practice of migrating services abroad. Over the past few years there has been a trend among call centres in industrialized affluent nations to relocate to countries such as India, for English-speaking companies, Morocco, Tunisia or Romania for the French equivalents, and so on. The primary reason for moving operations is the competitive advantage offered by the new locations in the form of lower labour costs, labour availability and a skilled educated flexible workforce (Taylor and Bain, 2003; Béranger, 2003). There is, however, a downside to offshoring, owing to difficulties with agents' language and accents and to cultural differences. To try and obviate problems, it is common practice to provide language and cultural training aimed at 'neutralizing' thick accents and inflections to bring accents into line with those of a particular client base (see Convergys, 2005). According to Granered (2005: 147), 'it takes from one to two months to train a college-educated Indian to handle calls with an acceptable accent and speech pattern. This involves taking on an interactional style that ranges from a lively give-and-take to a more matter-of-fact exchange of information.' Despite such efforts, agents often sound distinctly foreign and lack the depth of cultural knowledge and fluency required to deal with complex enquiries. This has led to reports of consumer dissatisfaction and the repatriation of some operations. Once again, problems are likely to be magnified in the case of less fluent customers, with both parties having difficulty understanding their interlocutor.

SMS

One of the most popular applications of the telephone in today's society is the use of mobile phones to send short text messages to other mobile users. Several features set SMS apart from the applications considered so far. The most conspicuous is the use of a non-voice service. In this respect, SMS marks a break with the past and the long-standing association between telephony and speech. Also unusual, and of direct relevance to this book, is the strategic replacement of conventional written forms with more economical transcriptions that offer an ingenious solution to the ergonomic shortcomings of the mobile phone as a writing environment. To these points must be added a different user profile with an over-representation of teenagers, the surprising ontogenesis of SMS, which contrasts with the planned top-down development of most other services, and the purposes for which people use SMS. SMS is used primarily to initiate and maintain relationships, with close-knit groups of friends developing their own lingo, to organize everyday activities, to pass on information when ringing is not possible or convenient (e.g. because it may entail a long conversation), and, increasingly, to respond to media invitations to give one's opinion on a programme or issue.

This is not to say that all aspects of SMS are wholly novel. The growth of SMS, for example, has parallels in the past. Originally used to inform customers of network problems, SMS was not intended for personal private communication but took off once it became possible to send messages between different networks (textually.org, 2003). Together with its appropriation by the young, this change of use recalls the way in which the adoption of the telephone by women turned what had been a business tool into a domestic device. Interestingly, both developments point the same way, in that they appear to be geared towards the satisfaction of a fundamental desire to communicate rooted in human beings' inherent sociability. Furthermore, neither development was anticipated by telephone companies, which only set about exploiting the commercial opportunities that had opened up once the trend became obvious. And, like other technologies, both have seen their expansion shaped by the influence of cost factors.

While SMS is a prime example of human beings' refusal to have their communication practices limited by the materiality of an artefact, SMS language is not without precedents. According to Kesseler and Bergs (2003: 82–3), nineteenth-century love letters and modern love text messages have 'surprisingly similar traits'. Among other things, 'the employment of orthographic symbols and secret written codes seems to be a stable feature of love letters across centuries and media'.

SMS may seem unlikely to be of interest to L2 speakers who may be thought to have enough to contend with using or learning conventional language. It is, however, very much part and parcel of today's cultural environment, as indicated by the inclusion of the term SMS and of lists of common abbreviations in recent editions of standard dictionaries, by neologisms like 'to text', and by the publication of SMS glossaries. It serves an important role, particularly for the young, in proclaiming and fostering membership of, and integration into, friendship groups and network communities. Depending on where a person lives, and who they interact with, there may well be a need or a strong incentive for them to have recourse to SMS in an L2, for example, to fit in with the practices of others. Lastly, while opaque to the uninitiated, SMS language is not intrinsically more difficult to master than most traditional orthographies. Moreover, it is a means of communication that many L2 speakers will have experience of in their mother tongue. There is a high degree of similarity between the strategies underpinning the saving of space in different languages: replacement of words or syllables with letters or numbers with a similar sound (b4 for before, 2m1 for 'demain' (tomorrow), rien 29 for 'rien de neuf' (nothing new), K7 for 'cassette', GN8 instead of 'gute Nacht' (goodnight)), omission of certain elements, use of fixed phrases, smileys, etc. L2 speakers used to SMS do not therefore come unprepared, but bring with them transferable relevant expertise and an awareness of what to expect. And in the case of non-native speakers of English, they will probably already have been using some English abbreviations in their own language (Anis, 2001: 107–9; Kasesniemi and Rautiainen, 2002: 184). Using SMS will require learning some aspects of the language that might otherwise be unnecessary, such as the sound of letters. But it is unlikely to have a negative effect on linguistic competence, provided learners are made aware of the degree of acceptability of SMS language outside an SMS environment. In fact, it can be argued that, just as SMS seems to trigger linguistic creativity in the fluent speakers among its users (Kesseler and Bergs, 2003), so attempts to puzzle out or compose messages are liable to provide useful practice that benefits the linguistic skills of L2 speakers. In addition, the sample messages offered by certain SMS websites can act as valuable resources by providing a ready-made source of vocabulary and authentic expressions (Flippo, 2006b).

The telephone in education and language learning

Conventional telephony

Telephone-based instruction has a long history stretching back to the invention of the telephone. It can, in fact, be argued that the connection between the telephone and language teaching started with Bell himself, since Bell was a teacher by profession. Like his father before him, he taught deaf children using a system for picturing speech sounds that had been devised by his father, called Visible Speech, together with 'time-combinations of signing, spelling, reading aloud and lipreading' (Hopper, 1992: 26). Speech would have been a second language for Bell's pupils, which arguably makes Bell an L2 teacher. Ironically, while Bell's knowledge of the human ear would help the development of the telephone, the people he taught would derive little benefit from his invention, which, as Hopper observes, only served to set them further apart by creating a means of communication they could not use.

An early ambitious educational use of the telephone was that pioneered by Theodore Puskas, a Hungarian entrepreneur who, in 1893, set up a system of telephone circuits in Budapest offering subscribers a regular programme that included linguistic lessons in English, Italian and French. In these lessons, which are reported to have been hailed as of great benefit to the young, a teacher would speak into a telephone transmitter at the central office, while subscribers listened with a copy of the book before them (Briggs, 1977). This kind of application was to disappear with the diffusion of radio, but it is indicative of the level of interest generated by the new invention. This interest is corroborated by the impact of the telephone on general linguistics. As Harris (1987, 215–16) observes, 'It can hardly be a coincidence that the illustration of A and B talking in the *Cours* [Ferdinand de Saussure's *Cours de linguistique générale*, first published in 1916] shows them schematically linked by what look suspiciously like telephone wires.' Since the 1930s, teaching by telephone has occurred mostly within the context of institutional distance learning, where it substitutes for face-to-face teaching for people unable to attend campus-based classes. Although the telephone initially continued to be used for relaying lectures (Rutter, 1987: 146), its role as a delivery medium has since been taken over by other media (radio, television/video, and lately, WWW). Its main function today is as a platform for tutorial support. It is used to provide individual feedback and support on a one-to-one basis, or to set up group tutorials that enable learners to participate in group activities and group discussions. Here, too, however, telephony finds itself increasingly replaced by more sophisticated alternatives, such as the Lyceum voice groupware of the Open University, a system combining voice conferencing and synchronous, visual workspace tools. Where it has not been ousted by integrated virtual learning environments (IVLEs), the telephone normally forms part of a suite of technologies, and is used for blended learning, alongside media and resources ranging from traditional written and audio-visual materials to online tuition and support.

While it is possible with facilities such as multiple cordless handsets and speakerphones for group activities to be delivered at a distance, typically by a tutor offsite to a campus-based class, audio group tutorials normally involve multi-site communication between geographically dispersed participants. Unlike one-to-one exchanges, audio conferencing requires access to special bridging equipment. This will often be booked for a precise slot, thereby imposing rigid time constraints, since contact between participants will cease at the appointed time, even if everyone wishes the session to be extended. The lack of temporal flexibility calls for good management skills on the part of the tutor and has both negative and positive consequences for learners. Aware that time is limited, students will tend to come properly prepared, but may feel inhibited and may refrain from speaking as much as they would like to. To the pressure of time constraints must be added the effect of the lack of visual information on group dynamics. Studies mention the need for the tutor to call the students by name when inviting contributions, the impossibility of using gestures to signal your wish to speak if you are one of the students, the need to follow the standard protocol of giving your name at the beginning of an unsolicited intervention, and the difficulty of gauging how things are being received in the absence of visual feedback. These constraints result in a more stilted form of interaction and a feeling that despite its usefulness, audio conferencing does not meet the same needs as conventional tutorial interaction (Macleod et al., 2000). Olgren (1997: 61) provides a list of the strengths and limitations of audio conferencing. Two-way verbal communication, accessibility, flexibility, cost, ease of use, and support for a variety of instructional activities make up the strengths, whereas the negative features are voice-only communication, increased interpersonal distance, a more formal climate, and a cause of tiredness.

By contrast with audio conferencing, one-to-one telephone tutorials can be conducted with standard equipment. This is a major selling point for commercial providers of telephone language tuition, which market the anywhere anytime aspect of telephone tutorials and the time saved by not having to travel to classes. All that is needed is access to a quiet place with a landline telephone (mobile telephony is discouraged due to the unreliability and lower sound quality of wireless connections). Stress is also laid on the fact that lessons are tailor-made to suit the individual's circumstances and their language needs and objectives (Cactus Language Training, 2006; Centro de estudios de lengua y cultura, 2006).

In all situations, one of the main advantages of telephone tuition, from a language learning point of view, is that it affords an opportunity to practise communicating in L2 in real time. It is therefore very valuable for enhancing listening and speaking skills, and can also help reduce anxiety about L2 telephone calls. However, it does require a high level of concentration, so that one-to-one telephone language lessons are normally limited to 30 minutes, as well as being generally regarded as unsuitable for complete beginners.

Mobile telephony

In a review of the capabilities and educational potential of mobile phones, Prensky (2005) makes a powerful case for employing mobile phones as learning devices, claiming that you can learn almost anything from a mobile phone. Learning via a mobile phone comes under the general umbrella of mobile learning or m-learning, an emergent paradigm that seeks to leverage mobile computational devices for learning, commonly a personal digital assistant (PDA) or mobile phone, but in fact 'any device that is small, autonomous and unobtrusive enough to accompany us in every moment in our everyday life and that can be used for some form of learning' (Trifonova and Ronchetti, 2003: 1794). Mobile learning is a phenomenon of our time that arises from the proliferation and popularity of handheld devices. It is very much attuned to the high value placed on flexibility and convenience in contemporary society due to its ability to deliver anytime, anyplace learning, and there have been a small number of innovative language learning applications (Chinnery, 2006).

Within mobile learning, distinctions should be made between different types of device. This is not simply a matter of properties but of availability, of the positioning of the device in the cultural milieu, and the psychological relationship users have with it. Noting that outside Asia, research into mobile learning has focused on PDAs, Prensky advocates paying more attention to the mobile phone:

> There are fewer than 50 million PDAs in the world but more than 1.5 billion cell phones. Of course PDA-based research will be useful, but we will not be on the right track until educators begin thinking of using the computing and communication device *currently in the students' pockets* to support learning. (Prensky, 2005)

In addition to being considerably less widespread than mobile phones, PDAs have evolved from personal organizers and retain business connotations, whereas mobile phones are customizable personal objects that are used for a variety of purposes and woven into the fabric of everyday life. As such, mobile phones offer good prospects for expanding social inclusion to learning, as investigated by a three-year EU initiative aimed at improving literacy and numeracy among disaffected young adult learners (Attewell, 2005).

As a learning platform, the mobile phone has a number of distinctive characteristics that offer opportunities for new pedagogical applications while restricting others. These distinctive features include portability, an ever-growing number of features and services, and the small size of the screen and keyboard. Portability is a huge asset in that it enables learning to occur virtually anywhere, anytime, for however long the learner wishes to study. This is seen as highly motivational: 'The reason that people quit Internet-based learning is that their motivation gets very low. They work all day, come home and they don't want to study. With mobile phones, you can study when your motivation is high' (McNicol, 2004). It also opens the way for opportunistic learning, making it possible to fill the interstices between other occupations with bite-size learning, or to combine learning with activities demanding low concentration (e.g. walking, waiting for a bus). In language learning, this may mean learning or revising some vocabulary items or listening to a short audio clip. Of perhaps greater interest, is the opportunity that portability gives for situated learning anchored in a real world setting. In allowing users immediate access to relevant knowledge on encountering an issue or practical problem in the field, whether by interrogating a database or consulting others, mobile technology provides an invaluable resource for a wide range of domains, from training and performance support in professions such as healthcare workers, service engineers and sales representatives, to the enhancement of biology field trips and just-in-time language learning. An early implementation of the latter can be found in Pincas (2004), who describes a system devised for people attending the Athens Olympic Games. It consisted in sending free SMS messages with useful Greek phrases to people's mobile phones several times a day and offering them the possibility of requesting SMS translations from and into Greek. It must be noted, however, that the advantages of portability are liable to be reduced by periods of no or low connectivity, and the use of a shared contested medium (broadcast radio). Hence the need to develop educational applications that can be used offline as well as online.

Singly and in combination, the functions supported by the mobile phone lend themselves to a myriad of pedagogical applications that can be divided along several intersecting and overlapping dimensions, including the following:

- central (to enhance subject expertise) versus peripheral (for practical or administrative matters, e.g. notification of room change)
- in-class versus out-of-class
- individual versus collaborative
- entailing receptive or productive practice
- interactive (voice communication, SMS or email, exchanging still or video pictures via multimedia messaging service (MMS)) versus

content based (accessing or responding to content that may be visual or audio, locally stored or external)
- connected mode (from always on to occasionally connected) or disconnected mode (offline)
- pull technology versus push technology.

Dichotomies do not necessarily imply sharply defined uses. Thus, while push technology sends out materials at specified times (sometimes in accordance with expressed preferences), there is no guarantee that learners will deal with them immediately. Indeed, one of the findings of Thornton and Houser (2004) was that while delivering vocabulary lessons at timed intervals was received positively, and was significantly more effective than encouraging learners to study identical materials on paper or via the Web, it had limited success in promoting carefully timed interval study.

There is a price to pay for portability, namely screen and keyboard miniaturization. As far as miniaturization is concerned, there are ways, as we know, of mitigating the drawbacks of a small keypad. Moreover, it can be argued that the inconvenience of typing on a mobile phone can be a useful incentive to hone your summarizing skills. It should be noted that not all learners will be equally affected. As pointed out by Kiernan and Aizawa (2004: 78), foreign students who have not yet learnt to type efficiently on a keyboard may, in fact, be more comfortable using a mobile phone keypad. Nevertheless, the dimensions of the mobile phone keypad remain a drawback that militates against requesting long answers, and orients developers towards single-stroke responses. In the same way, display finds itself restricted by the size of the screen. Again it is unwise to rule out possibilities, however improbable. The mobile phone may not seem a propitious environment for reading a digitalized book, but the success of phone-delivered novels in Japan, besides highlighting the existence of cross-cultural differences in the diffusion and use of technology, shows that the mobile phone is not ultimately incompatible with large amounts of text. Web Japan (2004) reports how 'Readers of these novels enjoy the medium for a variety of reasons, most having to do with the convenience and possibilities that mobile phones offer, such as not having to go to a bookstore, being able to read anywhere without carrying a book around, and being able to read in the dark.'

To date, mobile language learning research consists of little more than experimental studies involving discrete, easily manageable chunks of written materials, such as dictionary entries, basic phrases, example sentences and flashcards (e.g. BBC Quick Fix; TangoTown), sometimes with a sound accompaniment. Much of the potential of the mobile phone as a learning platform therefore remains to be investigated, although there is some evidence that pushing study opportunities at students can steer them towards learning (Levy and Kennedy, 2005). The practice may appear potentially intrusive, but is said to be appreciated by students as a means of keeping in contact, and is justified by educators on the grounds that regular exposure at spaced intervals is beneficial to retention. Mobile learning is acknowledged to be a highly fragmented experience liable to be fraught with distractions when students learn on the move: 'Users are in situations that place intermittent, unpredictable, yet critically important demands on their attention [...] The learning application must be designed with this in mind' (Brown, 2001). It is recognized that the mobile phone cannot provide an immersive experience, but it is seen as a useful adjunct within a strategy of blended learning, either for revision purposes, or as an additional form of input and support, possibly in tandem with another media such as interactive video (Pemberton and Fallahkhair, 2005).

Conclusion

As illustrated by this case study, the history of telephony epitomizes some important aspects of the evolution of technology and of its impact, from the progressive refinement and development of artefacts to the social concerns that innovations give rise to, and the way in which they are harnessed by education and language learning. Telephony currently occupies a very marginal place in language learning and prospects of growth seem limited, however attractive mobile language learning may appear, by the discrepancy between what the telephone can offer at present and the demanding multifaceted nature of language learning. The situation is likely to change, as advances such as voice recognition and moblogging (posting content to the Internet from a mobile device) become integrated into our everyday communication landscape, and automation easier to carry out. Finally, voice over the Internet (VoIP) is likely to have some interesting uses for language learning, which have yet to be fully explored. However, it is not immediately apparent how IP telephony per se (use of the Internet to carry telephone calls) will be different from traditional (fixed and mobile) telephony.

7
Conclusion

At the outset of this study I asked two questions: what has been the impact of the evolution of ICT on the experience of the language user/learner through the ages? What can we infer from this about how best to use ICT in language learning today? It can now be seen that one of the main effects of ICT has been to create more opportunities for language use. As these opportunities are seized, ICT turns into a centrifugal force, whose effect is tempered by that of centripetal forces, such as the need for mutual comprehension, or prescriptive attitudes favouring a particular set of forms. Over the past centuries, language learners have thus found themselves faced with a growing range of potential models soliciting their attention. This raises the important issue of which kind of language should be learnt and taught. Here, the analysis I have presented in terms of the effect of communication characteristics on participants and the importance of the social matrix provides a framework for making informed decisions by enhancing our understanding of the relative difficulty of different types of communication and the complex interplay of the factors at work.

As far as language pedagogy is concerned, the study has highlighted that while technological progress has affected the way in which languages are learnt and taught, it has not initiated paradigm shifts. Where there have been methodological changes, their origins are to be found elsewhere. Attention has been drawn to the existence of recurrent themes and parallels between previous eras and today, including concerns about the role of the teacher. One of the main implications for the use of ICT in language learning is the need to be discriminating and to build on what has gone before, on the findings of second language research, and on the ecological relevance of different options. In terms of future research, it means undertaking socially grounded studies into the use of media in L2 across different communities and the objectives of different kinds of learner. This should be done in parallel with SLA and CALL research and studies of mediated discourse.

Starting from the premise that L2 competence at the beginning of the twenty-first century includes the ability to communicate via contemporary media, from the telephone to the Internet, I have highlighted the polymorphous nature of the intersection of ICT with language learning. I have examined the various indirect and direct influences that together have shaped the evolution of language learning and teaching to make them what they are today. It has not been possible within the confines of a single work to consider all the factors in detail. Aspects such as the *sui generis* nature of English language teaching in a world increasingly dominated by English have only been treated in passing. But, by offering a wide-ranging account of the changing circumstances of language learning and use, I have sought to convey an idea of the huge array of complex, subtle influences liable to affect language study. Whether considered from the perspective of its impact on communication, on language or on education, ICT has been found to be associated with ever-widening choices that testify to the power of the human linguistic faculty.

In relation to current trends in language pedagogy, the analysis presented here serves to support the articulation of a more solid rationale for blended learning, or indeed any combination of face-to-face and/or different types of technology-enhanced learning, including mobile telephony. It also provides pointers to what needs to be taken into consideration, in order to ensure that the blends offered to learners are cognitively and affectively appropriate to individual needs and aspirations.

There is no doubt that the freedom of access to information and communication enjoyed by today's learners offers unprecedented opportunities to immerse oneself in a language. Faced with such abundance and versatility, it is tempting to use the term 'revolution'. But whether or not one describes the Internet in revolutionary terms, it is important to stress that what is new is the number of potentially useful tools and resources. Not only is there, in language learning as elsewhere, a significant risk of being overwhelmed by choice, but turning potentials into reality raises significant pedagogical issues. This is a crucial point. Teachers must have information on what does what, for what kind of learner, under what conditions, and with what result. It is therefore imperative to have thorough documentation, together with empirical evidence and reliable evaluation results. Only then will teachers be in a position to use their knowledge of the learning context in all its aspects to deliver language learning experiences that cater for the diverse, multi-faceted nature of language learning needs in what is a continually evolving communication landscape.

References

Adoni, H., Cohen, A.A. and Caspi, D. (2002). 'The Consumer's Choice: Language, Media Consumption and Hybrid Identities of Minorities', *Communications*, 27, 411–36.

Agar, J. (2003). *Constant Touch: a Global History of the Mobile Phone*. Cambridge: Icon Books.

Allen, O.E. (1990). 'The Power of Patents', *American Heritage Magazine*, 41(6).

Anis, J. (ed.) (2001). *Parlez-vous Texto? Guide des Nouveaux Langages du Réseau*. Paris: Le Cherche Midi Editeur.

Appel, M.C. (1999). *Tandem Language Learning by E-mail: Some Basic Principles and a Case Study*. Dublin: Trinity College, CLCS Occasional Papers, 54.

Ariès, P. (1979). *Centuries of Childhood*. Harmondsworth, Middx: Penguin.

Ariew, R. (1987). 'Integrating Video and CALL in the Curriculum: the Role of the ACTFL Guidelines'. In Flint Smith, W. (ed.), *Modern Media in Foreign Language Education: Theory and Implementation*. Lincolnwood, Ill.: NTC, pp. 41–66.

Aronson, S.H. (1977). 'Bell's Electrical Toy: What's the Use? The Sociology of Early Telephone Usage'. In Pool, I. (ed.), *The Social Impact of the Telephone*. Cambridge, Mass.: MIT Press, pp. 15–39.

Asher, J.J. (1969). 'The Total Physical Response Approach to Second Language Learning', *Modern Language Journal*, 53(1), 3–17.

Aston, G. (1995). 'Say "Thank You": Some Pragmatic Constraints in Conversational Closings', *Applied Linguistics*, 16(1), 57–86.

Attali, J. and Stourdze, Y. (1977). 'The Birth of the Telephone and Economic Crisis: the Slow Death of Monologue in French Society'. In Pool, I. (ed.), *The Social Impact of the Telephone*. Cambridge, Mass.: MIT Press, pp. 97–111.

Attewell, J. (2005). *Mobile Technologies and Learning: a Technology Update and M-Learning Project Summary*. London: Learning and Skills Development Agency.

Atwell, E. (1999). *The Language Machine*. London: British Council.

Ayto, J. (1999). *Twentieth Century Words*. Oxford: Oxford University Press.

Bakhtin, M.M. (1981). *The Dialogic Imagination*. Austin: University of Texas Press.

Bakhtin, M.M. (1986). *Speech Genres and Other Late Essays*. Austin: University of Texas Press.

Bardovi-Harlig, K. (2001) .'Evaluating the Empirical Evidence: Grounds for Instruction in Pragmatics?' In Rose, K.R. and Kasper, G. (eds), *Pragmatics in Language Teaching*. Cambridge: Cambridge University Press, pp. 13–32.

Bardovi-Harlig, K. and Mahan-Taylor, R. (2003). *Teaching Pragmatics*. Washington, DC: United States Department of State.

Baron, N.S. (1984). 'Computer Mediated Communication as a Force in Language Change', *Visible Language*, XVIII(2), 118–41.

Baron, N.S. (2000). *Alphabet to Email: How Written English Evolved and Where It's Heading*. London: Routledge.

Baron, N.S. (2003). 'Why Email Looks Like Speech: Proofreading, Pedagogy and Public Face'. In Aitchison, J. and Lewis, D.M. (eds), *New Media Language*. London: Routledge, pp. 85–94.

Bates, A.W. (2005). *Technology, E-Learning and Distance Education*, 2nd edn. London: Routledge.

Battarbee, K. (2002). 'Finnish'. In Görlach, M. (ed.), *English in Europe*. Oxford: Oxford University Press, pp. 261–76.

Baugh, A.C. and Cable, T. (1993). *A History of the English Language*, 4th edn. London: Routledge.

BBC Quick Fix. http://www.bbc.co.uk/languages/mobile

Beavis, C. (1998). 'Computer Games, Culture and Curriculum'. In Snyder, I. (ed.), *Page to Screen: Taking Literacy into the Electronic Era*. London: Routledge, pp. 234–55.

Bell, A. (1991). *The Language of News Media*. Oxford: Blackwell.

Bell, A. (1996). 'Text, Time and Technology in News English'. In Goodman, S. and Graddol, D. (eds), *Redesigning English: New Texts, New Identities*. London: Routledge, pp. 3–26.

Bell, D.M. (2003). 'TV News in the EFL/ESL Classroom: Criteria for Selection', *TESL-EJ*, 7(3), 1–17.

Belz, J.A. (2002). 'Social Dimensions of Telecollaborative Foreign Language Study', *Language Learning & Technology*, 6(1), 60–81.

Benczik, V. (2003). 'Communication as Source and Motivator of Language Evolution', *Language Problems & Language Planning*, 27(3), 249–68.

Béranger, A-L. (2003). *Frédéric Jousset* (Webhelp). http://www.journaldunet.com/0304/030403webhelp.shtml

Berlo, D.K. (1960). *The Process of Communication: an Introduction to Theory and Practice*. San Francisco: Rinehart.

Biber, D. (1995). *Dimensions of Register Variation: a Cross-Linguistic Comparison*. Cambridge: Cambridge University Press.

Biber, D. (2003). 'Compressed Noun-Phrase Structures in Newspaper Discourse: the Competing Demands of Popularization vs. Economy'. In Aitchison, J. and Lewis, D.M. (eds), *New Media Language*. London: Routledge, pp. 169–81.

Boden, D. and Molotch, H.L. (1994). 'The Compulsion of Proximity'. In Friedland, R. and Boden, D. (eds), *NowHere: Space, Time and Modernity*. Berkeley/Los Angeles: University of California Press, pp. 257–86.

Bolter, J.D. (1996). 'Ekphrasis, Virtual Reality, and the Future of Writing'. In Nunberg, G. (ed.), *The Future of the Book*. Berkeley: University of California Press, pp. 253–72.

Bolter, J.D. (1998). 'Hypertext and the Question of Visual Literacy'. In Reinking, D., McKenna, M.C., Labbo, L.D. and Kieffer, R.D. (eds), *Handbook of Literacy and Technology: Transformations in a Post-Typographic World*. Mahwah, NJ: Lawrence Erlbaum Associates, pp. 1–13.

Boyd-Barrett, O. (1990). 'Schools Computing Policy as State-Directed Innovation'. In Boyd-Barrett, O. and Scanlon, E. (eds), *Computers and Learning*. Wokingham, England: Addison-Wesley, pp. 3–22.

Brett, P. (1997). 'A Comparative Study of the Effects of the Use of Multimedia on Listening Comprehension', *System*, 25(1), 39–53.

Briggs, A. (1977). 'The Pleasure Telephone: a Chapter in the Prehistory of the Media'. In Pool, I. (ed.), *The Social Impact of the Telephone*. Cambridge, Mass.: MIT Press, pp. 40–65.

Briggs, A. and Burke, P. (2005). *A Social History of the Media: From Gutenberg to the Internet*, 2nd edn. Cambridge: Polity Press.

Broady, E. (ed.) (2000). *Second Language Writing in a Computer Environment.* London: AFLS/CILT.
Brooks, N. (1960). *Language and Language Learning: Theory and Practice.* New York: Harcourt, Brace and World.
Brown, E. (ed.) (2001). 'Mobile Learning Explorations at the Stanford Learning Lab', *Speaking of Computers,* Issue 55, January 8. http://sll.stanford.edu/projects/tomprof/newtomprof/postings/289.html
Brutt-Griffler, J. (2002). *World English: a Study of its Development.* Clevedon: Multilingual Matters.
Burbules, N.C. (1998). 'Rhetorics of the Web: Hyperreading and Critical Literacy'. In Snyder, I (ed.), *Page to Screen: Taking Literacy into the Electronic Era.* London: Routledge, pp. 102–22.
Busse, U. and Görlach, M. (2002). 'German'. In Görlach, M. (ed.), *English in Europe.* Oxford: Oxford University Press, pp. 13–36.
Byram, M. (1997). *Teaching and Assessing Intercultural Communicative Competence.* Clevedon: Multilingual Matters.
Cactus Language Training. http://www.cactuslanguagetraining.com/courses/telephone_courses.php
Cameron, D. (1995). *Verbal Hygiene.* London: Routledge.
Canale, M. (1983). 'From Communicative Competence to Communicative Language Pedagogy'. In Richards, J.C. and Schmidt, R.W. (eds), *Language and Communication.* London: Longman, pp. 2–27.
Carey, J.W. (1989). *Communication as Culture: Essays on Media and Society.* Boston: Unwin Hyman.
Castells, M. (1996). *The Rise of the Network Society.* Malden, Mass.: Blackwell.
Caxton, W. (1490). 'Eneydos – Preface', quoted in British Library: *Treasures in Full: Caxton's Chaucer.* http://www.bl.uk/treasures/caxton/english.html
Centro de Estudios de Lingua y Cultura. http://www.celc.com.ar/tutorias.html
Chalaby, J.K. (1998). *The Invention of Journalism.* Basingstoke: Macmillan Press.
Chambers, A., Conacher, J.E. and Littlemore, J. (eds) (2004). *ICT and Language Learning: Integrating Pedagogy and Practice.* Birmingham: University of Birmingham Press.
Chambers, J.K. (1998). 'TV Makes People Sound the Same'. In Bauer, L. and Trudgill, P. (eds), *Language Myths.* London: Penguin, pp. 123–31.
Chandler, D. with Munday, R. (1994). *Mediated Communication.* http://www.aber.ac.uk/media/Modules/MC10020/homepage.html
Chapelle, C.A. (1997). 'CALL in the Year 2000: Still in Search of Research Paradigms?', *Language Learning & Technology,* I(1), 19–43.
Chapelle, C.A. (2001). *Computers Applications in Second Language Acquisition: Foundations for Teaching, Testing and Research.* Cambridge: Cambridge University Press.
Chapelle, C.A. (2003). *English Language Learning and Technology: Lectures on Applied Linguistics in the Age of Information and Communication Technology.* Amsterdam: John Benjamins.
Chapelle, C.A. (2005). 'Computer-Assisted Language Learning'. In Hinkel, E. (ed.), *Handbook of Research in Second Language Teaching and Learning.* Mahwah, NJ: Lawrence Erlbaum, pp. 743–55.
Charlton, K. (1965). *Education in Renaissance England.* London: Routledge and Kegan Paul.

Chartier, R. (1999). 'Reading Matter and "Popular" Reading: From the Renaissance to the Seventeenth Century'. In Cavallo, G. and Chartier, R. (eds), *A History of Reading in the West*. Amherst: University of Massachusetts Press, pp. 269–83.

Chinnery, G.M. (2006). 'Emerging Technologies: Going to the MALL, Mobile Assisted Language Learning', *Language Learning and Technology*, 10(1), 9–16.

Clarke, A.C. (1992). *How the World Was One: the Turbulent History of Global Communications*. London: Victor Gollancz.

Clément, J. (2000). 'Écritures Hypermédiatiques: Remarques sur Deux Cédéroms d'Auteurs'. In Lancien, T. (ed.), *Multimédia: les Mutations du Texte*. Paris: Ophrys, pp. 27–39.

Coleman, J.A. (2005). 'CALL from the Margins: Effective Dissemination of CALL Research and Good Practices', *ReCALL*, 17(1), 18–31.

Collis, B. (1996). *Tele-Learning in a Digital World: the Future of Distance Learning*. London: International Thomson Computer Press.

Commission on Instructional Technology (1970). *To Improve Learning: a Report to the President and the Congress of the United States*. Washington, DC: US Government Printing Office.

Convergys (2005). Convergys Offshore Services: India. http://www.convergys.com/pdf/factsheets/offshore_india_fact.pdf

Cook, V. (2001). *Second Language Learning and Language Teaching*, 3rd edn. London: Arnold.

Council of Europe (ed.) (2001). *Common European Framework of Reference for Languages: Learning, Teaching, Assessment*. Cambridge: Cambridge University Press.

Crystal, D. (1988). *The English Language*. London: Penguin Books.

Crystal, D. (1997). *The Cambridge Encyclopedia of Language*. Cambridge: Cambridge University Press.

Crystal, D. (2001 and 2006). *Language and the Internet*, 2nd edn. Cambridge: Cambridge University Press.

Cummins, J. and Sayers, D. (1995). *Brave New Schools – Challenging Cultural Illiteracy through Global Learning Networks*. Basingstoke: Macmillan Press.

Davies, G. (ed.) (1999–2006). *Information and Communications Technology for Language Teachers (ICT4LT)*. Slough: Thames Valley University. http://www.ict4lt.org

Davis, B.H. and Brewer, J.P. (1997). *Electronic Discourse – Linguistic Individuals in Virtual Space*. State University of New York Press, Albany.

Dilts, R. and DeLozier, J. (2000). *Encyclopedia of Systemic NLP and NLP New Coding*. Scotts Valley, Calif.: NLP University Press.

Dominick, J.R. (1996). *The Dynamics of Mass Communication*. New York: McGraw-Hill.

Doughty, C. (1987). 'Relating Second-Language Acquisition Theory to CALL Research and Application'. In Flint Smith, W. (ed.), *Modern Media in Foreign Language Education: Theory and Implementation*. Lincolnwood, Ill.: NTC, pp. 133–67.

Eco, U. (1995). *Apocalypse Postponed*. London: Flamingo, HarperCollins.

EIAA (European Interactive Advertising Association) (2006a). *EIAA Press Releases: All on One, and One on All: Europe's 'Digital Generation' Embrace Media Convergence*. http://www.eiaa.net/news/eiaa-articles-details.asp?lang=1&id=97

EIAA (2006b). *Mediascope Europe – Digital Women Report.* http://www.eiaa.net/Ftp/casestudiesppt/EIAA%20Digital%20Women%20Presentation%20for%20website.pdf

Eisenstadt, M., Komzak, J. and Dzbor, M. (2003). 'Instant Messaging + Maprs = Powerful Collaboration Tools for Distance Learning', *Proceedings of TelEduc03*, Havana, Cuba. http://kmi.open.ac.uk/projects/buddyspace/docs/eisenstadt-komzak-dzbor-teleduc03.doc.

Eisenstein, E. (1979). *The Printing Press as an Agent of Change: Communications and Cultural Transformations in Early-Modern Europe*. Cambridge: Cambridge University Press.

Ellington, H., Percival, F. and Race, P. (1993). *Handbook of Educational Technology*, 3rd edn. London: Kogan Page.

Fairclough, N. (1995). *Media Discourse*. London: Arnold.

Febvre, L. and Martin, H-J. (1976). *The Coming of the Book – the Impact of Printing 1450–1800*. London: NLB.

Felix, U. (1999). 'Exploiting the Web for Language Teaching: Selected Approaches', *ReCALL*, 11(1), 30–7.

Felix, U. (2005). 'E-Learning Pedagogy in the Third Millennium: the Need for Combining Social and Cognitive Constructivist Approaches', *ReCALL*, 17(1), 85–100.

Fennell, B.A. (2001). *A History of English – a Sociolinguistic Approach*. Oxford: Blackwell.

Ferrara, K., Brunner, H. and Whittemore, G. (1991). 'Interactive Written Discourse as an Emergent Register', *Written Communication*, 8(1), 8–34.

Findahl, O. (1989). 'Language in the Age of Satellite Television', *European Journal of Communication*, 4, 133–59.

Fisher, E. (1993). 'Access to Learning: Problems and Policies'. In Scrimshaw, P. (ed.), *Language, Classrooms and Computers*. London: Routledge, pp. 75–90.

Fishman, J.A. (2001). 'Why is it so Hard to Save a Threatened Language'? In Fishman, J.A. (ed.), *Can Threatened Languages be Saved*? Clevedon: Multilingual Matters, pp. 1–22.

Fiske, J. (1987). *Television Culture*. London: Routledge.

Flippo, H. (2006a). 'Using the Telephone in German'. http://german.about.com/library/bltelvoc.htm

Flippo, H. (2006b) 'German SMS: Text Messaging auf Deutsch'. http://german.about.com/library/weekly/aa032601a.htm

Flowerdew, J. and Miller, L. (2005). *Second Language Listening Comprehension: Theory to Practice*. New York: Cambridge University Press.

Fowler, R. (1991). *Language in the News: Discourse and Ideology in the Press*. London: Routledge.

Fowler, R. (2000). 'Orality and the Theory of Mode in Advertisements'. In Guillot, M-N. and Kenning, M-M. (eds), *Changing Landscapes in Language and Language Pedagogy: Text, Orality and Voice*. London: AFLS/CILT, pp. 26–39.

Freud, S. (1920). 'The Psychogenesis of a Case of Homosexuality in a Woman'. In Freud, S. *Collected Papers*, vol. 2. London: Hogarth Press, pp. 202–31.

Gardner, E.C. and Lambert, W.E. (1972). *Attitudes and Motivation in Second Language Learning*. Rowley, Mass.: Newbury House.

Garner, R. and Gillingham M.G. (1998). 'The Internet in the Classroom: Is It the End of Transmission-Oriented Pedagogy?' In Reinking, D., McKenna, M.C.,

Labbo, L.D. and Kieffer, R.D. (eds), *Handbook of Literacy and Technology: Transformations in a Post-Typographic World.* Mahwah, NJ: Lawrence Erlbaum Associates, pp. 221–31.

Garrett, N. (1987). 'A Psycholinguistic Perspective on Grammar and CALL'. In Flint Smith, W. (ed.), *Modern Media in Foreign Language Education: Theory and Implementation.* Lincolnwood, Ill.: NTC, pp. 169–96.

Gauntlett, D. and Hill, A. (1999). *TV Living: Television, Culture and Everyday Life.* London: Routledge.

Gee, J.P. (2003). *What Video Games have to Teach us about Learning and Literacy.* New York: Palgrave Macmillan.

Godwin-Jones, R. (2005). 'Emerging Technologies: Messaging, Gaming and Peer-to-Peer Sharing: Language Learning Strategies and Tools for the Millennial Generation', *Language Learning and Technology*, 9(1), 17–22.

Goffman, E. (1981). *Forms of Talk.* Oxford: Blackwell.

Görlach, M. (2002). 'Introduction'. In Görlach, M. (ed.), *English in Europe.* Oxford: Oxford University Press, pp. 1–12.

Gouin, F. (1896). *The Art of Teaching and Studying Languages.* London: George Philip and Son.

Graddol, D. (1994). 'What is a Text?' In Graddol, D. and Boyd-Barrett, O. (eds), *Media Texts: Authors and Readers.* Clevedon: Multilingual Matters, pp. 40–50.

Graddol, D. (1996). 'Global English, Global Culture?' In Goodman, S. and Graddol, D. (eds), *Redesigning English: New Texts, New Identities.* London: Routledge, pp. 181–217.

Granered, E. (2005). *Global Call Centers: Achieving Outstanding Customer Service across Cultures and Time Zones.* Boston: Nicholas Brealey.

Green, P.S. (1996). 'The Tape Recording Revolution'. In Hawkins, E. (ed.), *30 Years of Language Teaching.* London: CILT, pp. 211–22.

Guillot, M-N. (1999). *Fluency and its Teaching.* Clevedon: Multilingual Matters.

Gumpert, G. (1987). *Talking Tombstones and Other Tales of the Media Age.* New York: Oxford University Press.

Haas, C. (1989). 'Does the Medium Make a Difference? Two Studies of Writing with Pen and Paper and with Computers', *Human–Computer Interaction*, 4(2), 149–69.

Haas, C. (1996). *Writing Technology: Studies on the Materiality of Literacy.* Mahwah, NJ: Lawrence Erlbaum.

Halliday, M.A.K. (1989). *Spoken and Written English*, 2nd edn. Oxford: Oxford University Press.

Halliday, M.A.K. (1994). 'Spoken and Written Modes of Meaning'. In Graddol, D. and Boyd-Barrett, O. (eds), *Media Texts: Authors and Readers.* Clevedon: Multilingual Matters, pp. 51–73.

Halliday, M.A.K., McIntosh, A. and Strevens, P. (1964). *The Linguistic Sciences and Language Teaching.* London: Longman.

Halmari, H. (1993). 'Intercultural Business Telephone Conversations: a Case of Finns vs. Anglo-Americans', *Applied Linguistics*, 14(4), 408–30.

Hampel, R. (2006). 'Rethinking Task Design for the Digital Age: a Framework for Language Teaching and Learning in a Synchronous Online Environment', *ReCALL*, 18(1), 105–21.

Harris, R. (1987). *Reading Saussure: a Critical Commentary on the* Cours de Linguistique Générale. London: Duckworth.

Harris, R. and Taylor, T.J. (1997). *Landmarks in Linguistic Thought 1: The Western Tradition from Socrates to Saussure*, 2nd edn. London: Routledge.
Havelock, E.A. (1963). *Preface to Plato*. Oxford: Basil Blackwell.
Hawisher, G.E. (1988). 'Research Update: Writing and Word Processing', *Computers and Composition*, 5(2), 7–27.
Hawkins, E. (1994). 'Percept before Precept'. In King, L. and Boaks, P. (eds), *Grammar! A Conference Report*. London: CILT, pp. 109–28.
Headrick, D.R. (1991). *The Invisible Weapon: Telecommunications and International Politics 1851–1945*. New York: Oxford University Press.
Heppell, S. (2000). 'Foreword'. In Gamble, N. and Easingwood, N. (eds), *ICT and Literacy*. London: Continuum, pp. xi–xv.
Hermerén, L (1999). *English for Sale: a Study of the Language of Advertising*. Lund: Lund University Press.
Herring, S.C. (2003). 'Media and Language Change: Introduction', *Journal of Historical Pragmatics*, 4(1), 1–17.
Hesse, C. (1996). 'Books in Time'. In Nunberg, G. (ed.), *The Future of the Book*. Berkeley: University of California Press, pp. 21–36.
Hill, B. (1991). 'Satellites and Language Teaching'. In Gilbert, J.K., Temple, A. and Underwood, C. (eds), *Satellite Technology in Education*. London: Routledge.
Hinkel, E. (ed.) (1999). *Culture in Second Language Teaching and Learning*. Cambridge: Cambridge University Press.
Holtzer, G. (2003). 'Learning Culture by Communicating: Native–Non-Native Speaker Telephone Interactions'. In Byram, M. and Grundy, P. *Context and Culture in Language Learning and Teaching*. Clevedon: Multilingual Matters, pp. 43–50.
Honey, J. (1997). *Language is Power: the Story of Standard English and its Enemies*. London: Faber and Faber.
Hopper, R. (1992). *Telephone Conversation*. Bloomington: Indiana University Press.
Hot Potatoes. http://hotpot.uvic.ca/
Howatt, A.P.R. with Widdowson, H.G. (2004). *A History of English Language Teaching*, 2nd edn. Oxford: Oxford University Press.
Hughes, G. (1988). *Words in Time: a Social History of the English Vocabulary*. Oxford: Blackwell.
Hulstijn, J.H. (1993). 'When do Foreign-Language Readers Look up the Meaning of Unfamiliar Words? The Influence of Task and Learner Variables', *The Modern Language Journal*, 77, 139–47.
Hulstijn, J.H. (2000). 'The Use of Computer Technology in Experimental Studies of Second Language Acquisition: a Survey of Some Techniques and Some Ongoing Studies', *Language Learning & Technology*, 3(2), 32–43.
Hulstijn, J.H. and Trompetter, P. (1998). 'Incidental Learning of Second Language Vocabulary in Computer-Assisted Reading and Writing Tasks'. In Albrechtsen, D., Henrikse, B., Mees, I.M. and Poulsen, E. (eds), *Perspectives on Foreign and Second Language Pedagogy*. Odense, Denmark: Odense University Press, pp. 191–200.
Humbley, J. (2002). 'French'. In Görlach, M. (ed.), *English in Europe*. Oxford: Oxford University Press, pp. 108–27.
Hutchby, I. (2001). Conv*ersation and Technology: From the Telephone to the Internet*. Cambridge: Polity Press.
Hutchins, J. (1998). 'Translation Technology and the Translator', *Machine Translation Review*, 7, 7–14.

Hymes, D.H. (1972). 'Toward Ethnographies of Communication: the Analysis of Communicative Events'. In Giglioli, P. (ed.), *Language and Social Context*. Harmondsworth, England: Penguin Education, pp. 21–44.

Hymes, D. (1977). *Foundations in Sociolinguistics*. London: Tavistock Publications.

IJMLO (*International Journal of Mobile Learning and Organisation*). www.inderscience.com/ijmlo/

Illich, I. (1971). *Deschooling Society*. London: Marion Boyars.

Ishii, H. (1993). 'Cross-Cultural Communication and CSCW'. In Harasim, L.M. (ed.), *Global Networks: Computers and International Communication*. Cambridge, Mass.: MIT Press, pp. 143–51.

Jahandarie, K. (1999). *Spoken and Written Discourse: a Multi-Disciplinary Perspective*. Stamford: Ablex.

Jakobson, R. (2000). 'Linguistics and Poetics (1960)'. In L. Burke, T. Crowley and A. Giruin (eds), *The Routledge Language and Cultural Theory Reader*. London: Routledge, pp. 334–9.

Jensen, K.B. (ed.) (2002). *A Handbook of Media and Communication Research: Qualitative and Quantitative Methodologies*. London: Routledge.

Jerman, J.A. (1965). 'Audio-Visual Methods in Modern Language Teaching'. In Dutton, B. (ed.), *A Guide to Modern Language Teaching Methods*. London: Cassell, pp. 1–83.

Jespersen, O. (1904). *How to Teach a Foreign Language*. London: George Allen and Unwin.

Johns, T. and King, P. (eds) (1991). 'Classroom Concordancing', *English Language Research Journal*, 4, Birmingham: Birmingham University Press.

Johnson, K. (1996). *Language Teaching and Skill Learning*. Oxford: Blackwell.

Johnson, K. (2001). *An Introduction to Foreign Language Learning and Teaching*. Harlow: Longman.

Johnson, S. (1755). *Preface to the Dictionary*. http://andromeda.rutgers.edu/~jlynch/Texts/preface.html

Johnston, J. (1987). *Electronic Learning: From Audiotape to Videodisc*. Hillsdale, NJ: Lawrence Erlbaum Associates.

Jones, A. and Mercer, N. (1993). 'Theories of Learning and Information Technology'. In Scrimshaw, P. (ed.), *Language, Classrooms and Computers*. London: Routledge, pp. 11–26.

Jones, B. (1986). 'CALL – a Teacher, a Class and a Computer Program'. In Kexkes, I. and Papp, F. (eds), *Linguistics and Methodology in CALL*. Budapest: Hungarian Academy of Sciences Press, pp. 19–36.

Jones, G. (1986). 'Computer Simulations in Language Teaching – the KINGDOM Experiment', *System*, 14, 179–86.

Joyce, P. (1991). *Visions of the People: Industrial England and the Question of Class 1848–1914*. Cambridge: Cambridge University Press.

Jung, U.O.H. (1994). 'Experiential Learning: What Educational Technology can Contribute'. In Jung, H. and Vanderplank, R. (eds), *Barriers and Bridges: Media Technology in Language Learning*. Frankfurt: Peter Lang, pp. 1–14.

Kasesniemi, E.-L. and Rautiainen, P. (2002). 'Mobile Culture of Children and Teenagers in Finland'. In Katz, J.E. and Aakhus, M. (eds), *Perpetual Contact: Mobile Communication, Private Talk, Public Performance*. Cambridge: Cambridge University Press, pp. 170–92.

Katz, J.E. and Aakhus, M. (2002). 'Introduction: Framing the Issues'. In Katz, J.E. and Aakhus, M. (eds), *Perpetual Contact: Mobile Communication, Private Talk, Public Performance*. Cambridge: Cambridge University Press, pp. 1–13.

Katz, J., Aspden, P. and Reich, W.A. (1997). 'Public Attitudes towards Voice-Based Electronic Messaging Technologies in the United States: a National Survey of Opinions about Voice Response Units and Telephone Answering Machines', *Behaviour and Information Technology*, 16 (3), 125–44.

Kaufer, D.S. and Carley, K.M. (1993). *Communication at a Distance: the Influence of Print on Sociocultural Organization and Change*. Hillsdale, NJ: Lawrence Erlbaum.

Kelly, L.G. (1969). *25 Centuries of Language Teaching*. Rowley, Mass.: Newbury House.

Kempster, G. (2000). 'Skills for Life: New Meanings and Values for Literacies'. In Gamble, N. and Easingwood, N. (eds), *ICT and Literacy*. London: Continuum, pp. 25–30.

Kendon, A. (1988). 'How Gestures can Become Like Words'. In Poyatos, F. (ed.), *Cross-Cultural Perspectives in Nonverbal Communication*. Toronto: Hogrefe, pp. 131–41.

Kenning, M.J. and Kenning, M-M. (1983). *An Introduction to Computer Assisted Language Teaching*. Oxford: Oxford University Press.

Kenning, M-M. (1999). 'Effective Language Learning and the Media: a Study of the Implications of Current Theories for the Exploitation of Technology'. In Hogan-Brun, G. and Jung, U.O.H. (eds), *Media, Multimedia, Omnimedia*. Frankfurt: Peter Lang, pp. 1–8.

Kenning, M-M. and Kenning, M.J. (1990). *Computers and Language Learning: Current Theory and Practice*. London: Ellis Horwood.

Kesseler, A. and Bergs, A. (2003). 'Literacy and the New Media: Vita Brevis, Lingua Brevis'. In Aitchison, J. and Lewis, D.M. (eds), *New Media Language*. London: Routledge, pp. 75–84.

Kiddle, L.B. (1949). 'The Laboratory of the Department of Romance Languages at Michigan', *Language Learning*, 1949, II(4), 121–7.

Kiernan, P.J. and Aizawa, K. (2004). 'Cell Phones in Task Based Learning – Are Cell Phones Useful Language Learning Tools?', *ReCALL*, 16, 71.

Kirkup, G. and Jones, A. (2000). 'Information and Communication Technologies in Distance and Lifelong Learning'. In Ducatel, K., Webster, J., and Herrmann, W. (eds), *The Information Society in Europe: Work and Life in an Age of Globalization*. Lanham, Md: Rowan and Littlefield, pp. 201–31.

Klapper, J. (2005). 'Teaching Grammar'. In Coleman, J.A. and Klapper, J. (eds), *Effective Learning and Teaching in Modern Languages*. London: Routledge, pp. 67–74.

Knobel, M., Lankshear, C., Honan, E. and Crawford, J. (1998). 'The Wired World of Second-Language Education'. In Snyder, I. (ed.), *Page to Screen: Taking Literacy into the Electronic Era*. London: Routledge, pp. 20–50.

Kramsch, C. (1993). *Context and Culture in Language Teaching*. Oxford: Oxford University Press.

Kress, G. (1998). 'Visual and Verbal Modes of Representation in Electronically Mediated Communication: the Potential of New Forms of Text'. In Snyder, I. (ed.), *Page to Screen: Taking Literacy into the Electronic Era*. London: Routledge, pp. 53–79.

Kress, G. (2003). *Literacy in the New Media Age*. London: Routledge.

Kress, G. and Van Leeuwen, T. (2001). *Multimodal Discourse*. London: Arnold.

Kvaran, G. and Svavarsdóttir, Á. (2002). 'Icelandic'. In Görlach, M. (ed.), *English in Europe*. Oxford: Oxford University Press, pp. 82–107.

Lado, R. (1964). *Language Teaching: a Scientific Approach*. New York: McGraw-Hill.

Lamizet, B. (2000). 'Les Défilés de la Communication Multimédiatée'. In Lancien, T. (ed.), *Multimédia: Les Mutations du Texte*. Paris: Ophrys, pp. 13–26.

Lamy, M-N. (2004). 'Oral Conversations Online: Redefining Oral Competence in Synchronous Environments', *ReCALL*, 16(2), 520–38.

Landlow, G.P. (1996). 'We are Already Beyond the Book'. In Chernaik, W., Deegan, M. and Gibson, A. (eds), *Beyond the Book: Theory, Culture and the Politics of Cyberspace*. Office for Humanities Communication, University of London, pp. 23–32.

LanguagesICT (2004). http://www.languages-ict.org.uk/default.htm

Larsen-Freeman, D. and Long, M.H. (1991). *An Introduction to Second Language Acquisition Research*. London: Longman.

Lasswell, H.D. (1960). 'The Structure and Function of Communication in Society (1948)'. In Schramm, W. (ed.), *Mass Communications*. Urbana: University of Illinois Press, pp. 117–30.

Laurillard, D. (2002). *Rethinking University Teaching: a Conversational Framework for the Effective Use of Learning Technologies*, 2nd edn. London: Routledge.

Leith, D. (1996). 'English – Colonial to Postcolonial'. In Graddol, D., Leith, D. and Swann, J. (eds), *English: History, Diversity and Change*. London: Routledge, pp. 180–221.

Leith, D. and Graddol, D. (1996). 'Modernity and English as a National Language'. In Graddol, D., Leith, D. and Swann, J. (eds), *English: History, Diversity and Change*. London: Routledge, pp. 136–79.

Leitner, G. (1980). 'BBC English and Deutsche Rundfunksprache: a Comparative and Historical Analysis of the Language on the Radio', *International Journal of the Sociology of Language*, 26, 75–100.

LeLoup, J. and Ponterio, R. (2003). 'Second Language Acquisition and Technology: a Review of the Research', *Digest*. http://www.cal.org/resources/digest/0311leloup.html

Lemke, J.L. (1998). 'Metamedia Literacy: Transforming Meanings and Media'. In Reinking, D., McKenna, M.C., Labbo, L.D. and Kieffer, R.D. (eds), *Handbook of Literacy and Technology: Transformations in a Post-Typographic World*. Mahwah, NJ: Lawrence Erlbaum Associates, pp. 283–301.

Levinson, S.C. (1988). 'Putting Linguistics on a Proper Footing: Explorations in Goffman's Concepts of Participation'. In Drew, P. and Wootton, A. (eds), *Erving Goffman: Exploring the Interaction Order*. Cambridge: Polity Press, pp. 161–227.

Levy, M. (1997). *Computer-Assisted Language Learning: Context and Conceptualization*. Oxford: Clarendon Press.

Levy, M. and Kennedy, C. (2005). 'Learning Italian via Mobile SMS'. In Kukulska-Hulme, A. and Traxler, J. (eds), *Mobile Learning: a Handbook for Educators and Trainers*. London: Routledge, pp. 76–83.

Licoppe, C. and Heurtin, J-P. (2002). 'France: Preserving the Image'. In Katz, J.E. and Aakhus, M. (eds), *Perpetual Contact: Mobile Communication, Private Talk, Public Performance*. Cambridge: Cambridge University Press, pp. 94–109.

Liddicoat, A. (1994). 'Discourse Routines in Answering Machine Communication in Australia', *Discourse Processes*, 17, 283–309.

Little, D. (1996). 'Freedom to Learn and Compulsion to Interact: Promoting Learner Autonomy through the Use of Information Systems and Information Technologies'. In Pemberton, R., Li, E.S.L., Or, W.W.F. and Pierson, H.D. (eds), *Taking Control: Autonomy in Language Learning*. Hong Kong: Hong Kong University Press, pp. 193–209.

Little, D. (1998). *Technologies, Media and Foreign Language Learning*. Trinity College, Dublin: Authentik.

Little, G.D. (1994). 'Visual Style'. In Little, G.D. and Montgomery, M. (eds), *Centennial Usage Studies*. Tuscaloosa: University of Alabama Press, pp. 40–7.

Liu, M., Moore, Z., Graham, L. and Lee, S. (2003). 'A Look at the Research on Computer Based Technology Use in Second Language Learning: a Review of the Literature from 1990–2000', *Journal of Research on Technology in Education*, 34(3), 250–73.

Lodge, D. (1991). *Paradise News*. London: Secker and Warburg.

Loonen, P. (1994). 'The Influence of Comenius on Modern Language Teaching: the Case of Nathanael Duez', *Paradigm*, 15.

Lyons, M. (1999). 'New Readers in the Nineteenth Century: Women, Children, Workers'. In Cavallo, G. and Chartier, R. (eds), *A History of Reading in the West*. Amherst: University of Massachusetts Press, pp. 313–44.

McFarlane, A. (2000). 'Communicating Meaning – Reading and Writing in a Multimedia World'. In Gamble, N. and Easingwood, N. (eds), *ICT and Literacy*. London: Continuum, pp. 19–24.

Macleod, H., Barrowcliff, D., Crook, C., McAteer, E., Musselbrook, K. and Tolmie, A. (2000). 'Telephone Tutorials in Distance Learning Programmes'. http://www.gla.ac.uk/lncs/main/FOURTEEN.HTM

McLuhan, M. (1964). *Understanding Media: the Extensions of Man*. London: Routledge and Kegan Paul.

McNicol, T. (2004). 'Language E-Learning on the Move', *Japan Media Review*. http://ojr.org/japan/wireless/1080854640.php

Marvyn, C. (1988). *When Old Technologies were New: Thinking about Electric Communication in the Late Nineteenth Century*. Oxford: Oxford University Press.

Marx, G.T. (1994). 'New Telecommunications Technologies Require New Manners', *Telecommunications Policy*, 18(7), 538–51.

Marx, L. (1994). 'The Idea of "Technology" and Postmodern Pessimism'. In Smith, M.R. and Marx, L. (eds), *Does Technology Drive History? The Dilemma of Technological Determinism*. Cambridge, Mass.: MIT, pp. 237–57.

Marx, L. and Smith, M.R. (1994). 'Introduction'. In Smith, M.R. and Marx, L. (eds), *Does Technology Drive History? The Dilemma of Technological Determinism*. Cambridge, Mass.: MIT, pp. ix–xv.

Matheson, H. (1933). *Broadcasting*. London: Thornton Butterworth.

Meinhof, U.H. (1998). *Language Learning in the Age of Satellite Television*. Oxford: Oxford University Press.

Mey, J.L. (2001). *Pragmatics: an Introduction*. Oxford: Blackwell.

Microsoft (2004). Microsoft Local Language Quote Sheet: *Feature Stories*. http://www.microsoft.com/presspass/features/2004/mar04/03-16llp.mspx

Mikulecky, L. and Kirkley, J.R. (1998). 'Changing Workplaces, Changing Classes: the New Role of Technology in Workplace Literacy'. In Reinking, D., McKenna, M.C., Labbo, L.D. and Kieffer, R.D. (eds), *Handbook of Literacy and Technology: Transformations in a Post-Typographic World*. Mahwah, NJ: Lawrence Erlbaum Associates, pp. 303–20.

Milroy, J. and Milroy, L. (1985). 'Linguistic Change, Social Network and Speaker Innovation', *Journal of Linguistics*, 21, 339–84.

Milroy, J. and Milroy, L. (1999). *Authority in Language: Investigating Standard English*, 3rd edn. London: Routledge.

Misa, T.J. (1994). 'Retrieving Sociotechnical Change from Technological Determinism'. In Smith, M.R. and Marx, L. (eds), *Does Technology Drive History? The Dilemma of Technological Determinism*. Cambridge, Mass.: MIT, pp. 115–41.

Mishan, F. (2004). 'A Task-Based Approach to Web Authoring for Learning Languages'. In Chambers, A., Conacher, J.E. and Littlemore, J. (eds), *ICT and Language Learning: Integrating Pedagogy and Practice*. Birmingham: Birmingham University Press, pp. 121–44.

Mochet, M-A. and O'Neil, C. (2000). 'Mise en Page, Mise en Texte – Encyclopédies Paper et Multimedia'. In Lancien, T. (ed.), *Multimédia: Les Mutations du Texte*. Paris: Ophrys, pp. 87–118.

Moores, S. (2000). *Media and Everyday Life in Modern Society*. Edinburgh: Edinburgh University Press.

Morsbach, H. (1988). 'Nonverbal Communication and Hierarchical Relationships: the Case of Bowing in Japan'. In Poyatos, F. (ed.), *Cross-Cultural Perspectives in Nonverbal Communication*. Toronto: Hogrefe, pp. 189–99.

Moyal, A. (1992). 'The Gendered Use of the Telephone: an Australian Case Study', *Media, Culture and Society*, 14, 51–72.

Muhr, R. (2003). 'Language Change via Satellite: the Influence of German Television Broadcasting on Austrian German', *Journal of Historical Pragmatics*, 4(1), 103–27.

Murray, D.E. (1989). 'When the Medium Determines Turns: Turn-Taking in Computer Conversation'. In Coleman, H. (ed.), *Working with Language: a Multidisciplinary Consideration of Language Use in Work Contexts*. Berlin: Mouton de Gruyter, pp. 319–37.

Murray, D.E. (2000). 'Protean Communication: the Language of Computer-Mediated Communication', *TESOL Quarterly*, 34(3), 397–421.

Myles, F. (2002). 'Second Language Acquisition (SLA) Research: Its Significance for Learning and Teaching Issues'. http://www.lang.ltsn.ac.uk/resources/goodpractice.aspx?resourceid=421

New London Group (1996). 'A Pedagogy of Multiliteracies: Designing Social Futures', *Harvard Educational Review*, 66(1), 60–92.

Norris, J.M. and Ortega, L. (2000). 'Effectiveness of L2 Instruction: a Research Synthesis and Quantitative Meta-Analysis', *Language Learning*, 50(3), 417–528.

Nunberg, G. (2000). 'Will the Internet Always Speak English?' *The American Prospect*, March 27.

O'Donnell, J.J. (1996). 'The Pragmatics of the New: Trithemius, McLuhan, Cassiodorus'. In Nunberg, G. (ed.), *The Future of the Book*. Berkeley: University of California Press, pp. 37–62.

O'Dowd, R. (2004). 'Intercultural E-Mail Exchanges in the Foreign Language Classroom'. In Chambers, A., Conacher, J.E. and Littlemore, J. (eds), *ICT and Language Learning: Integrating Pedagogy and Practice*. Birmingham: Birmingham University Press, pp. 145–64.

O'Dowd, R. and Eberbach, K. (2004). 'Guides on the Side? Tasks and Challenges for Teachers in Telecollaborative Projects', *ReCALL*, 16(1), 5–19.

Olgren, C.H. (1997). 'Teaching by Telephone', *New Directions for Teaching and Learning*, 71, 59–66.

Olson, D.R. (1994). *The World on Paper*. Cambridge: Cambridge University Press.
Ong, W.J. (1967). *The Presence of the Word: Some Prolegomena for Cultural and Religious History*. New Haven: Yale University Press.
Ong, W.J. (1982). *Orality and Literacy: the Technologizing of the Word*. London: Routledge.
ONS (Office for National Statistics) (2000). *Family Spending: a Report on the 1999–2000 Family Expenditure Survey*. London: Stationery Office.
ONS (2004). *Family Spending: a Report on the 2002–2003 Expenditure and Food Survey*. London: Stationery Office.
Oxford English Dictionary (1989). 2nd edn. Online. http://dictionary.oed.com
Passy, P. (1899). 'De la Méthode Directe dans l'Enseignement des Langues', *Le Maître Phonétique*, May Special Supplement.
Pattanayak, D.P. (1981). *Multilingualism and Mother-Tongue Education*. Delhi: Oxford University Press.
Pavlidou, T.-S. (2000). 'Telephone Conversations in Greek and German: Attending to the Relationship Aspect of Communication'. In Spencer-Oatey, H. (ed.), *Culturally Speaking – Managing Rapport through Talk across Cultures*. London: Continuum, pp. 122–42.
Pederson, K.M (1987). 'Research on CALL'. In Flint Smith, W. (ed.), *Modern Media in Foreign Language Education: Theory and Implementation*. Lincolnwood, Ill.: NTC, pp. 99–131.
Pemberton, L. and Fallahkhair, S. (2005). 'Design Issues for Dual Device Learning: Interactive Television and Mobile Phone'. http://www.mlearn.org.za/CD/papers/Pemberton&Fallahkhair.pdf
Pennington, M.C. (1993). 'Exploring the Potential of Word Processing for Non-Native Writers', *Computers and the Humanities*, 27, 149–63.
Perry, C.R. (1977). 'The British Experience 1876–1912: the Impact of the Telephone during the Years of Delay'. In Pool, I. (ed.), *The Social Impact of the Telephone*. Cambridge, Mass.: MIT Press, pp. 69–96.
Phillips, D. and Filmer-Sankey, C. (1993). *Diversification in Modern Language Teaching: Choice and the National Curriculum*. London: Routledge.
Phillipson, T. (2003). *English-Only Europe?* London: Routledge.
Pickering, J. (1996). 'Hypermedia: When Will They Feel Natural?' In Chernaik, W., Deegan, M. and Gibson, A. (eds), *Beyond the Book: Theory, Culture and the Politics of Cyberspace*. Office for Humanities Communication, University of London, pp. 43–55.
Pile, S. (2001). 'Radio Times View of the Nation Television Survey', *Radio Times*, 1–7 September 2001, pp. 30–4.
Pincas, A. (2004). 'Using Mobile Phone Support for Use of Greek during the Olympic Games 2004 (The INLET Project)'. http://www.itdl.org/Journal/Jun_04/article01.htm
Pioneers of Psychology (2001). 'John Amos Comenius'. http://educ.southern.edu/tour/who/pioneers/comenius.html
Piper, A. (1986). 'Conversation and the Computer: a Study of the Conversational Spin-Off Generated among Learners of English as a Foreign Language Working in Groups', *System*, 14, 187–98.
Pool, I. (1977). 'Introduction'. In Pool, I. (ed.), *The Social Impact of the Telephone*. Cambridge, Mass.: MIT Press, pp. 1–9.
Pool, I. (1983). *Forecasting the Telephone: a Retrospective Technology Assessment*. Norwood, NJ: Ablex.

Postman, N. (1987). *Amusing Ourselves to Death: Public Discourse in the Age of Show Business*. London: Methuen.

Prensky, M. (2005). 'What Can you Learn from a Cell Phone? Almost Anything!', *Innovate*, 1 (5). http://www.innovateonline.info/index.php?view=article&id=83

Pujolà, J-T (2002). 'CALLing for Help: Researching Language Learning Strategies Using Help Facilities in a Web-Based Multi-Media Program', *ReCALL*, 14 (2), 235–62.

Purushotma, R. (2005). 'Commentary: You Are Not Studying, You're Just...', *Language Learning and Technology*, 9(1), 80–96.

Quaterman, J.S. (1993). 'The Global Matrix of Minds'. In Harasim, L.M. (ed.), *Global Networks: Computers and International Communication*. Cambridge, Mass.: MIT Press, pp. 35–56.

Quinault, R.J. (1947). 'English by Radio', *ELT*, I(5), 119–25.

Rebillard, F. (2000). 'L'Hypertextualité, Dispositif Central de la Presse sur Cédérom et sur le Web. Le Cas des Publications Consacrées au Thème du Multimédia'. In Lancien, T. (ed.), *Multimédia: Les Mutations du Texte*. Paris: Ophrys, pp. 41–55.

Reith, J.C.W. (1924). *Broadcast over Britain*. London: Hodder and Stoughton.

Robinson, G.L. (1989). 'The CLCCS CALL Study: Methods, Error Feedback, Attitudes, and Achievement'. In Flint Smith, W. (ed.), *Modern Technology in Foreign Language Education: Applications and Projects*. Lincolnwood, Ill.: NTC, pp. 119–34.

Rogers, E.M. (1983). *Diffusion of Innovations*. New York: The Free Press.

Rogers, E.M. (1986). *Communication Technology: the New Media in Society*. New York: The Free Press.

Rogers, E.M. and Shoemaker, F.F. (1971). *Communication of Innovations*, 2nd edn. New York: Free Press.

Rose, K.R. and Kasper, G. (eds) (2001). *Pragmatics in Language Teaching*. Cambridge: Cambridge University Press.

Rosengren, K.E. (2000). *Communication: an Introduction*. London: SAGE Publications.

Ross, N.J. (1995). 'Dubbing American in Italy', *English Today*, 41(1), 45–8.

Royis, P. and Parpette, C. (2000). 'Le Dédoublement Discursif dans le Discours Pédagogique'. In Guillot, M-N. and Kenning, M-M. (eds), *Changing Landscapes in Language and Language Pedagogy: Text, Orality and Voice*. London: AFLS/CILT, pp. 209–26.

Rutter, D.R. (1987). *Communicating by Telephone*. Oxford: Pergamon.

Salaberry, R.M. (1996). 'A Theoretical Foundation for the Development of Pedagogical Tasks in Computer Mediated Communication', *CALICO Journal*, 14(1).

Salaberry, R.M. (2000). 'Pedagogical Design of Computer Mediated Communication Tasks: Learning Objectives and Technological Capabilities', *The Modern Language Journal*, 84(1), 28–37.

Salomon, G. (1979). *Interaction of Media, Cognition, and Learning: an Exploration of How Symbolic Forms Cultivate Mental Skills and Affect Knowledge Acquisition*. San Francisco: Jossey-Bass Publishers.

Sasseville, B. (2004). 'Integrating Information and Communication Technology in the Classroom', *Canadian Journal of Learning and Technology*, 30(2).

Saussure, F. de (1972 (1916)). *Cours de Linguistique Générale*. Paris: Payot.

Savignon, S.J. (1983). *Communicative Competence: Theory and Classroom Practice*. Reading, Mass.: Addison-Wesley.

Scannell, P. (1996). *Radio, Television and Modern Life: a Phenomenological Approach*. Oxford: Blackwell.

Schegloff, E.A. (1977). 'Identification and Recognition in Interactional Openings'. In Pool, I. (ed.), *The Social Impact of the Telephone*. Cambridge, Mass.: MIT Press, pp. 415–50.

Schegloff, E.A. (1986). 'The Routine as Achievement', *Human Studies*, 9, 111–51.

Schneller, R. (1988). 'The Israeli Experience of Crosscultural Misunderstanding: Insights and Lessons'. In Poyatos, F. (ed.), *Cross-Cultural Perspectives in Nonverbal Communication*. Toronto: Hogrefe, pp. 153–73.

Scragg, D.G. (1974). *A History of English Spelling*. Manchester: Manchester University Press.

Sebeok, T.A. (1994). *An Introduction to Semiotics*. London: Pinter.

Shannon, C. and Weaver, W. (1949). *The Mathematical Theory of Communication*. Urbana: University of Illinois Press.

Shield, L. (2003). 'MOO as a Language Learning Tool'. In Felix, U. (ed.), *Language Learning Online: Towards Best Practice*. Lisse: Swets and Zeitlinger, pp. 97–122.

Sinclair, J.M. (ed.) (2004). *How to Use Corpora in Language Teaching*. Amsterdam: John Benjamins.

Smith, A. (1979). The *Newspaper: an International History*. London: Thames and Hudson.

Smith, M.R. (1994). 'Technological Determinism in American Culture'. In Smith, M.R. and Marx, L. (eds), *Does Technology Drive History? The Dilemma of Technological Determinism*. Cambridge, Mass.: MIT, pp. 1–35.

Smith, R. and Curtin, P. (1998). 'Children, Computers and Life Online: Education in a Cyber-World'. In Snyder, I. (ed.), *Page to Screen: Taking Literacy into the Electronic Era*. London: Routledge, pp. 211–33.

Smoreda, S. and Licoppe, C. (2000). 'Gender-Specific Use of the Domestic Telephone', *Social Psychology Quarterly*, 63(3), 238–52.

Snyder, I. (1998). 'Beyond the Hype: Reassessing Hypertext'. In Snyder, I. (ed.), *Page to Screen: Taking Literacy into the Electronic Era*. London: Routledge, pp. 125–43.

Squires, D. (2000). 'Peripatetic Electronic Teachers in Higher Education'. In Squires, D., Conole, G. and Jacobs, G. (eds), *The Changing Face of Learning Technology*. Cardiff: University of Wales Press, pp. 167–79.

Standage, T. (1998). *The Victorian Internet: the Remarkable Story of the Telegraph and the Nineteenth Century's Online Pioneers*. London: Phoenix.

Steffens, L. (1958). *The Autobiography of Lincoln Steffens*. New York: Harcourt, Brace and World.

Stevenson, J. (1991). 'Resource Systems for Education'. In Gilbert, J.K., Temple, A. and Underwood, C. (eds), *Satellite Technology in Education*. London: Routledge, pp. 171–92.

Strang, B.M.H. (1970). *A History of English*. London: Methuen.

Stuart-Smith, J. (2004). 'Is Television a Contributory Factor in Accent Change in Adolescents?' Economic and Social Research Award R000239757, Non-Technical Summary.http://www.arts.gla.ac.uk/SESLL/EngLang/phonetics/index.html

Stuart-Smith, J. and Tweedie, F. (2000). 'Accent Change in Glaswegian: a Sociophonetic Investigation'. *Final Report to the Leverhulme Trust* (Grant no. F/179/AX):http://www.arts.gla.ac.uk/SESLL/EngLang/research/accent/accent1.htm

Sweet, H. (1899 (1964)). *The Practical Study of Languages: a Guide for Teachers and Learners*. Dent: London, republished by Oxford: Oxford University Press.

TangoTown. http://www.tangotown.jp/tangotown

Taylor, P. and Bain, P. (2003). 'Call Centres in Scotland and Outsourced Competition from India'. Scottish Economic Policy Network. http://www.scotecon.net/publications/Call%20Centres%20Scotland.pdf#search=%22Scotecon%20%2B%20Taylor%22

Textually.org (2003). *SMS celebrates 10th Birthday*. http://www.textually.org/textually/archives/2003/02/000040.htm

Thompson, J. (2005). 'Computer-Assisted Language Learning (CALL)'. In Coleman, J.A. and Klapper, J. (eds), *Effective Learning and Teaching in Modern Languages*. London: Routledge, pp. 148–52.

Thompson, J.B. (1995). *The Media and Modernity: a Social Theory of the Media*. Cambridge: Polity Press.

Thorne, S.L. (2003). 'Artifacts and Cultures-of-Use in Intercultural Communication', *Language Learning & Technology*, 7(2), 38–67.

Thorne, S.L. and Payne, J.S. (2005). 'Evolutionary Trajectories, Internet Mediated Expression, and Language Education', *CALICO Journal*, 22(3), 371–97.

Thornton, P. and Houser, C. (2004). 'Using Mobile Phones in Education'. In Roschelle J., Chan T-W., Kinshuk and Yang S.J.H. (eds), *Proceedings of the 2nd IEEE International Workshop on Wireless and Mobile Technologies in Education*. Los Alamitos, Calif.: IEEE Computer Society, pp. 3–10.

Tiffin, J. and Rajasingham, L. (1995). *In Search of the Virtual Class: Education in an Information Society*. London: Routledge.

Townsend Hall, B. (2000). 'Telephone Language'. http://www.suite101.com/article.cfm/tesol/51702

Trifonova, A. and Ronchetti, M. (2003). 'Where is Mobile Learning Going?' *Proceedings of the World Conference on E-learning in Corporate, Government, Healthcare, & Higher Education (E-Learn 2003)*, Phoenix, Ariz., pp. 1794–801.

Trudgill, P. (1983). *On Dialect: Social and Geographical Perspectives*. New York: New York University Press.

Trudgill, P. (1986). *Dialects in Contact*. Oxford: Blackwell.

Trudgill, P. (1990). *The Dialects of England*. Oxford: Blackwell.

Turkle, S. (1984). *The Second Self – Computers and the Human Spirit*. New York: Simon and Schuster.

Twain, M. (1996). *The $30,000 Bequest and Other Stories*. New York: Oxford University Press.

UNESCO (1999). *Statistical Yearbook 1999*. Paris: UNESCO.

Vaugelas, C.F. de (1970 (1643)). *Remarques sur la Langue Françoise*. Geneva: Slatkine Reprints.

Vincent, D. (2000). *The Rise of Mass Literacy: Reading and Writing in Modern Europe*. Cambridge: Polity Press.

Vygotsky, L.S. (1978). *Mind in Society: the Development of Higher Psychological Processes*. Cambridge, Mass.: Harvard University Press.

Walter, H. (2001). *Honni Soit qui Mal y Pense*. Paris: Laffont.

Warschauer, M. (1997). 'Computer-Mediated Collaborative Learning: Theory and Practice', *Modern Language Journal*, 81, 470–81.

Warschauer, M. (1998). 'Researching Technology in TESOL: Determinist, Instrumental, and Critical Approaches', *TESOL Quarterly*, 32(4), 757–61.

Warschauer, M. (2003). 'Demystifying the Digital Divide', *Scientific American*, 289(2), 42–7.

Warschauer, M. and Healey, D. (1998). 'Computers and Language Learning: an Overview', *Language Teaching*, 31, 57–71.

Watson, D.M. (1984). 'The Role of CAL in Decision-Making in the Humanities', *Computers and Education*, 8, 31–4.

Web Japan (2004). *Novels Delivered to your Phone*. http://web-japan.org/trends/lifestyle/lif040310.html

Williams, R. (1980). *The Long Revolution*. Harmondsworth: Penguin.

Windeatt, S., Hardisty, D. and Eastment, D. (2000). *The Internet*. Oxford: Oxford University Press.

Winston, B. (1998). *Media Technology and Society, a History: From the Telegraph to the Internet*. London: Routledge.

Wright, S. (2000). *Community and Communication*. Clevedon: Multilingual Matters.

All websites were verified on 28.10.06.

Index

Aakhus, M., 172, 173
access to ICT, 54–6, 117, 131
  current attitudes, 1, 171
  importance of decision-makers, 18, 97
  and language learning, 96, 196
  and literacy, 120–1
accommodation, 80–3
  and action orientation, 52
action orientation, 50–2
  dynamic nature of, 51, 113
  impact on participants, 51–2
  and interpersonal vs mass communication, 50–1
  and L2 users, 52
  and other communication variables, 51–2, 113
  and support for learning, 113
  and the telephone, 178, 179, 180
  see also interpersonal specificity
Adoni, H., 57
affordances
  as an influence on use, 20, 129, 164, 169
  varied nature of, 112
Africa, 55, 131, 174
Agar, J., 175
Aizawa, K., 193
Allen, O.E., 11
Anis, J., 188
answering machines, 179, 183–4
Appel, M.C., 158
applied linguistics, 135, 142, 148–9, 154
  see also language teaching, SLA research
Ariès, P., 107, 108, 138
Ariew, R., 163
Aronson, S.H., 173, 174
Asher, J.J., 147
Asia, 8, 55, 191
  see also individual countries
Aspden, P., 185
assessment, 36–7, 124, 169
Aston, G., 48
asynchronous communication, 42, 43, 49, 52–3, 178–9
Attali, J., 75
Attewell, J., 191
Atwell, E., 12, 141
audio cassettes, *see* audio technologies
audio technologies, 111, 128, 131, 146–9, 181–90
  see also individual media
Audiolingual Method, 148
Audiovisual Method, 145, 149
Australia, 175, 182
autonomous learning, 104–6, 108, 133–4
awareness, 79–80, 116, 164, 165, 167, 188
Ayto, J., 87

Bain, P., 186
Bakhtin, M.M., 35, 47, 67
Bardovi-Harlig, K., 165
Baron, N.S., 20, 66, 77, 91
Bates, A.W., 114, 130, 131
Battarbee, K., 58
Baugh, A.C., 68, 73
BBC (British Broadcasting Corporation), 13, 51, 68, 79, 88, 111
Beavis, C., 117
Bell, A., 16, 35, 100
Bell, Alexander Graham, 11, 14, 173, 188
Bell, D.M., 169
Belz, J.A., 167
Benczik, V., 82
Béranger, A-L., 186
Bergs, A., 61, 187, 188
Berlo, D.K., 47
Biber, D., 72, 77, 92
blended learning, 134, 189, 196
Boden, D., 29, 56, 57

body language, 30, 44–6, 47, 128
Bolter, J.D., 32, 124, 126
books
  availability of, 73, 108–9, 115, 118–19, 130, 144
  digital books, 33–4, 193
  and education, 108–9, 114, 116–17, 166
  in former times, 33, 108–9, 118–19, 123
  and language, 33–4, 73, 75–6, 92, 95–6
  and language learning, 137, 140, 143–4, 156, 189
  see also print
Boyd-Barrett, O., 18
Brett, P., 169
Brewer, J.P., 51
Briggs, A., 15, 73, 173, 174, 175, 189
Broady, E., 168
Brooks, N., 149
Brown, E., 194
Brunner, H., 93
Brutt-Griffler, J., 138
Burbules, N.C., 125
Burke, P., 73, 174, 175
Busse, U., 86
Byram, M., 165

Cable, T., 68, 73
CALL (computer-assisted language learning), 154, 157–8, 165, 168, 169
call centres, 184–6
Cameron, D., 78
Canale, M., 150
Carey, J.W., 16, 64
Carley, K.M., 17
Castells, M., 20, 54, 158
Caxton, W., 90, 92, 95–6
CDs, *see* audio technologies
CEF (Common European Framework), 24
centrifugal forces, *see* diversification
centripetal forces, *see* unification
Chalaby, J.K., 7
Chambers, A., 168
Chambers, J.K, 82–3
Chandler, D., 27
channel, 27, 28–34, 50
  differences between channels, 29–31, 70–2
  as instructional variable, 112, 113, 128–9
  vs mode, 28, 30
  multichannel communication, 28–9, 34
  and simultaneous feedback, 48–50
  and technological progress, 31–2
Chapelle, C.A., 3, 24, 99, 154, 157–8, 168, 169
Charlton, K., 109, 140
Chartier, R., 118–19
China, 8
Chinnery, G.M., 191
Clarke, A.C., 11, 26, 174
Clément, J., 33–4
CMC (computer-mediated communication), 36, 41–2, 91
  and language learning, 155, 157, 158, 160, 162, 163, 166–9
  see also individual tools, tandem learning
Coleman, J.A., 168
collaborative learning, 121–2, 158, 166–9
Collis, B., 109, 110, 114
Comenius, J.A., 144–5
communication models, 27, 38
communication patterns, changes in, 23, 31–2
  in contemporary society, 54–7
  implications for communicative competence, 24–5
  and L2 users, 23, 24, 25, 53–4, 57–60
  and language change, 84, 99
communication variables, 38–53
  impact on participants, 39–44, 45–6, 47–8, 49–50, 51–2, 180
  interactions between, 52, 113
  and pedagogical applications, 156–7
  and the telephone, 177–80
communicative competence, 150
  changes in the nature of, 24–5, 59–60
communicative language teaching, 24

computers
in education, 18, 110, 123–5, 127, 132
as an evolving technology, 31–2, 36, 123
impact on language, 87, 98–9
and language learning, 151–3, 157, 160, 162–3, 165, 168–9
and SLA research, 153–4
and social inclusion, 8, 99, 127–8
see also Internet, multimedia, WWW
Conacher, J.E., 168
convergence
technological, 26, 172
of trends, 19
Cook, V., 164
costs
cost-effectiveness, 7, 151–2
as an influential factor, 7, 9, 19, 33, 74, 127, 145, 151–2, 159, 186, 187, 190
cross-national comparisons, 8, 55, 97, 119, 174, 175
Crystal, D., 74, 77, 78, 86–7, 91, 93, 140
cultural differences
between home and school, 116–17, 133
impact on communication, 45, 48, 166, 167–8, 181
see also intercultural competence
Cummins, J., 106, 120–1, 122
curricula
place of language in, 116, 136, 137, 145
and popular culture, 116–17
Curtin, P., 105

Davies, G., 169
Davis, B.H., 51
deductive vs inductive approaches, 143–4
DeLozier, J., 110
Denmark, 18, 119
diffusion of innovations, 7–9
in language, 79–86
and social inclusion, 127–8
and social and political factors, 8–9, 17–20, 74
Dilts, R., 110
Direct Method, 145–8
distance learning, 126, 163, 189
distance, physical, 16, 26, 39, 58
and the telephone, 177–8
see also distance education
diversification, 66–9
and the emergence of new registers, 92–3
and L2 users, 100–1
Dominick, J.R., 11, 27, 35, 56, 98
Doughty, C., 154
Dzbor, M., 169

Eastment, D., 168
Eberbach, K., 167
Eco, U., 69, 76–7
educational technology
differences between media, 128–30, 162–4
historical overview, 126–7, 152–3
in language learning, 151–70
and purpose of education, 105–7
see also individual media
Eisenstadt, M., 168
Eisenstein, E., 67, 96, 108, 118
Ellington, H., 152
email
and L2 users, 44
in language learning, 23, 158, 167–8
use of language in, 13, 19–20, 61, 74, 77, 84, 93
English
American English, 66, 88
and its development as a lingua franca, 19, 58, 95–9, 137–40
influence on other languages, 66, 84, 87, 90
and register variation, 72, 92–4
and standardization, 65, 68, 69, 73, 76, 90–1
Europe, 8, 55, 75–6, 95, 96, 108, 118–19, 138, 143, 145, 174, 175
explicit vs implicit approaches, 154, 166

external environment, importance of, 7, 8, 17, 19–20, 34, 69, 77, 127, 167–8

face-to-face
  characteristics of, 28, 30, 31, 42, 44, 45–6, 47, 50, 113
  in education, 113, 115, 134, 158
  primacy of, 28–9, 56–7
  vs technology-mediated contact, 45, 74, 158, 169, 178
Fairclough, N., 94
Fallahkhair, S., 194
Febvre, L., 33, 96
feedback, simultaneous, 48–50
  impact on participants, 49–50
  vs reciprocity, 47
Felix, U., 169, 170
Fennell, B.A., 63, 66, 95, 96, 99, 118
Ferrara, K., 93
Filmer-Sankey, C., 137
film
  and education, 127
  and language, 80–1, 84, 97, 98
  and language learning, 149, 165
Findahl, O., 98
Finland, 58, 119, 175
Fisher, E., 115
Fishman, J.A., 100
Fiske, J., 56
Flowerdew, J., 168
fluency, 42, 184, 186
  in education and language learning, 121, 149, 157
Fowler, R., 28, 93
France, 18, 74–5, 96, 97, 98, 119, 120–1, 145, 149, 167, 174, 182
Freinet, C., 120–1
Freire, P, 120
French, 65, 87, 90, 95, 96, 97, 98, 121, 137–8, 139–40, 142, 143, 145, 189
Freud, S., 10–11

Gardner, E.C., 138
Garner, R., 132
Garrett, N., 164
Gauntlett, D., 56
Gee, J.P., 33, 117
gender differences, 108, 136, 182
German, 82, 86, 97, 138, 181, 188
Germany, 97, 119, 173
Gillingham, M.G., 132
globalization
  and education, 109, 159
  impact on language and language use, 86, 98, 100, 101–2, 141–2, 159, 186
  see also Internet, satellite TV
Godwin-Jones, R., 169
Goffman, E., 35
Görlach, M., 86, 90
Gouin, F., 146, 147
Graddol, D., 19, 96, 123
grammar in language teaching, 143–4, 145–7, 150, 155–6, 164–5
Grammar–Translation Method, 145–7
Granered, E., 186
Greek, 137, 181, 192
Green, P.S., 15
Guillot, M-N., 42
Gumpert, G., 174, 176

Haas, C., 4, 15, 69, 125
Halliday, M.A.K., 31, 92
Halmari, H., 181
Hampel, R., 169
Hardisty, D., 168
Harris, R., 75, 96, 189
Havelock, E.A., 70
Hawisher, G.E., 125
Hawkins, E., 37
Headrick, D.R., 63–4, 96
Healey, D., 24, 158, 163
Heppell, S., 122, 123
Hermerén, L., 94
Herring, S.C., 61, 101
Hesse, C., 10
Heurtin, J-P., 177–8
Hill, A., 56
Hill, B., 168
Hinkel, E., 165
historical precedents, 15–16, 97, 109, 114, 121–2, 182–3, 187
Holtzer, G., 181
Honey, J., 65, 75, 79
Hopper, R., 188, 189
Houser, C., 193

Howatt, A.P.R., 90, 91, 137–8, 140, 143, 144, 145–6
Hughes, G., 63, 92, 94
Hulstijn, J.H., 154
Humbley, J., 90
Hutchby, I., 20, 173, 181
Hutchins, J., 141
Hymes, D., 24, 27, 35
hybrid media, 31, 129
see also individual media
hypertext, 4, 6, 125–6

Iceland, 98, 119
Illich, I., 105–6, 109, 120
individualization, 105, 129, 153
inductive vs deductive approaches, 143–4
Industrial Revolution, 97
innovations
consequences of, 6, 9–14, 15, 17, 19–20
diffusion of, 7–9, 74–5, 79–80, 83, 84
examples of linguistic innovations, 84–5, 86–8, 90, 91–4
genesis of, 14–15
as an influence on applied linguistics, 147, 148–50
interactivity, 46–50
and other communication variables, 47, 51–2, 113
and support for learning, 112–13, 127, 129
and the telephone, 178, 179, 180
see also feedback, reciprocity
intercultural competence, 45, 120–2, 159, 162, 163, 165–8
Internet
diffusion and use of, 54, 56, 117, 194
and education, 106, 109–10, 115, 132
and language, 67, 69, 78, 93
and language learning, 100, 166–8, 170, 194
and language status, 99–100, 140–1
see also CMC, email, WWW
interpersonal communication, 81, 176
vs mass communication, 47, 50, 68, 75, 76, 80, 83, 113
interpersonal specificity, 50, 51–2
and education, 113, 129
and the telephone, 179, 185–6
see also action orientation
Ishii, H., 44
Italian, 82, 84–5, 138, 189
Italy, 69, 76–7, 84–5, 121

Jahandarie, K., 72
Jakobson, R., 27
Japan, 8, 166, 193
Jensen, K.B., 46
Jerman, J.A., 149
Jespersen, O., 146, 147–8
Johns, T., 165
Johnson, K., 60, 157
Johnson, S., 76
Johnston, J., 128
Jones, A., 115, 127
Jones, B., 153
Jones, G., 153
Joyce, P., 89
Jung, U.O.H., 156

Kasesniemi, E-L., 177, 188
Kasper, G., 48, 165
Katz, J. E., 172, 173, 185
Kaufer, D.S., 17
Kelly, L.G., 144, 145, 153
Kempster, G., 115, 120, 128
Kendon, A., 44–5
Kennedy, C., 194
Kenning, M.J., 116, 153, 170
Kenning, M-M., 116, 153, 156, 170
Kesseler, A., 61, 187, 188
Kiddle, L.B., 152–3
Kiernan, P.J., 193
King, P., 165
Kirkley, J.R., 122–3, 124
Kirkup, G., 127
Klapper, J., 164–5
Knobel, M., 13
Komzak, J., 168
Kramsch, C., 165

Kress, G., 19–20, 28, 29, 30, 32, 33, 42, 43
Kvaran, G., 98

L2 users
 and communication variables, 44, 46, 52
 compared with L1 users, 25, 40, 78, 101, 185
 and language variation and change, 78, 100–1
 media use by, 53–4, 57–8
 needs of, 23, 24, 25, 52, 58, 60, 94, 159, 184, 187
Lado, R., 149
Lambert, W.E., 138
Lamizet, B., 125
Lamy, M-N., 169
Lancelot, C., 145
Landlow, G.P., 73
language acquisition
 and instruction, 155–6, 164
 vs language learning, 103
 see also SLA research
language change
 causes of, 63–6
 examples of, 84–5, 86–8, 90, 91–4
 impact on participants, 41
 and L2 users, 100–1
language laboratories, 111, 149, 152–3
language learners, 67, 77–8
 see also language learning, L2 users
language learning
 evolutionary dimension of, 124, 136, 139–40, 194
 informal vs formal, 1–2, 103
 and the media, 162–8
 and the telephone, 177, 178, 188–94
 vs use, 155
language processing, 154, 164, 169
 and time coordinates, 41, 42–4, 71–2, 179
language skills, 162–3
 see also individual skills
language spread
 and language learning, 137–8, 139–40
 reasons for, 95–9
language status
 and language learning, 60
 and the media, 40, 58, 99–100, 140–1
language teaching
 innovations in, 120–1, 144
 issues, 24, 34, 36–7, 40, 58–9, 60, 160, 161
 overview of methodological changes, 142–51
language use vs language learning, 155
language variation
 and L2 users, 40, 67, 78, 100–1
 and physical distance, 39–40
 see also language change
Larsen-Freeman, D., 155–6
Lasswell, H.D., 27
Latin, 90, 95, 96
 and language learning, 138, 143, 145
Laurillard, D., 109, 129–30, 133
learner control, 129, 130, 132, 162, 163
learning networks, 122
learning paradigms, 106–9
Leith, D., 96
Leitner, G., 68
LeLoup, J., 158
Lemke, J.L., 30, 105, 106, 116, 140
less widely spoken languages, 99–100, 140–1
Levinson, S.C., 35
Levy, M., 135, 161, 194
Licoppe, C., 177–8, 182
Liddicoat, A., 183–4
listening
 in contemporary society, 54
 in language learning, 36–7, 162, 163, 190
 vs reading, 71–2
 see also oral communication, reception
literacy
 and education, 118, 120–1
 multiple nature of, 34, 118, 120, 122–3
 spread of, 75, 118–19
Little, D., 24, 156

Little, G.D., 91
Littlemore, J., 168
Liu, M., 158, 160
Lodge, D., 166
Lodi, M., 121
Long, M.H., 155–6
Loonen, P., 145
Lyons, M., 119, 123

Macleod, H., 190
Mahan-Taylor, R., 165
many-to-many communication, 36
many-to-one communication, 36
Martin, H-J., 33, 96
Marvyn, C., 17, 183
Marx, G.T., 173
Marx, L., 4–5, 6
mass communication, 36
  vs interpersonal communication, 47, 50, 68, 75, 76, 80, 83, 113
mass media, 68–9, 79, 83, 100
  see also individual media, mass communication
Matheson, H., 51, 80, 114
McFarlane, A., 116–17
McIntosh, A., 92
McLuhan, M., 4, 38, 39
McNicol, T., 192
media
  educational potential of, 128–33
  overview of developments, 26
  overview of strengths and weaknesses for language learning, 161–4
media use
  and bilingualism, 53–4, 57–8
  consumption patterns, 54, 55–6
  and face-to-face, 56–7
  implications for language learning, 59
  importance of, 54
mediated communication
  and face-to-face, 28–9, 38, 45, 57, 81, 134, 141, 178
  implications for language learning, 58, 60
  importance of, 158–9
  and language status, 40, 58
  and support for learning, 110, 111–12, 134
Meinhof, U.H., 123, 168
Mercer, N., 115
methodology
  see under language teaching
Mey, J.L., 48, 166
Mikulecky, L., 122–3, 124
Miller, L., 168
Milroy, J., 78–9, 83, 88–9
Milroy, L., 78–9, 83, 88–9
Misa, T.J., 17
Mishan, F., 125
m-learning, mobile learning, 132–3, 191
  and language learning, 192, 193–4
  platform issues, 191
  strengths and weaknesses of, 191–3
mobile phones
  early history of, 175
  and education, 191–4
  in language learning, 192, 193–4
  see also telephones
mobility, importance of, 159
Mochet, M-A., 34
mode
  vs channel, 28
  in education, 112, 169
  and language competence, 34
  multimodal communication, 29, 46
  and shifts in usage, 31–2, 33–4
  and technological progress, 32
Molotch, H.L., 29, 56, 57
Moores, S., 57, 59
Morsbach, H., 166
motivation, 2, 101, 120–1, 124–5, 136–7, 138–40, 192
Moyal, A., 176, 182
Muhr, R., 86
multimedia, 34, 132, 169
Murray, D.E., 41
Myles, F., 157

needs analysis, need for, 24, 58–60, 159
New London Group, 120
newspapers, 6–7, 8, 13–14, 18, 61, 77, 93–4

Norris, J.M., 154
Nunberg, G., 140

O'Donnell, J.J., 9
O'Dowd, R., 167
Olgren, C.H., 190
Olson, D.R., 33, 70, 86
O'Neil, C., 34
one-to-many communication, 26, 36
one-to-one communication, 26
one-way communication, 41
  vs two-way communication, 40, 47, 113
Ong, W.J., 13, 29, 31, 70, 71–2, 108
oral communication, 31, 34, 47, 57, 70, 71, 121, 141, 178–80
  in education and language learning, 130, 146–7, 149
oral cultures, 29, 70
Ortega, L., 154

paradigm shifts in education and language learning, 24, 107–8, 109–10
Parpette, C., 31
participant roles
  categories of, 34–5, 177
  and channel possibilities, 49–50
  implications for language learning, 36–7
  number of incumbents, 36
  and reciprocity vs feedback, 46–7
  see also under receiver, source
Passy, P., 146–7
Pattanayak, D.P., 104
Pavlidou, T-S., 181
Payne, J.S., 169
Pederson, K.M., 153
Pemberton, L., 194
Pennington, M.C., 125
Percival, F., 152
Perry, C.R., 174–5
Phillips, D., 137
Phillipson, T., 99
Piaget, J., 115
Pickering, J., 126
pictures, 30, 32, 33–4, 46, 87–8, 144–5
Pile, S., 56
Pincas, A., 192
Piper, A., 153
Ponterio, R., 158
Pool, I., 11, 174
Postman, N., 4, 5, 56
Prensky, M., 191
prestige, 65–6, 95, 137–8
print
  and education, 107–9, 114, 126, 130–1, 132
  and language, 63, 65–6, 67, 69, 73, 75, 82, 90–1, 92, 95–6
  and language learning, 144, 146, 162, 163
  and society, 10, 15, 18, 19, 33
  vs writing, 31, 73, 111
production
  blurring of boundary with reception, 125–6
  and channel availability, 49, 50
  vs reception, 36–7
  and space coordinates, 39–40
  and time coordinates, 42–4, 179
pronunciation, 88–90
  and language learning, 111, 147–8, 152, 164
Pujolà, J-T., 154
punctuation, 91, 101
Purushotma, R., 169

Quaterman, J.S., 36
Quinault, R.J., 131

Race, P., 152
radio
  in contemporary society, 54, 55, 56, 117
  early history of, 11, 13–14, 26, 51
  and education, 127, 131–2
  and language, 66, 68, 76–7, 80, 87, 88, 93
  and language learning, 152, 162, 163
Rajasingham, L., 46, 58, 104, 134
Rautiainen, P., 177, 188
reading
  in contemporary society, 54, 115, 124, 193
  as language learning skill, 162, 163, 164

as process, 43, 71–2, 125–6
see also literacy, production
Rebillard, F., 113
receiver, 27, 34–8, 40, 41, 45, 46, 50, 52, 177, 180, 182
as active participant, 47, 49
reception
blurring of boundary with production, 125–6
and channel availability, 50
vs production, 36–7
and space coordinates, 39–40
and time coordinates, 41, 42–4, 179
reciprocity, 46–8
vs feedback, 47
impact on participants, 47–8
issues with, 53
register variation, 64, 72, 92–4
and L2 users, 34, 101
Reich, W.A., 185
Reith, J.C.W., 13, 14, 68, 111–12, 152
Robinson, G.L., 154
Rogers, E.M., 7–8, 8–9, 26–7, 79, 83, 118, 127–8, 174
Ronchetti, M., 191
Rose, K.R., 48, 165
Rosengren, K.E., 55–6
Ross, N.J., 84–5
Royis, P., 31
Rutter, D.R., 180, 189

Salaberry, R.M., 161, 169
Salomon, G., 112
Sasseville, B., 4, 127
satellite TV, 54, 77, 86, 98, 168
Saussure, F. de, 27, 189
Savignon, S.J., 25
Sayers, D., 106, 120–1, 122
Scannell, P., 51
Schegloff, E.A., 45, 176, 180–1
Schneller, R., 30, 45
Scotland, 119, 142
Scragg, D.G., 76, 90, 91
Sebeok, T.A., 165–6
Shannon, C., 27, 28, 35
Shield, L., 168
Shoemaker, F.F., 79
Sinclair, J.M., 165
situated learning, 107, 117, 192
see also tandem learning, Vygotsky
SLA (second language acquisition) research, 153–4, 155–6, 157
Smith, A., 7, 8, 119
Smith, M.R., 4, 6
Smith, R., 195
Smoreda, S., 182
SMS (short message service), 61, 179, 186–9, 192
Snyder, I., 6
social inclusion and computers, 8, 99, 117, 127–8
social matrix, *see* external environment
source, 27, 34–8, 49–50, 71, 180
as main partner, 42, 45, 47, 48, 49–50
space coordinates, 38–40
impact on participants, 39–40
independence from time coordinates, 38–9
and other communication variables, 47
and support for learning, 109, 111–12
and the telephone, 177–8
Spain, 75, 174
Spanish, 82, 121, 138
speaking
in language learning, 36–7, 162, 163, 190
vs writing, 31, 71–2
see also fluency, oral communication, production
speech vs written language, 34, 78, 91
see also register variation
spelling, 75–6, 90–1
Squires, D., 110
Standage, T., 15–16
standard varieties, 65, 68, 75–6, 76–7, 78, 90–1, 96
states
and education, 108, 118
and language, 76
and language learning, 136, 137, 138
and the media, 17–18, 68, 74–7
Steffens, L., 85

Stevenson, J., 163
Stourdze, Y., 75
Strang, B.M.H., 88
Strevens, P., 92
Stuart-Smith, J., 81
Svavarsdóttir, Á., 98
Sweden, 55, 98, 119, 174
Sweet, H., 146–8
symbolic cues, 44–6
  impact on participants, 45–6, 180
  and other communication variables, 49–50, 52
  and support for learning, 46, 112
  and the telephone, 178–80
synchronous communication, 42, 43, 49, 52–3, 178–80

tandem learning, 158, 166–8, 181–2
Taylor, P., 186
Taylor, T. J., 75, 96
teacher's role
  in a digital world, 110, 114–15, 170
  facets of, 110–11
  importance of, 114
  and psychological underpinning of education, 115–16
technological determinism
  factors conducive to, 5
  origins of, 4–5
  problems with, 6–16
telegraph
  and language, 64, 85, 96–7
  and social change, 6–7, 15–16
telephones, traditional
  and education, 131, 189–90
  vs face-to-face, 57, 178, 180–1
  and gender, 182
  and L2 users, 46, 181, 182
  and language, 45–6, 97, 180–1
  and language learning, 162, 163, 171–2, 181–2, 189, 190
  see also answering machines, call centres, mobile phones, SMS
telephony
  diffusion and use of, 54
  early history of, 11, 74–5, 97, 173, 174–5, 183, 189
  evolutionary dimension of, 176
  as one-way technology, 75, 173
television
  and communication variables, 31, 46, 51, 117, 129, 131
  in contemporary society, 54, 55, 56, 58, 117
  and education, 105, 127, 129, 130, 132
  and language, 58, 66, 69, 81, 84, 85, 86, 87, 88, 91, 93
  and language learning, 162, 163
  see also satellite television
Thompson, J., 168
Thompson, J.B., 16, 38, 45, 54
Thorne, S.L., 167–8, 169
Thornton, P., 193
Tiffin, J., 46, 58, 104, 134
time coordinates, 40–4
  impact on participants, 40–4
  independence from space coordinates, 38–9
  and support for learning, 112
Townsend Hall, B., 181
translation
  and language, 18, 84, 87, 96
  and language learning, 143–4, 145–7, 192
  machine translation, 140–1
Trifonova, A., 191
Trompetter, P., 154
Trudgill, P., 64, 66, 80, 80–1, 83, 88, 89
Turkle, S., 124
turn-taking, 42, 45, 46, 48
Twain, M., 182
Tweedie, F., 81
two-way communication, 46, 49
  vs one-way communication, 40, 47, 113

unification, 66–9, 75
  see also English, standard varieties
USA, 97, 98, 116, 150, 151, 174, 175

Van Leeuwen, T., 28, 42
Vaugelas, C.F. de, 65
verbal vs non-verbal information, 30–1, 32–4, 44–6, 47, 128, 144
vernaculars, 18, 67, 96, 142–3, 145
  see also individual languages

video cassettes/recorders
  in contemporary society, 54, 55
  and education, 130, 132, 192
  and language learning, 162, 163
Vincent, D., 75, 108, 119
virtual reality, 93, 130, 153, 155, 166, 168
visual media, 71, 128
  see also individual media
vocabulary, 64–5, 85, 86–8
  in language teaching, 139, 144–5, 165
voicemail, 179, 183–4
Vygotsky, L.S., 115

Walter, H., 87
Warschauer, M., 3, 8, 24, 158, 163
Watson, D.M., 124–5
Weaver, W., 27, 28, 35
Welsh, 96
Whittemore, G., 93
Williams, R., 85
Windeatt, S., 168
Winston, B., 14, 15, 173
word processors, 73, 124–5
Wright, S., 138, 140
writing
  in education, 107, 120–1, 122
  and language, 82, 86
  as language learning skill, 162, 163, 168
  as major landmark, 26, 31, 70–2
  as process, 43, 71, 72, 124–6
  vs speech, 31, 71, 72
  see also literacy, production, register variation
written language
  vs pictures, 29
  vs spoken language, 71, 78, 82
  see also register variation
WWW (World Wide Web), 93, 105, 109–10, 162, 163, 165, 169